Residential Schools and Indigenous Peoples

Residential Schools and Indigenous Peoples provides an extended multi-country focus on the transnational phenomenon of genocide of Indigenous peoples through residential schooling. It analyses how such abusive systems were legitimised and positioned as benevolent during the late nineteenth century and examines Indigenous and non-Indigenous agency in the possibilities for processes of truth, restitution, reconciliation, and reclamation.

The book examines the immediate and legacy effects that residential schooling had on Indigenous children who were removed from their families and communities in order to be 'educated' away from their 'savage' backgrounds, into the 'civilised' ways of the colonising societies. It brings together Indigenous and non-Indigenous authors from Aotearoa/New Zealand, Australia, Greenland, Ireland, Norway, the United Kingdom, and the United States in telling the stories of what happened to Indigenous peoples as a result of the interring of Indigenous children in residential schools.

This unique book will appeal to academics, researchers, and postgraduate students in the fields of Indigenous studies, the history of education, and comparative education.

Stephen James Minton is a British chartered psychologist and an Associate Professor in Applied Psychology at the School of Psychology, University of Plymouth, UK.

Routledge Research in International and Comparative Education

This is a series that offers a global platform to engage scholars in continuous academic debate on key challenges and the latest thinking on issues in the fast-growing field of International and Comparative Education.

Titles in the series include:

Informal Learning and Literacy among Maasai Women
Education, Emancipation and Empowerment
Taeko Takayanagi

Parental Involvement Across European Education Systems
Critical Perspectives
Edited by Angelika Paseka and Delma Byrne

Transculturalism and Teacher Capacity
Professional Readiness in the Globalised Age
Niranjan Casinader

Residential Schools and Indigenous Peoples
From Genocide via Education to the Possibilities for Processes of Truth, Restitution, Reconciliation, and Reclamation
Edited by Stephen James Minton

Transnational Perspectives on Curriculum History
Edited by Gary McCulloch, Ivor Goodson, and Mariano González-Delgado

For more information about this series, please visit: https://www.routledge.com/Routledge-Research-in-International-and-Comparative-Education/book-series/RRICE

Residential Schools and Indigenous Peoples

From Genocide via Education to the Possibilities for Processes of Truth, Restitution, Reconciliation, and Reclamation

Edited by Stephen James Minton

LONDON AND NEW YORK

First published 2020
by Routledge
2 Park Square, Milton Park, Abingdon, Oxon OX14 4RN

and by Routledge
52 Vanderbilt Avenue, New York, NY 10017

Routledge is an imprint of the Taylor & Francis Group, an informa business

© 2020 selection and editorial matter, Stephen James Minton; individual chapters, the contributors

The right of Stephen James Minton to be identified as the author of the editorial material, and of the authors for their individual chapters, has been asserted in accordance with sections 77 and 78 of the Copyright, Designs and Patents Act 1988.

All rights reserved. No part of this book may be reprinted or reproduced or utilised in any form or by any electronic, mechanical, or other means, now known or hereafter invented, including photocopying and recording, or in any information storage or retrieval system, without permission in writing from the publishers.

Trademark notice: Product or corporate names may be trademarks or registered trademarks, and are used only for identification and explanation without intent to infringe.

British Library Cataloguing-in-Publication Data
A catalogue record for this book is available from the British Library

Library of Congress Cataloging-in-Publication Data
A catalogue record has been requested for this book

ISBN: 978-1-138-61558-8 (hbk)
ISBN: 978-0-429-46304-4 (ebk)

Typeset in Bembo
by Cenveo® Publisher Services

'Sequoyah, the Gift' (painting by Daniel Milton Horsechief)

This book is dedicated to all survivors of the types of residential schools, and other similar institutions, that we have described in this book; to their families, and their descendants. We honour them, and also all of those who live with the legacy and contemporary effects of the attempts to forcibly assimilate Indigenous peoples in post-colonial nation states.

Contents

List of figures x
List of tables xi
List of contributors xii
Preface xv
Acknowledgements xix
List of abbreviations xxi

1 Setting the scene 1
STEPHEN JAMES MINTON

The scope of this book 1
The structure of this book 6
Some initial thoughts on the possibilities for processes
 of truth, restitution, reconciliation, and reclamation 8
Notes 14
References 19

2 Some theoretical touchstones 24
STEPHEN JAMES MINTON

Indigenous as 'Other' 24
Educational systems as agents of (cultural) genocide 30
The residential school as a 'total institution' 34
Assimilation and nation state identity 38
Notes 41
References 45

3 Aotearoa/New Zealand 48
TANIA KA'AI

Historical contexts 48
The operation of the residential schools system 54

The legacy of the residential schools system 55
Processes of truth, restitution, reconciliation, and reclamation 57
A final note 61
Notes 62
References 64

4 Australia's native residential schools   66
ROSEMARY NORMAN-HILL

Introduction 66
Historical contexts 68
The establishment of the residential schools system in Australia 70
The legacy of the residential schools system in Australia 78
Processes of truth, restitution, reconciliation, and reclamation 82
A final note 86
Notes 90
References 90

5 Greenland   95
STEPHEN JAMES MINTON AND HELENE THIESEN

Historical contexts 95
'The experiment' 103
Efforts towards processes of truth, restitution,
   reconciliation, and reclamation 105
Notes 107
References 109

6 The colonisation of Sápmi   113
JENS-IVAR NERGÅRD

Key elements of Norwegianisation 115
Internal colonisation 120
An inferno takes shape 122
Bleak fate at a boarding school in the 1970s 127
Destructive consequences 135
The milestones of reconstruction 137
References 139

7 **Colliding Heartwork: The space where
our hearts meet and collide to process
the boarding school experience** 141
NATAHNEE NUAY WINDER

Introduction 141
A brief history of Indian boarding schools in the United States 143
*Overview of 'Southwestern University' students
   and the dissertation study 146*
Methods and methodology 148
Findings 151
Concluding remarks 159
Notes 160
References 160

8 **Punishing poverty: The curious case
of Ireland's institutionalised children** 163
JEREMIAH J. LYNCH

Historical contexts 163
The operation of the residential schools system 166
Ireland's Travelling community and the industrial schools 170
The legacy of the residential schools system 174
Processes of truth, restitution, reconciliation, and reclamation 177
Notes 182
References 185

9 **Reflections** 191
JULIE VANE, STEPHEN JAMES MINTON, TANIA KA'AI,
ROSEMARY NORMAN-HILL, AND NATAHNEE NUAY WINDER

A reflection by Julie Vane and Stephen James Minton 191
*Reflections by Tania Ka'ai, Rosemary Norman-Hill,
   and Natahnee Nuay Winder 209*
Notes 216
References 218

Index 220

Figures

6.1	John in the kitchen of his house	124
6.2	Collection of knives made by John	125
6.3	John fishing on a summer night	127
6.4	Mollesjohka Fjellstue	128
6.5	Mollesjohka Fjellstue today	128
6.6	Fishing on Iesjávri in spring	129
6.7	Per and his brother visiting Grensen boarding school as adults	131
6.8	An open and endless world	132
6.9	An open and endless world	133
6.10	Gifts from nature	134
6.11	Gifts from nature	135
6.12	Freedom	139
7.1	Love/hate relationship	152
7.2	Keep gate closed	153
7.3	Right on target	153
7.4	Lost in the classroom	154
7.5	Isolation	155
7.6	Not all is washed away – intergenerational trauma	156
7.7	Breath of prayer	157
7.8	Symbol of my identity	158

Tables

3.1 The Waitangi Tribunal assessment of te reo Māori 2010   60
3.2 Recommendations of the Waitangi Tribunal (2011)   60
7.1 Participants' characteristics   147

Contributors

The contributing authors to this book are (alphabetically, by surname):

Tania Kaʻai, who is of New Zealand Māori (Ngāti Porou and Ngāi Tahu), Hawaiian (Kanaka Māoli), Cook Island Māori and Sāmoan descent, and is a world-renowned Indigenous author and academic. She heads *Te Whare o Rongomaurikura* [The International Centre for Language Revitalisation], which is based at *Te Ipukarea* [The National Māori Language Institute], Auckland University of Technology, Aotearoa/New Zealand. She is the author of the third ('Aotearoa/New Zealand') chapter of this book, and a co-author of the ninth ('Reflections') chapter.

Jeremiah J. Lynch, who has recently (2019) completed his doctoral research on survivors' experiences of the notorious (at least, to Irish readers) St. Joseph's Christian Brothers School, in Co. Galway, Ireland. He brings his considerable experience of psychotherapeutic work with survivors of this, and other institutions, to bear in his authoring of the eighth ('Ireland') chapter of this book.

Stephen James Minton, who is a British chartered psychologist, and an Associate Professor in Applied Psychology at the School of Psychology, University of Plymouth in the United Kingdom. He is the author of the first ('Setting the Scene') and second ('Some Theoretical Touchstones') chapters; a co-author of the fifth ('Greenland') and ninth ('Reflections') chapters of this book; and served as the book's editor.

Jens-Ivar Nergård, who is a Professor at the Department of Education and Teacher Education at the University of Tromsø, and a Professor II at the Centre for Professional Studies, Bodø University College. An educational ethnographer of national and international importance, Professor Nergård brought his four decades of research experience with the Sámi people, the Indigenous people of Scandinavia, to bear in his authoring of the sixth ('The Colonisation of Sápmi') chapter of this book.

Contributors xiii

Rosemary Norman-Hill, who is a Darug woman, and has recently (2019) completed her doctoral research (at Gnibi College of Indigenous Australian Peoples, Southern Cross University) on the Parramatta Native Institution, the first of its kind in Australia, where her great-great-great grandmother was in the founding group of Aboriginal students. She is the author of the fourth ('Australia's Native Residential Schools') chapter of this book, and a co-author of ninth ('Reflections') chapter.

Helene Thiesen, who is a Greenlandic Inuit author. She was one of twenty-two Greenlandic Inuit children who, in 1951, were forcibly taken from their homes and families in Greenland, to families and institutions located in Greenland's colonial ruler, Denmark, to be re-educated as 'model Danish citizens', and after a year's schooling in Denmark to return to Greenland as 'Danish cultural bearers'. She is the author of '*For flid og god opførsel: vidnesbyrd fra et eksperiment*' ['For Diligence and Good Behaviour: Testimony from an Experiment'] (2011), in which she documents her experiences at the time, her subsequent reflections, and her quests for the truth since. She is a co-author of the fifth ('Greenland') chapter of this book.

Julie Vane, who is a British woman, and is a practicing clinical psychologist, who previously worked with people with learning disabilities. She is curious about ways to understand and address the positions and needs of marginalised populations. She is a co-author of the ninth ('Reflections') chapter of this book.

Natahnee Nuay Winder, who is a citizen of the Duckwater Shoshone Nation, and is Paiute, Ute, Navajo, and African American; she identifies herself as a strong and passionate mixed-heritage Indigenous and Black warrior woman. She is an Assistant Professor at the Department of First Nations Studies and the School of Public Policy, Simon Fraser University, Canada. She has recently (2019) completed her doctoral research, in which she elucidated her development of the '*Colliding Heartwork*' framework, which explains how Indigenous descendants of boarding and residential school survivors empathise through storytelling, and how they are impacted differently and intersect, creating a space where hearts meet to heal, talk, and share how they feel about the ongoing effects of colonialism. She is the author of the seventh ('Colliding Heartwork – The Space where our Hearts Meet and Collide to Process the Boarding School Experience') chapter of this book, and a co-author of the ninth ('Reflections') chapter.

The painting at the front of this book, '*Sequoyah, the Gift*', is an original work by **Daniel Milton Horsechief,** who is a native Pawnee/Cherokee artist from Oklahoma. *Sequoyah* (also rendered *Ssiquoya*, and *Se-quo-ya;* b. ca. 1770, d. 1843), was a Cherokee silversmith who developed a Cherokee syllabary, which was officially adopted by the Cherokee Nation in 1825, and used in the *Cherokee Phoenix* (1828–1834), the newspaper of the Cherokee Nation.

Within a few years of the adoption of the syllabary, the literacy rate amongst the Cherokee became higher than that of the surrounding settler populations. Furthermore, Sequoyah's development of the Cherokee syllabary also inspired the creation of Cree syllabics, and other native syllabaries across North America. Given Sequoyah's historical prominence, and the fact that this book contains many accounts of Indigenous agency and reclamation, I felt that the image has a special significance to this work, and I am exceptionally grateful to Daniel for giving me his permission to use it.

Preface

The story of how this book came to be compiled is, for me, the book's editor, necessarily personal; it involves many people (some of whom I will name, some of whom I won't), and several places. That being the case, it will probably seem to be a less than straightforward story; however, I will do my best to tell it. I am a British psychologist of education, and have been simultaneously engaged as a researcher, practitioner and some-time campaigner in the prevention of violence (especially bullying) in school communities for almost two decades. In the autumn of 2012, two significant events occurred which drew me towards looking at schools not only as locations where violence could and did take place between children, but also as schools and schooling systems as institutions in which powerful members of societies, including governments, could and did implement practices and policies of violence against children, and the populations of which those children formed a part. The first of these events was my initial meeting with Dr Jeremiah J. Lynch, whose doctoral research I was honoured to go on to supervise. Jerry's doctoral research involved his skilful and sensitive investigation of the lived experiences of six survivors of the most notorious of Ireland's industrial schools, St. Joseph's Christian Brothers School, Letterfrack, Co. Galway. (Jerry's deep humanism, expressed in his sheer abilities as a narrator, and his energies as an advocate, are tangible in the eighth chapter of this book, which I was delighted that he could contribute). A matter of weeks after first meeting Jerry, a chance previous e-mail contact I had had with Professor Hadi Strømmen Lile (now at the University College of Østfold, Norway) prompted him to invite me to Tromsø, Norway, where I met with him, and other Sámi (the Indigenous[1] people of Scandinavia) scholars. There I was informed, for the first time – and Hadi was generous and well-prepared enough to provide me with references, thankfully in English – that residential schools had played an important part in the forcible assimilation, or 'Norwegianisation', of the Sámi people. Through my general reading and some personal contacts, I had known for decades past that the children of the native peoples of what are now the Americas, and of what are now Aotearoa/New Zealand and Australia, had been interred in residential schools, as part of the assimilation and genocidal efforts made against Indigenous peoples by those post-colonial nation states. But what crystallised for me in a moment in October 2012 – I recall that at the time, I was sitting alone on a converted barrel seat outside a pub in Tromsø, smoking my pipe – was that these processes had gone on, around the world, at more or less the same time. The obvious questions of 'How?' and 'Why?' sprang into my mind, and my own work on this book marks the beginning of an attempt to answer them.

I devoted a chapter in my last book, '*Marginalisation and Aggression from Bullying to Genocide*', to a historical comparison of experiences of Indigenous people in residential schools in Norway and the United States. However, I was painfully aware of two limiting factors in my writing of that chapter: first, due to the confines of space imposed by a book devoted to a more general subject matter, I had told, in a heavily summarised form, the stories of only two sets of experiences that I knew to have been repeated all over the world. Second, and more importantly, I had approached that chapter as an 'outsider' – as a British person, I could not have possibly, and in no way would want to pretend to have, been directly affected by the issues that I was writing about. I felt that a better path – better in every sense of the word – lay in my noting the similarities and repetitions in histories and experiences, and then inviting more informed others to provide their own authentic accounts of what had gone on. Suffice it to say, the limitations that I saw in what I had written previously meant that I was determined to be part of something more respectful and meaningful in the future.

In a review of this book's potential at the proposal stage, one of the referees stated that the collective multi-disciplinary, trans-Indigenous, Western/Indigenous authorship of this book would be a strength; furthermore, the referee's comment that, '….it's not a book on Indigenous peoples, but a book for, with and by Indigenous peoples' was a perfect summary of many of my intentions for the book. (I hope that the referee will not be disappointed with the finished product.) I do hope that the book will be read by Indigenous peoples, and that they will experience it as having been written for, with and by them. I also hope that Indigenous readers may take an interest in, and perhaps even drawn strength from, reading about certain commonalities in experience; such is the structure and multi-location nature of this book, I believe that the possibility for recognising those commonalities exists. Even in my all-too limited experience, I have seen some indications that the 'taking-an-interest-in' and 'drawing-strength-from' aspects of this ambition could, can and do exist in other contexts. I have had, for example, the privilege of discussing my joint work with Sámi scholars on Sámi experiences of historical forcible assimilation and contemporary discrimination, and the experiences of Irish people in industrial schools, with native people from what is now North America, some of whom had not previously heard of these experiences (and also, with some of those who had). I have also had discussions with survivors of industrial schools and Magdalen laundries in

Ireland, many of whom, knowing little about the experiences of Indigenous peoples, had not previously realised that systems of austere institutions run by so-called men and women of God, in which deprivation and neglect were constant, and vile incidents of abuse were almost everyday occurrences, were neither unique to Roman Catholicism, nor to Ireland. On a personal note, my attempts to understand, as an outsider, the lived experiences of those realities have been immeasurably enriched by the time that I have spent listening to the native peoples of all of the countries featured in this book – Indigenous men and women of Aotearoa/New Zealand, Australia, Canada, Greenland, Norway, and the United States – as well as survivors of institutions in Ireland. I am profoundly grateful to those people for their kindness and willingness to spend some time in conversation with me. In some of these conversations, recognitions of shared past and present suffering, shared grief, shared determinations, and something that I can only describe (and here, I am running up against the limits of my facility with the English language) as feelings of kinship were expressed. Such expressions started with statements like, 'I thought it was only me', or 'I thought it was only our people', or, 'I didn't know that things like we've gone through had happened anywhere else'. For me to say more here – to say where these discussions ended up; or to try to authentically and respectfully render in print those moments in which the tender recognitions of mutuality emerged, sometimes seeming (to me) to hang in the ether, like hands and hearts extended across time and space – would not only be indelicate, but also, I must own, elude my skill as a writer.

I also believe that non-Indigenous people can learn something of value from this book. As the European that I am, I hold that my people (Europeans, and settler populations of European descent) must truly come to realise, without equivocation, that our ancestors committed atrocious, genocidal actions against the ancestors of Indigenous peoples; that the power imbalances set in play by those actions prevail to this day in post-colonial nation states; and that the effects of these actions and inequalities have been, and still are, lived realities for Indigenous peoples. We must come to really know this – and to feel, accept and meaningfully address the consequences of these truths. It is perhaps far too late, and certainly far too inadequate, for settler populations to offer meaningless gestures of apology, and under the delusory yet pervasive influence of our Abrahamic faith understandings, to expect, or even to demand, guilt-assuaging forgiveness. I believe that one of the first things that Europeans, and settler populations of European descent, must do in approaching or effecting any type of meaningful change is to stop hiding, disavowing and mythologising these truths. And if reading some of the accounts of the events and experiences in this book elicits feelings of shock, horror or shame in Europeans, and those of European descent, then in some senses, I say so much the better. This is *not* because I wish to shock, horrify, or shame the non-Indigenous reader – I have no such wish – but rather, because I believe and hope that those feelings can be signifiers that the functions of unveiling, owning and demythologising truths may be served. Having expressed so many hopes in this preface, it is my most earnest hope of all that this book can, and in some small and yet hopefully tangible way will, mark a step along the road to truth, as a foundation stone in the effecting of the type of change that will be meaningful to Indigenous peoples.

Stephen James Minton
Dublin, April 2019

Note

1. Out of respect for Indigenous scholars who use the same convention, and in solidarity with the reasons that they do so, I capitalise the word 'Indigenous' throughout, except where directly quoting from sources where this word is not capitalised.

Acknowledgements

As the editor of the book, first and foremost, I would like to offer my sincere thanks to the contributing authors, five of whom (i.e. Tania Ka'ai, Jens-Ivar Nergård, Rosemary Norman-Hill, Helene Thiesen, and Natahnee Winder) I was not personally acquainted with when I first asked them to contribute to this book. I am profoundly honoured by them placing their trust in me – a non-Indigenous stranger, who presumably seemed to have had a reasonably good idea – as an editor. I thank them, and Jeremiah J. Lynch and Julie Vane, for their contributions. I also wish to express my gratitude to the artist Daniel Milton Horsechief, whose painting, 'Sequoyah, the Gift', appears at the front of this book.

In a similar respect, I would like to give special thanks to my colleague Professor Shawn Wilson, who helped me to find Dr Rosemary Norman-Hill as an author for the fourth ('Australia's Native Residential Schools') chapter. It was also Shawn who suggested that I attend the *International Congress for Qualitative Inquiry*, at the University of Illinois Urbana-Champaign, in May 2018, where I was welcomed into the work of that conference's *Indigenous Inquiries Circle*. I would like to offer my sincere thanks to the members of that Circle, especially to Professor Roe Bubar, who helped me to find Dr Natahnee Nuay Winder as an author for the seventh ('Colliding Heartwork – The Space where our Hearts Meet and Collide to Process the Boarding School Experience') chapter. I would also like to thank Dr Astrid Nonbo Andersen, for our discussion of the fifth ('Greenland') chapter at an early stage of the book's development, and for suggesting Helene Thiesen as a co-author for that chapter. Similarly, I would like to thank Dr Rachel Ka'ai-Mahuta, who correctly identified her mother, Professor Tania Ka'ai, as the best possible person to write the third ('Aotearoa/New Zealand') chapter.

I have greatly appreciated the opportunities to discuss the progress of this book as a whole provided by four very valued people, whom I feel fortunate to count as both friends and colleagues: Professor Hadi Strømmen Lile, Professor Willy Aagre, and two of my former doctoral students, Dr Martin Kelly and Dr Jeremiah J. Lynch (the latter of whom is the author of the eighth chapter ['Punishing Poverty – The Curious Case of Ireland's Institutionalised

Children']). Although I never had the pleasure of meeting her, I feel it is important to acknowledge the contribution of Dr Karen Sherlock, who died in 2018. She was a friend of my partner, Julie. She worked, she cared, and she shared her books, many of which have been cited in this work. I hope that she would have liked this book, and understood the efforts taken, and how they have been made.

I would also like to thank the publishers of this book, Routledge, and in particular, the editor, Emilie Coin; the editor who originally commissioned this work, Aiyana Curtis; and the editorial assistants with whom I have worked, Will Bateman and Swapnil Joshi. Their professionalism, courtesy, and assistance have been everything I could have wished for as a contributing author to, and as an editor of, a co-authored work. The insights of the reviewers of this book at its proposal stage were also extremely helpful, and I thank them for these.

In terms of 'conflicts of interest', I can state that no direct financial assistance, from any source whatsoever, was forthcoming in supporting the researching, writing, or editing of this book. The more time that I spend learning from Indigenous friends and colleagues about the contemporary issues of marginalisation that their peoples continue to experience, and about the history of Indigenous genocide, assimilation, and epistemocide, the less this fact surprises me.

Finally, I have the very great pleasure of being able to offer my genuine and formal thanks to my daughter, Anna Minton, for her proofreading of, and her making of editorial suggestions for, the first four chapters of this book, and her research assistance on the fifth chapter. I would also like to thank my partner, Julie Vane (represented here as the lead author of the book's ninth chapter, 'Reflections'), in this instance, for everything that she has done to make this book possible. My thanks also go to my mother, Rosemary Fox, who encouraged my thinking and learning from my very earliest years. Her genuine compassion for, and interest in, all those who have struggled for dignity and social justice, have been values which I hope that I too have come to embody. *'For a' that, an' a' that, it's coming yet for a' that – that Man to Man, the world o'er, shall brothers be for a' that!'* So to Anna, to Julie, and to Mum; and also, no less, to my son, Conor Minton, and my sister, Sarah Minton – my love to you all, forever and always.

Abbreviations

AICCA	Aboriginal and Islander Child Care Agency (Australia)
AIM	American Indian Movement (United States and Canada)
ATSICPP	Aboriginal and Torres Strait Islander Child Placement Principle (Australia)
BBC	British Broadcasting Corporation
BCE	Before Common/Current Era
BIA	Bureau of Indian Affairs (United States)
BPP	Black Panther Party for Self-Defense (United States)
CBC	Canadian Broadcasting Corporation
CBS	Christian Brothers School (Ireland)
CE	Common/Current Era
CICA	Commission to Inquire into Child Abuse (Ireland)
DNZM	Dame Companion of The New Zealand Order of Merit
DKK	Danish krone (unit of currency in Denmark and Greenland)
EEC	European Economic Community
EMRIP	(United Nations') Expert Mechanism on the Rights of Indigenous Peoples
ERO	Education Review Office (Aotearoa/New Zealand)
EU	European Union
FBI	Federal Bureau of Investigation (United States)
GDP	Gross Domestic Product
IRM	Indigenous Research Methods
ISPCC	Irish Society for the Prevention of Cruelty to Children (Ireland)
LGBTQ+	Lesbian, Gay, Bisexual, Transgender, Queer / Questioning, plus (other non-heterosexual orientation, other non-binary gender expression/identity)
MBE	Member of the Most Excellent Order of the British Empire
MS	Motor Ship
NARF	Native American Rights Fund (United States)
NOK	Norwegian krone (unit of currency in Norway)
NRK	*Norsk rikskringkasting* [Norwegian Broadcasting Corporation]

NSPCC	National Society for the Prevention of Cruelty to Children (United Kingdom)
NSW	New South Wales (Australia)
NSWAM	New South Wales Aborigines' Mission (Australia)
NT	Northern Territories (Australia)
PAR	Participatory Action Research
PMLD	Profound and Multiple Learning Disabilities
QLD	Queensland (Australia)
RIRB	Residential Institutions Redress Board (Ireland)
SA	South Australia
SGA	Self-Government Act (Greenland)
Tas	Tasmania (Australia)
TJ	Transitional Justice
TRC	Truth and Reconciliation Commission (Canada)
UK	United Kingdom (of Great Britain and Northern Ireland)
UN	United Nations
UNCAT	United Nations Committee Against Torture
UNDRIP	United Nations' Declaration on the Rights of Indigenous Peoples
UNPFII	United Nations' Permanent Forum on Indigenous Issues
US/USA	United States (of America)
Vic	Victoria (Australia)
WA	Western Australia
WHO	World Health Organization

Chapter 1

Setting the scene

Stephen James Minton

My task is threefold in this chapter, and this is reflected in its structure. In the first place, I want to say something about the subject matter with which my fellow authors and I will be concerned – in other words, the scope of this book. Second, I want to outline the structure of this book. In the third and final section of this chapter, I will present some of my initial thoughts on the possibilities that might exist for processes of truth, restitution, reconciliation, and reclamation.

The scope of this book

In a number of countries around the world, a system of residential schools in which Indigenous children were compulsorily enrolled was operational by the late nineteenth century, and continued to be so for at least a further century. These schools were, in many cases, run by Christian religious orders on behalf of, but with relative independence from, the governments of post-colonial nations, with the usually expressed intention of 'solving' the 'problem' of Indigenous peoples. This 'solution' was often implemented in the deliberate and forceful removal of Indigenous children from their families and communities, and them being 'educated' away from their 'savage' backgrounds, into the 'civilised' ways of the colonising societies. As these truths have begun to be recognised, a horrifying history of abuse and neglect has emerged, and the legacy that has been left by the operation of these residential schools systems has, in many cases, been one of significant individual and cultural trauma. In bringing together Indigenous and non-Indigenous authors from Aotearoa/New Zealand, Australia, Greenland, Ireland, Norway, the United Kingdom, and the United States, this book marks an attempt to tell the stories of what happened to Indigenous peoples as a result of the interring of Indigenous children in residential schools, to say how and why the schools were set up and run, to document the patterns of abuse and neglect, and to examine the legacies that the residential schools systems have had on Indigenous peoples. As attempts are made to move from the horrors of the past to a position in the future, where truths can be fully acknowledged, and where processes of restitution, reconciliation, and reclamation might become possible, we must ensure that the efforts that are made are thoughtful and genuine, and cannot serve, or be made to serve, as further negations of the historical experiences and contemporary rights of Indigenous peoples. We will, therefore, also be concerned with considering how such progress can and could be made.

In assessing the potential overall value of this book, it must first be acknowledged that the processes of genocide perpetrated against Indigenous peoples, and the attempts to assimilate them made by colonising peoples, extended far beyond the compulsory enrolment of Indigenous children in residential schools. The physical slaughter, torture, enslavement, imprisonment, open warfare, and sterilisation of Indigenous peoples; the forcible separation of Indigenous children from their families of origin, and the adoption of these children by non-Indigenous parents, or the placing of such children in other institutions; the theft of land, and the deliberate destruction of long-established ways of life, such as societal and family structures, child-rearing, and livelihoods; the desecration of cultural artefacts and traditionally sacred spaces, and the forcible conversion of Indigenous peoples to the religious faiths of the colonisers; the purposeful exclusion of Indigenous peoples from the social structures (including the right to buy, sell, or own land and housing, or property of the most basic kind) in the nation states to which they now, voluntarily or involuntarily, found themselves to belong; the removal of individual liberties and the fundamentals of personal and social identity, including being forbidden to speak one's own language, or even to use one's own given name – all of these things were part of the genocidal processes. So too were the belief and value systems of the colonisers which, especially when formulated and codified into systems of legislature, made such horrific actions permissible, and in the colonisers' eyes, 'right', moral, and even charitable, benevolent, and philanthropic. In some cases, some of these atrocities were perpetrated within the residential schools systems; in others, they were perpetrated before, outside, or alongside these systems. The confines of any single book, I feel, can permit telling only one part of this history. But it is my hope that by telling this part well, my fellow authors and I will be able to indicate what part the system of residential schooling played, and to situate it within those broader contexts.

It is true to say that no overt physical war was made on Norway's Indigenous Sámi people (unlike, say, what was the case in the United States), and that the government policy of the forcible assimilation of the Sámi and Kven[1] peoples in Norway (*fornorsking*, or in English, 'Norwegianisation'), which was operational between 1850 and 1980, was carried out primarily through the compulsory education of children at residential schools. Indeed, the 'Norwegianisation' policy has been characterised by Sámi scholars as having been '... introduced in the field of culture, *with school as the battlefield and teachers as frontline soldiers*' (Niemi, 1997 in Minde, 2005, p. 7).[2] However, even given the fact that no physical war was made, Scandinavia's Indigenous people have experienced physical and spiritual privations of the most serious kind. Indeed, attempts made by the Scandinavians to physically displace the Sámi people date back as far as the arrival in Norway of bubonic plague in 1349 (Urbanczyk, 1980), as have incursions into the traditional spiritual space of the Sámi people.[3] For example, in the eighteenth century, in the conversion efforts made by Lutheran missionaries, the traditionally pagan Sámi were forcibly converted to Christianity, their sacred sites were destroyed, and their drums were burnt (Somby, 2015). Indeed, well into the twentieth century, any person who wanted to buy or lease state lands for agriculture in Norway's northernmost county of Finnmark, a traditional Sámi area, had first to prove their knowledge of the Norwegian language, and had to register with a Norwegian name (Minde, 2005). Hence, whilst the histories that have been written regarding the forcible assimilation of the Sámi and Kven peoples in Norway have focussed largely on 'Norwegianisation' through education (which will also be one of the focuses of the truth commission in Norway, see Minton & Lile, 2018, 2019), historical experiences of forcible assimilation certainly took on other forms. In terms of legacy issues, there is also compelling empirical evidence, based on large-scale representative surveys, that Sámi people in Norway continue to experience discrimination to the present day (see Hansen et al., 2008, 2016).

However, in other parts of the world, it is evident that the genocide perpetrated against Indigenous peoples via means of education accompanied, followed on from, and may be considered to have completed the grim task of physical genocide (Adams, 1995; Minton, 2016).[4] It has been estimated that between 90 and 98 per cent of the Indigenous populations of what are now known as the Americas were physically exterminated in the first four centuries that followed the arrival of Columbus in Hispaniola (Stannard, 1992).[5] From the late nineteenth century, in the landmass that was claimed by the United States, the outright and overt killing of the Indigenous peoples by the military at first augmented and then, following the Massacre at Wounded Knee,[6] was replaced by the enrolment of Indigenous children in what were called Indian Boarding Schools. In illustrating the intent behind such schools, a phrase coined by Captain Richard Henry Pratt, who after serving as an officer in the Tenth Cavalry Regiment founded the United States' first Indian Boarding School,[7] is often referred to. Pratt's (in)famous summary of his social and pedagogical position was (Pratt, 1892 in Bruchac & Smelcer, 2013)

> A great general has said that the only good Indian is a dead one.[8] In a sense, I agree with the sentiment, but only in this: that all the Indian there is in the race should be dead. Kill the Indian in him, and save the man. (p. 2)

Hence, during the late nineteenth and the twentieth centuries, the four-century-long practice of killing the 'Indian' was to be replaced by 'saving' him, by killing the 'Indian within', through the process of education (Adams, 1995; Minton, 2016).[9] Via a process of aphorism honing similar to that to which Sheridan's statement was subject (see endnote 8), and as I have already suggested, the phrase 'Kill the Indian, save the man' became almost equally well known.[10] As this section (and indeed, this book as a whole) will go on to show, these experiences were not unique to Indigenous peoples within the United States.[11] Nor are they unique to North America, nor even to the Americas as a whole. I have spent some time here reflecting upon Pratt's phrase, as it has become deservedly infamous as one of the most overt statements of the 'desirability' of the forcible assimilation of Indigenous peoples. But whilst I could not countenance using the word 'desirability' in the previous sentence without the irony-laden quotation marks, it is worth noting here that in his own days, Pratt reckoned himself to be, and was generally recognised as, a humanitarian educational and social reformer.[12] We shall return to this seemingly intractable and inexplicable paradox in Chapter 2, in the section 'Assimilation and Nation State Identity'.

A key point that will emerge over the course of this book, particularly in the individual country chapters (Chapters 3–8), is that the outcomes of the legislature and social and educational policies and provisions (which were, and still are, made for Indigenous peoples by the powers that governed, and still govern, post-colonial nation states) are often very different indeed from the outcomes of legislature, policies, and provisions made *by* or, at the very least, *with* Indigenous peoples. Whilst it is indeed instructive to reflect upon the facts that (for example) the appalling conditions that existed in Indian Boarding Schools were recognised in a US federal government report as early as 1928,[13] there are other means by which today's reader can learn about these experiences – she or he can directly hear, or rather read, the voices of the ones interred. Indeed, a number of first-hand survivor accounts have already been written by Indigenous people who were interred in residential schools, particularly in Canada[14] – Theo Fontaine's *Broken Circle: The Dark Legacy of Indian Residential Schools: A Memoir* (2010), Celia Haig-Brown's *Resistance and Renewal: Surviving the Indian Residential School* (1989), and Bev Sellars' *They Called Me Number One: Secrets and Survival at an Indian Residential School* (2013) provide some pertinent examples.

Scholars too, some of them Indigenous, have weighed in with historical overviews of the residential school systems in individual country contexts. Again, in Canada, these include Roland Chrisjohn and his colleagues' *The Circle Game: Shadows and* Canada *Substance in the Indian Residential School Experience in Canada* (1994) and John Milloy's *A National Crime: The Canadian Government and the Residential School System* (1999). David Wallace Adams' remarkable and classic work, *Education for Extinction*, covers similar historical ground in the United States. In addition to, other single-country critical historical treatments, to which the authors of the individual country chapters will refer to, some inter-country comparative accounts have also been published.

For example, Andrew Armitage (1995) has contributed his *Comparing the Policy of Aboriginal Assimilation: Australia, Canada, and New Zealand*, Margaret Jacobs (2006) has compared experiences in Australia and the United States, and a relatively short comparative report (47 pages, excluding references) on Indigenous peoples and boarding schools was prepared for the Secretariat of the United Nations Permanent Forum on Indigenous Peoples by Andrea Smith (2009). This book, then, continues and expands the inter-country comparative focus begun by the likes of Armitage (1995) and Jacobs (2006) (see above).

As we have already seen, first-hand accounts written by Indigenous survivors of residential schools in Canada exist (e.g. Fontaine, 2010; Haig-Brown, 1989; Sellars, 2013); and, as is discussed below (see the section 'Some Initial Thoughts on the Possibilities for Processes of Truth, Restitution, Reconciliation and Reclamation'), in recent years, the Truth and Reconciliation Commission of Canada (2015) has published its final report, after four years of work. Furthermore, critical scholarly accounts already exist of the histories of the residential schools in Canada (e.g. Chrisjohn et al., 2002; Chrisjohn, Young & Maraun, 1994, 2006; Milloy, 1999), the potential value of the Truth and Reconciliation Commission of Canada (e.g. Chrisjohn & Wasacase, 2009), as does the final report of Truth and Reconciliation Commission of Canada (2015), and any number of media commentaries on it (e.g. CBC News, 2015; Palmater, 2015a, 2015b). So, whilst we will reference the Canadian experience in this and the following chapter (Chapter 2), and to an extent in other chapters, we see no point in covering ground that has already been so ably covered elsewhere. The reader with a specific interest in the Canadian experience is, therefore, referred to these aforementioned sources. In this book, we will be endeavouring to tread if not new, perhaps in many cases, at least less thoroughly documented ground. We will be considering what happened with respect to institutional schooling in six countries (Aotearoa/New Zealand, Australia, Greenland, Ireland, Norway, and the United States) across three continents (Australasia, Europe, and North America). In order to provide the best possible documentation of, and commentary on, such histories, as an editor, I believe that I have been exceptionally fortunate in terms of the contributing authors involved in this book; I feel genuinely humbled to be in such company, and I am profoundly grateful to them. Any success that we have in this book in addressing the issues posed in this opening chapter would, I am certain, be due primarily to their contributions; and the responsibility for any mistakes or shortfalls, I am equally certain, would be mine alone.

On a personal note, and to build somewhat on what I had to say in the book's preface, as a non-Indigenous editor and contributing author, I have had to look hard at my own motivations for compiling and contributing to this book, and my very involvement in this subject area. Often, the 'white saviour' myth[15] and position are all too persuasive to attempt to enter into for some non-Indigenous/white people, and all too 'marketable' to others who fall into those categories. Whilst I do not feel this to be true in my case, I must own that nearly two decades of involvement in anti-bullying research and practice (a specialism that I did not, of course, choose at random) has compounded my lifelong feelings of affinity with those who find themselves to be, in any way, marginalised. My interest in what lies behind the apparently school-based phenomenon of bullying, which in my opinion is a manifestation of broader patterns of prejudice and discrimination,[16] has led me to concern myself as a researcher with the situation of groups of people who find themselves to be the targets of aggressive marginalisation and violence inside and outside the school gates – LGBTQ+ people, those with special educational needs, and the Indigenous Sámi people of northern Europe (see Minton, 2014, 2016, 2017 for overviews). My reason for doing so – as a white, male, heterosexual, university-educated individual who, whilst having working class origins, is now living something approaching a middle-class lifestyle, with its attendant personal and societal privilege – is that I do not believe that it is in anyway justifiable to leave the addressing of the endemic problems and manifestations of individual and societal disempowerment, and differential privilege, to the disempowered and non-privileged.[17] Hence, I am in full agreement with the feminist scholars and activists who advocate that the women's movement needs men – that men can, and should, be feminists (I certainly identify, and am usually identified, as such), and the LGBTQ+ scholars and activists who similarly value their straight allies (again, I identify, and am usually identified, as such). I feel that my stance here, therefore, is not a condescending one of 'standing up for' those who do not enjoy the privileges that I do, but rather an attempt to 'stand *with*'. As my colleague Patrick Lewis (2018) wrote, 'Ally is not an identity, it is an action'.[18] So at a personal level, I hope that my own contributions to this book, and to this area, would be understood as an as-yet all-too small contribution along these lines.[19]

The structure of this book

As we have seen, the first two sections of Chapter 1 are (i) 'The Scope of this Book' and (ii) 'The Structure of this Book'. The third section, (iii) 'Some Initial Thoughts on the Possibilities for Processes of Truth, Restitution, Reconciliation, and Reclamation', builds on the fact that the results of the practices of (cultural) genocide via 'education' are now gradually being recognised (albeit in an all-too limited number of quarters). In some countries, explicit calls for processes of truth, restitution, reconciliation, and reclamation have been made; and in a smaller number of countries, the beginnings of patterns of restitution and reclamation are becoming tangible. Following this expression of my initial thoughts, further country-specific details are provided in Chapters 3–8 inclusively.

Setting the scene   7

In Chapter 2, four broad theoretical frameworks (or as I refer to them, 'touchstones') are included in the following four sections:

i 'Indigenous as "Other"' (i.e. the idea that Indigenous peoples have been seen and understood by those of European descent, and socially/historically/politically positioned by them, as 'Other' [in the sense that the term is used in phenomenological and existential philosophy]).
ii 'Educational Systems as Agents of (Cultural) Genocide' (this encompasses a critical view of those who planned, implemented, and obscured the true workings of residential schools systems as agents of [cultural] genocide, and indeed, whether the use of term 'cultural genocide' is helpful or, in fact, has the potential to further obfuscate the emergence of truth).
iii 'The Residential School as a "Total Institution"' (in the sense that Goffman (1961/1991) used the term 'total institution'; this in itself permits an analysis of how, in some cases, abuse and neglect continued to occur unabated, and how it was possible to conceal and recast intentions, actions, and inactions, permitting oppressive individuals, organisations, and nation states to position themselves as benevolent influences).
iv 'Assimilation and Nation State Identity' (in the expansion or consolidation of 'their' lands, post-colonial nations invariably met national security concerns in positioning their state as a 'homeland' for a single people, into which Indigenous peoples were to be assimilated). As might be expected, these are sometimes referred to by the authors of the individual country chapters (Chapters 3–8 inclusively), and also inform some of the viewpoints expressed in Chapter 9.

A common, but non-restrictive and certainly non-prescriptive, format was offered to the contributing authors of Chapters 3–8 inclusively. As the editor, I suggested that the contributing authors make inclusions on:

- *Historical contexts:* Accounts of the historical patterns of colonisation pertinent to the country in question; the appropriation by the colonisers of Indigenous lands and resources; and an account of the overall implementation, or attempts to implement, processes of physical and cultural genocide against the Indigenous peoples in the country in question.
- *The operation of the residential schools systems:* Accounts of the setting up and running of the residential schools systems; the overt and covert, avowed and disavowed intentions behind the setting up of the systems and schools; and an account of what actually went on. This was expected to include the documentation of abuse and neglect.
- *The legacies of the residential schools systems:* As well as the impact that the residential schools systems had on Indigenous peoples historically (at the time of their operation), these systems have continued to exert an influence today. This includes the continuing impact on those alive today

who experienced these systems, and somewhat broader influences. There are competing discourses around these issues of legacy, and these are reflected in these sections.
- *Processes of truth, restitution, reconciliation, and reclamation:* Whether there has been a call for, a move towards, or direct experience of processes of truth, restitution, reconciliation, and reclamation will vary considerably, according to country under consideration. Hence, experiences of how Indigenous peoples have attempted to negotiate the legacy of the residential schools will similarly vary across country contexts, and this is reflected in these sections.

As the editor, my intention was that the authors of the individual chapters would use this rather loose common format to reflect the situation *as they and their peoples had understood and lived it* in those countries. That is to say, whilst the chapter authors would have the freedom to write their own accounts, the book was to retain an overall coherence that would permit the possibilities of comparative understandings being made across country contexts.

Some initial thoughts on the possibilities for processes of truth, restitution, reconciliation, and reclamation

I would like to begin this section with an example from the world of sports. In 1995, followers of rugby union[20] witnessed a sight that just a few years earlier would have seemed almost unimaginable: Nelson Mandela, the then President of South Africa, presenting the William Web Ellis Cup (the world championship trophy) to the South African national team, the Springboks. Due to sporting boycotts, South Africa had been permitted to return to international competition only four years back; and Mandela had been released from a twenty-seven-year period of imprisonment only five years back (having been convicted of conspiring to overthrow, and initiating guerrilla warfare against, the then-apartheid South African State). The significance of what has been called one of the 'greatest moments in world sport'[21] did not lie, of course, in anything so trivial as the *Bokke*'s overcoming a recent run of poor form, and their achievement of a narrow-margin victory over their heavily fancied opponents, the New Zealand All Blacks, but rather in the iconic reflection of the monumental changes that had occurred in South Africa over the preceding five years. The apartheid state had been dismantled; and just one year back, Mandela had been elected, in the country's first multiracial elections, as the President of a new 'rainbow nation'. The factors that precipitated these changes were of course, multiple: Growing international pressure, the isolation of South Africa, the comparative progressiveness of the former President F.W. de Klerck (who had ordered Mandela's release from prison), and fears of racial civil war, all undoubtedly had their part to play. But a key element of the operative process of the dismantling of the apartheid regime, and the institutionalisation of multiracial representative democracy in its place, is often held to be the now-famous processes of 'truth and reconciliation'.

Rather than prosecuting people for past crimes, as had been the function of the Nuremberg Trials, the aim for the truth and reconciliation process in South Africa, chaired by Archbishop Desmond Tutu, was to uncover the truth about the human rights violations that had occurred during the apartheid period. Over 22,000 statements were taken, concerning experiences of torture, killings, disappearances and abductions, and severe ill-treatment. Despite certain challenges and limitations (e.g. the top echelons of the military did not cooperate; many felt that the policies and political economy of apartheid did not receive sufficient attention, and the post-Mandela government was slow to implement the TRC's recommendations), the processes were generally regarded as having been successful, and received global attention (Tutu, 2016). To an extent, that image of President Mandela presenting the William Webb Ellis Cup in Johannesburg, dressed for the occasion in a Springboks rugby jersey and cap, seemed to symbolise the extraordinary possibilities that can emerge when people commit to talking and listening to one another.

In the fifteen years that followed the truth and reconciliation processes in South Africa, over twenty truth and reconciliation commissions were established around the world. Hayner (2010) has defined a truth commission as (i) being focussed on past, rather than ongoing, events; (ii) investigating 'a pattern of events that took place over a period of time'; (iii) engaging directly and broadly with the affected population, gathering information on their experiences; (iv) being 'a temporary body, with the aim of concluding with a final report'; and (v) 'officially authorised or empowered by the state under review'. In terms of their application to addressing the historical problems of the residential schooling of Indigenous children, after a four-year period of operation, the Truth and Reconciliation Commission of Canada published its final report in 2015 (Truth and Reconciliation Commission of Canada, 2015). Based heavily on the 'Canadian example', Greenland established a Reconciliation Commission in 2014, with the aim of initiating a process of reconciliation with its long-time colonial ruler, Denmark (DIIS [Danish Institute for International Studies], 2015; Jacobsen, 2014). There have been calls (as yet unheeded) for the establishment of a similar governmentally mandated process in the United States (see, e.g. Lakota People's Law Project, 2015), and the calls for truth processes to be implemented in Norway (to address the past forcible assimilation of the Sámi and Kven peoples; see Andersen, Idivuoma & Somby, 2016; Lile, 2011) were approved by the Norwegian national government in June 2017 (see Minton & Lile, 2018, in press; Verstad, Larsson & Idivuoma, 2017).

Such processes, however, are not universally acclaimed. Drawing examples from Australia, Canada, Guatemala, and Peru, and noting that Indigenous peoples are disproportionately the target of state violence, as well as neoliberal reforms (such as government apologies and truth commissions), Corntassel and Holder (2008) offered compelling evidence that such commissions '.... have not lived up to their potential for transforming inter-group relations when applied in 24 different countries around the world' (p. 469). The fact that reconciliation itself is a neoliberal construct is particularly problematic in the case of Indigenous peoples because, as de Costa (2009) puts it:

> Neoliberalism certainly comprises a range of market-based mechanisms for redistribution – privatisation, liberalisation, structural adjustment – but as a political and ideological project, these policy mechanisms rely on the erosion or outright suppression of collective sources of opposition and alternative systems of social allocation. Within a culture of neoliberalism, then, are social phenomena that valorise autonomous individuals and rational market-agents, or collectives that do not and cannot provide a systematic opposition to a reorientation of policy towards market allocations. (p. 1)

Reconciliation processes permit powerful agencies (such as post-colonial nation states) to effectively place '.... rigid material and symbolic limits upon apologies and truth commissions to promote political and legal stability' (Corntassel & Holder, 2008, p. 465). Their very operation requires the victim(s) of (say) colonisation to become

> .... reconciled to loss, and this is no basis for a sustainable settlement .... We contend that decolonisation and restitution are necessary elements of reconciliation because these are necessary to transform relations with Indigenous communities in the way justice requires. Whether the mechanism attempting to address injustice to Indigenous peoples and remedy wrongs is an apology or a truth and reconciliation commission, it must begin by acknowledging Indigenous peoples' inherent powers of self-determination. [Furthermore] .... If apologies and truth commissions cannot effectively address historic and ongoing injustices committed against indigenous peoples, then they are fundamentally flawed mechanisms for transforming inter-group relations. (pp. 466–467)

Furthermore, and with particular relevance for this book, de Costa (2009) made the observation that

> Neoliberalism shares with Residential Schools policy the objective of undermining collective experiences and identities deemed contrary to economic development and nation-building. Residential schools sought both to deracinate Indigenous children, thereby preparing them for agricultural, industrial and domestic labour, and to erase Indigenous

communities as the loci of alternative economies. Can restitution for this policy then address fully its intentions and consequences? (p. 1)

It is quite understandable that Chrisjohn and Wasacase (2009) (who had the specific example of the Truth and Reconciliation Commission of Canada in mind) were sharply critical of what *could* actually be achieved by processes of truth and reconciliation. They argued that the outcomes of such processes do not, and *cannot*, constitute the *justice* that survivors of residential schools want and deserve, especially given that such processes are often characterised by, and limited to, '... a succession of individuals [the survivors] testifying publicly about painful personal memories' (p. 202). Furthermore, they pointed out that 'In general, the perpetrators of a crime do not get to enforce their own sentence', and asked whether '"having to listen to the victim" [would] be sufficient castigation for rape, child abuse, enslavement, or other more specific abuses associated with residential schooling?' (p. 202), stating that such a process

> ... looks and sounds like some bizarre confessional, where one confesses what was done to him or her, instead of what he or she did, and, in a further perversion, confesses to representatives of those who committed the original offences. Somehow, the crimes of clergy are absolved, not by them accepting responsibility for their actions, but by listening (if they so choose) to victims accuse them of those actions. (p. 203)

What is even more objectionable, according to Chrisjohn and Wasacase (2009), is the assumption or direct suggestion that such public testimony will act as a *catharsis* (in other words, the so-called healing agenda). We must be acutely aware that the crimes of residential school systems cannot be reduced to the injuries experienced by surviving individuals – for residential schools systems were not aimed at *individuals*, but rather entire *peoples*. Even if it is possible that for some individuals '... excoriating one's oppressors [or their successors] in public (even if they are not there) will feel good and validate the marginalised lives the victims of the abuse of Indian residential school have had to live' (p. 203), Chrisjohn and Wasacase (2009) stated that we must ask ourselves

> ... how many days or how many hours will it be before those who testify find themselves back where they started, with the additional task of having to face the enormity of the realisation that public castigation of an identified personal oppressor has not only done nothing to resolve personal issues, but it has let the offending party and the institution standing behind him or her off the hook? (p. 203)

Chrisjohn and Wasacase (2009, p. 204) concluded that the Canadian Truth and Reconciliation Commission was set to be '... a dismissible process that resolves nothing, clarifies nothing, and permits the offenders yet another layer of obscurantism .... Residential school Survivors deserve better'. At the vantage point of just over four years since the publication of the Truth and Reconciliation Commission of Canada's (2015) final report, it is not possible to answer the question of how well that particular body can be said to have delivered (or even, how well it is delivering) its recommended outputs (its ninety-four 'Calls to Action') with any degree of certainty. However, in April 2017, Tracy Bear and Chris Andersen (who are, respectively, an assistant professor, and the dean at the Faculty of Native Studies, University of Alberta) described a 'vigorous' debate having opened up regarding '… the gap between the Canadian federal government's promises to Indigenous peoples, and what might charitably be termed the muted delivery on those promises'. It seems that much remains to be seen and learnt – not least of all by the advocates of truth and reconciliation processes elsewhere that are to be based on the 'Canadian example'.

State apologies made to Indigenous peoples by representatives of the governments of post-colonial states have also been a feature of the last two decades. Indeed, the political scientist Matt James (2008) offered a model via which the authenticity (or otherwise) of state apologies could be adjudicated (three categories may be assigned: (i) apologies, (ii) quasi-apologies, and (iii) non-apologies). According to James (2008), the degree of 'authenticity' can be ascertained according to eight criteria: (i) recording the apology officially in writing, (ii) naming the wrongs, (iii) accepting responsibility, (iv) stating regret, (v) promising non-repetition, (vi) not demanding forgiveness, (vii) non-arbitrariness, and (viii) undertaking, through ceremony or reparation, efforts to indicate sincerity. An 'authentic' (or 'genuine') apology should satisfy all eight criteria; 'quasi-apologies' and 'non-apologies' meet progressively fewer of the criteria. However, in her review of such settler-state apologies, Sheryl Lightfoot (2015) made the following point:

> A state apology to Indigenous peoples must meet two criteria in order to be meaningful in this way. It must, first, fully and comprehensively acknowledge the wrongs of the past and/or the present. Second, the state must make a credible commitment to do things differently, to make substantial changes in its policy behaviour, in the future. Any state apology that fails to deliver both of these two elements will not be meaningful in the eyes of Indigenous recipients, regardless of how 'authentically' it is delivered by the state, as judged by the James criteria. (p. 17)

Furthermore,

> A meaningful apology cannot serve to solidify the status quo of a colonial set of power relations in Indigenous–state relationships. It cannot be a one-sided gesture of the state that serves its own needs for guilt

alleviation while ignoring the needs of the victims, or even expecting their automatic forgiveness simply because an apology has been offered. In moving beyond Judeo-Christian traditions and toward a more worldly view of reconciliation and restoration of just relationships, forgiveness by the victim should not be the goal of an apology. Rather, a meaningful apology must move beyond rhetoric. It must serve as a gesture of change, and it should be the fulcrum of a credible commitment to change the Indigenous–state relationship. (p. 35)

So having introduced the respective hopes of some, and the concerns and criticisms of others, for state apologies, and processes of truth and reconciliation, our thinking should surely not be confined to such types of measures; surely, even the most ardent supporters of state apologies and truth and reconciliation processes would be loath to conceive of them as panaceas. What of reclamation, then? To bookend this section somewhat, let us return to that late June day in Johannesburg in 1995, and think about the victorious Springboks' aforementioned opponents, the New Zealand All Blacks. That day, immediately before the start of the match, and as has been the case in all their Test match appearances since 1905, the All Blacks performed a *haka*.[22] This traditional opening challenge is world-famous, even amongst people who pay little or even no attention whatsoever to rugby union. Whilst Māori players have always featured strongly in All Blacks rugby, so too do New Zealanders of other ethnic origins (including those of European ancestry, and those of Pacific Islands birth or heritage) who, of course, always perform the opening *haka* alongside their Māori teammates. Hence, the post-colonial, multi-ethnic[23] country of Aotearoa/New Zealand precedes the playing of its national sport (which international results show, it generally does so without parallel) with a demonstration of unity and challenge in an *Indigenous* ceremony. A perhaps optimistic interpretation of this sporting tradition is that it is a very internationally visible example of how at least some Indigenous 'space' has been reclaimed in a post-colonial society. In the Aotearoa/New Zealand chapter of this book (Chapter 3), other (less internationally visible) examples of Māori reclamation of culture and cultural artefacts within historical, and especially contemporary, Aotearoa/New Zealand society, and the often troublesome paths that have been taken towards negotiating and effecting such reclamation, will be reviewed.

A polar opposite position, perhaps, to such processes of Indigenous cultural reclamation within post-colonial societies, has been called for and actions taken towards Indigenous separatism and the establishment of sovereign states – a logical correlate, or perhaps realisation, it seems, of the more generally upheld right to Indigenous self-determination.[24] Again, in terms of international visibility, perhaps the most famous example of such an effort was the formal declaration, in 1973, that the territory of Wounded Knee, South Dakota was the 'Independent Oglala Nation'; Indeed, a delegation travelled to New York in an unsuccessful attempt to have its sovereign nation status recognised by the United Nations (Crow Dog & Erdoes, 2011; Means, 1996; Reinhardt, 2007).[25] A similar strike for sovereign status for the Lakota people was raised by a body known as the 'Lakota Freedom Delegation' (led by Russell Means, who was a leader within the American Indian Movement before, famously during and after the 1973 'Wounded Knee Incident', see endnote 25), which travelled to Washington DC in December 2007 in order to declare the independence of the 'Republic of Lakotah'.[26] To date, however, this independence has not been recognised by any sovereign state, or by any elected tribal government within the United States. Yet if the only solution which apparently presents itself is a continuance of 'living within' post-colonial countries, the extent to which 'reclamation' can be fully realised, and also what is meant, and can actually be meant, when this term is used, will remain, to at least some, highly questionable.

As a diverse set of individuals, Lakota people do not, nor can they be expected to, speak with one voice on this, or any other issue. As noted above, the Lakota People's Law Project has petitioned the United States Congress to establish a governmentally mandated body similar to the Canadian Truth and Reconciliation Commission, and in doing so, stated their belief that 'Formally *acknowledging the painful truth* will prepare the way for a new era of reconciliation and healing' (Lakota People's Law Project, 2015, p. 4; italics mine). Again, as another diverse set of individuals, the authors of Chapters 3–8 will, of course, see different possibilities (including, sometimes, the non-possibilities) for the processes of reconciliation, restitution, and reclamation. However, it is hoped that through this book, the unvarnished *truth* of *what happened* to Indigenous children in residential schools across a variety of contexts can emerge; and that the light of truth can also be shed on *why* it happened, *what that has meant* and *still means* for Indigenous peoples, and perhaps also *what can be done now* to untangle and address these experiences – in reconciliation, restitution, reclamation, or whatever else that 'untangling' and 'addressing' might look like.

Notes

1. The Kven people are the descendants of emigrants to Norway from neighbouring northern parts of Sweden and Finland in the eighteenth and nineteenth centuries, who were escaping poverty and famine. The present day Kven population in Norway is estimated to be between 10,000 and 15,000. In the English language, an interesting article on the history and language of the Kven people has been written by Marjut Aikio (1989).
2. It is instructive to compare Niemi's comment here with Adams' citation (1995, p. 27) of the American Merrill Gates' (who was the president of the 1883 Lake Mohonk Conference of prominent philanthropists, missionaries, social and educational reformers, and politicians) words in 1891: 'The time for fighting the Indian tribes is passed .... We are going to conquer the Indians by a standing army of school-teachers, armed with ideas, winning victories by industrial training, and by the gospel of love and the gospel of work'.

3. It is notable that fatal consequences of such spiritual incursions were evident in the witchcraft trials of the seventeenth century – of the 150 people who were executed for sorcery in northern Norway between 1621 and 1663, all of the males were Sámi (Hagen, 2015).
4. As Adams (1995, p. 5) puts it: 'As the Iriquois, the Shawnee, and the Arapaho would eventually all discover, the white man's superior technology, hunger for land, and ethnocentrism seemingly know no bounds. The white threat to Indians came in many forms: Smallpox, missionaries, Conestoga wagons, barbed wire, and smoking locomotives. *And in the end, it came in the form of schools*' [emphasis mine].
5. Historian David Stannard suggested a best working estimate of 95 per cent (although he also opined that '… even figures of 95 and 98 and 99 per cent destruction may time and again be too low' (Stannard, 1992, p. 129)), and a conservative estimate of the pre-Columbus Indigenous population of the Americas of between 75 and 100 million (Stannard, 1992). Elsewhere, I have suggested that in order to avoid being overwhelmed by these numbers, and thereby losing the human sense of the destruction, a modern-day European equivalent of the reduction of the combined populations of France, Belgium, the Netherlands, and Switzerland to that of the single city of Paris (Minton, 2016). Stannard also took issue with the emphasis that many historians have placed on the spreading of 'Old World' diseases (to which Indigenous peoples in the Western Hemisphere had no inborn resistance) in accounting for the decline in the native population: '… by focussing almost entirely on disease, by displacing responsibility for the mass killing onto an army of invading microbes, contemporary authors increasingly have created the impression that the eradication of those tens of millions of people was inadvertent …. The near total destruction of the Western Hemisphere's native people was neither inadvertent nor inevitable. From almost the instant of first human contact between Europe and the Americas firestorms of microbial pestilence *and* purposeful genocide began laying waste the American natives' (Stannard, 1992, p. xii).
6. This took place on 29 December 1890, and involved the slaughter of 153 (although most of the wounded died, so in all, almost 300) of a band of 350 Minneconjou and Hunkpapa Lakota (120 men, 230 women and children) in the act of surrender by four divisions of the US Army's Seventh Cavalry Regiment. Subsequently, the Congressional Medal of Honor, the US Army's highest commendation, was awarded to eighteen of the soldiers responsible for the massacre (Green, 1994) which, despite intermittent campaigns, have never been rescinded. This atrocity marked the end of the so-called Indian Wars, as thereafter, none of the surviving Indigenous peoples in the territory claimed by the United States could be deemed to be living freely; aside from a few so-called outlaws, most had by then been confined to reservations (Brown, 1970/1991; Stannard, 1992). A moving eyewitness account of these events has been provided by Black Elk (b. 1863, d. 1950), an Oglala medicine man, who arrived shortly after the massacre, and helped to rescue some of the wounded (see Black Elk, 1972).
7. The Carlisle Indian Industrial School was located in Carlisle, Pennsylvania, and between its founding in 1879 and its closure in 1918, enrolled over 10,000 Indigenous children from 140 peoples. Whilst only 158 of these children ever fully graduated (Hunt, 2012), around 180 were buried on the school premises (these were the ones who had died of tuberculosis, and due to fears of contagion, their bodies were not sent home to the families, as was the practice with other causes of death (Witmer, 1993)).
8. This refers to General Philip A. Sheridan's reply to Tosawi [Silver Knife], who, in 1864, was bringing in his band of Comanche to surrender. When presented to Sheridan, Tosawi spoke his own name, and two words of broken English:

'Tosawi, good Indian'. Sheridan's reply was, 'The only good Indians I ever saw were dead'. In Brown's (1970/1991, p. 172) words, Sheridan's statement was subsequently '… honed into an American aphorism: "The only good Indian is a dead Indian"'.

9. Adams (1995, p. 274) records that one Carlisle school commencement, Reverend J.A. Lippincott proclaimed, 'The Indian is DEAD in you. Let all that is Indian within you die! You cannot become truly American citizens, industrious, intelligent, cultured, civilised until the INDIAN within you is DEAD'. On hearing this, Pratt jumped to his feet, with the words, 'I never fired a bigger shot and never hit the bull's eye more centre'.

10. For example, in addition to its persistence in the popular memory, the phrase appears as the title of four publications in my possession. Three of these made deliberate ironic use of the phrase, in setting out their critical treatments (Altaha & Kraus, 2012; Bess, 2000; Churchill, 2004), whilst a 1923 report made use of it as an already well-known starting point (Green, 1923).

11. The Canadian federal government has estimated that approximately 30 per cent of its Indigenous children – 150,000 individuals – were enrolled in its residential schools (Truth and Reconciliation Commission of Canada, 2015). The Chair of Canada's Truth and Reconciliation Commission, Justice Murray Sinclair, stated that at least 6,000 aboriginal children had died while in the residential school system (CBC News, 2015). However, in its final report, whilst the Commission could confirm the deaths of 2,040 named individuals and those of a further 1,161 unnamed individuals (hence, a total of 3,201 reported deaths), it stated that the final number was '… not likely ever to be known in full' (Truth and Reconciliation Commission of Canada, 2015, p. 99).

12. It is evident from his memoirs, and much that has been written about Pratt, that he genuinely considered himself to be a 'friend of the Indian', and above all, in the 'noble cause' of saving the Indians from physical extinction by removing their children from the reservations, and educating them into what he considered to be *civilised* ways (see Adams, 1995; Pratt, 2004). As shall hopefully become apparent throughout this book, Pratt's social and educational philosophies, and his famous aphorism, look very different indeed today when viewed through Indigenous eyes, or the lens of genocide.

13. This was the so-called Meriam Report (nicknamed for Dr Lewis Meriam, who led the survey team), whose title was *The Problem of Indian Administration*. (Although widely referred to, it has not, to the best of my knowledge, been digitised, but it is available from the website National Indian Law Library (2017)). Bear (2008) highlighted the following passages: '"The survey staff finds itself obliged to say frankly and unequivocally that the provisions for the care of the Indian children in boarding schools are grossly inadequate" …. "At a few, very few schools, the farm and the dairy are sufficiently productive to be a highly important factor in raising the standard of the diet, but even at the best schools these sources do not fully meet the requirements for the health and development of the children. At the worst schools, the situation is serious in the extreme" …. "The term 'child labour' is used advisedly. The labour of children as carried on in Indian boarding schools would, it is believed, constitute a violation of child labour laws in most countries"' (Bear, 2008, pp. 8–9). The 'Recommendations for Immediate Action' made in Chapter 2 of the Meriam Report do not appear to have been acted upon.

14. Canada is perhaps unusual in the number of books which have been written on the subject, this having been sustained largely through the activities of independent publishers in the western part of the country.

15. A 'white saviour' is a white person who acts to help non-white people, but with a strong element of self-interest (most often, the expectation of being congratulated for having done so) (see Cole, 2012, for review). The phrase has been applied in a variety of contexts, including some of those (largely privileged, middle class) white people who spend time volunteering in developing countries during 'gap years' prior to and within their university and professional careers – and heavily document their experiences in social media posts directed at the folks back home. Indeed, it was reported recently that the Norwegian Students' and Academics' International Assistance Fund has created a guide for such potential volunteers called '*How Not to Act Like a White Saviour while volunteering in Africa*' (see Quartz Media, 2017). That being said, the term 'white saviour' is probably most often used in describing certain film narratives, that is, where a white lead character somehow 'rescues' non-white people from their plight – commercially successful twenty-first-century examples include *The Blind Side, Blood Diamond, Django Unchained, Gran Torino, The Soloist,* and *Twelve Years a Slave*. Russell Means, an Oglala Lakota, and a high-profile Indian activist from the late 1960s until his death in 2012, described *Dances with Wolves* as a 'terrible white saviour movie': 'Remember "*Lawrence of Arabia*"? That was "Lawrence of the Plains"' (Means, 2009).

16. This point of view is, seemingly, not shared by the overwhelming majority of researchers and practitioners in the field of anti-bullying, including those who are responsible for the design, implementation, and evaluation of anti-bullying programmes. The view that 'bullying can happen to anyone' – which is true, and is helpful in defusing the feelings of self-blame so often internalised by targets of abuse – seems to have been maintained above, beyond, and at the expense of the observation that any child could make (and which is substantiated in a considerable body of empirical research) that bullying happens more frequently to certain groups of people than it does to other groups of people. As a consequence, the operations of existing broad-scale anti-bullying programmes are principally characterised by 'awareness raising' and 'behaviour management', rather than by addressing underlying features such as prejudice and discrimination. I feel that a shift in focus may well help to improve the documented limited effectiveness of such interventions. Whilst few people, other than some of my students and closest colleagues, share my opinions in this respect, I have expanded on them at various lengths elsewhere (see, e.g. Minton, 2014, 2016, 2017).

17. In Ireland, the type of attitude I have implied here as being non-justifiable is sometimes referred to as '*mé féin-ism*' (from the Irish, '*mé féin*', 'myself'), and someone who holds such an attitude might be known as a '*mé féin-er*' (The British English phrase 'the "I'm alright, Jack" attitude' is conceptually the same). Increasingly, in my experience, people in Ireland, the United Kingdom, and the United States (and this might well be true of other countries) seem to be encouraged by the mass media towards *mé féin-ism*, for example, in considering the decision-making of their political representatives solely on the basis of how it will affect them personally. To further elucidate, potential decisions around budgets by governments are usually presented in the news in terms of how the various proposed measures will affect the take-home pay of various categories of individuals – 'What the budget will mean for you/your pocket', and the like. Far less frequently, it seems to me, is the ordinary citizen in a Western country asked to reflect upon political decisions in the context of thinking about to what sort of a society she or he wishes to belong.

18. This quote comes from the second of the two typically insightful articles entitled, *What Does It Mean to Be an Ally* (Parts I and II), which were based on a presentation he had given at the 11th International Congress of Qualitative Inquiry. Lewis

18 Stephen James Minton

(2018, p. 46) continued, 'Non-Indigenous white settlers must learn this, understand this and act it. As Chelsea Vowel once said, "Hope when things start going down that non-Indigenous allies remember to stay in their own canoe on discussions of community accountability"'.
19. My colleague, Shawn Wilson (an Opaskwayak Cree from northern Manitoba, who is currently Director of Research at Gnibi College of Indigenous Australian Peoples, Southern Cross University, Australia), has illustrated, with his usual insight and clarity another disturbing reality, which began in what he calls the 'assimilationist' phase of Indigenous research (1940–1970): 'Non-Aboriginal people became experts on Aboriginal people. Anthropologists, archaeologists, physicians, psychologists, historians, professors, and classroom teachers who had studied Aboriginal people, or who might even have read a study *about* Aboriginal people, felt qualified to pass on their learning .... In Canada, this practice continues. In some universities, entire departments of native studies or of anthropology are staffed by non-Aboriginal faculty members who claim to be, and are recognised as, "Indian experts" by their colleagues .... The study *of* and *on* (but never *by*) Aboriginal people became and remains profitable business for academics who want to advance their careers' (Wilson, 2008, p. 49). In my own far more limited experience, I have been struck by how often it is the case amongst the Indigenous scholars I know who are employed in university departments of Indigenous or Native Studies, that the bulk of their departmental colleagues are non-Indigenous. I can also confirm that I have no such career-advancement aspirations; and, being based at a British university, neither would any such 'opportunities' be foreseeable, even if I were to be of such an exploitative mindset.
20. I am aware of the somewhat perverse irony in citing an example drawn from a sport that was spread via patterns of European (and in this case, British Imperial) colonisation, and ask the reader to bear with me.
21. In the retrospective 'best ever' lists that made up so many television programmes at the turn of the twenty-first century, this 'moment' made regular appearances in the 'sports' categories. It was also the subject of a 2009 American/South African film entitled, *Invictus*, which was directed by Clint Eastwood, and starred Morgan Freeman and Matt Damon.
22. War *haka* (the word is plural, too, in both the English and Māori languages) were, in traditional Māori culture, the dances performed by warriors prior to battle in order to intimidate opponents. However, there are many types of *haka*, which can be performed in order toto welcome guests, to acknowledge significant achievements, or on other special occasions (including funerals). The *haka* performed most frequently by the All Blacks (and performed at the afore-mentioned 1995 match) is a traditional war *haka* known as '*Ka Mate*' (which is usually translated into English as 'This is death', or sometimes, 'I may die'), although since 2005, the team has also performed a specifically composed *haka* called '*Kapa o Pango*' (which is translated into English as 'Team in Black'). *Haka* are performed by many Aotearoa/New Zealand groups, including their national representative teams in other sports (Australian rules football; basketball; ice hockey; a modified version in paralympic rugby, which is also sometimes known as 'murderball'; and rugby league).
23. New Zealanders of Māori descent are a population minority, and New Zealanders of European descent are a population majority. Specifically, the 2013 Aotearoa/New Zealand Census revealed that 74.0 per cent of New Zealanders were of European descent, 14.9 per cent Māori, 11.8 per cent Asian, 7.4 per cent Pacific Islanders, 1.2 per cent Middle Eastern/Latin American/African, and 1.7 per cent of 'other' descent. The cumulative totals reveal, of course, that a significant proportion of the country's inhabitants are of mixed ethnicity (Stats, 2017).

24. The content of this right is, in fact, rather unclear in the international legislative and policy frameworks. Article 1 of the Covenant on Civil and Political Rights (CCPR), and the Covenant on Economic, Social, and Cultural Rights (CESCR), includes the wording, 'All peoples have the right of self-determination. By virtue of that right they freely determine their political status and freely pursue their economic, social, and cultural development'; and, in the UN Declaration on the Rights of Indigenous Peoples (UNDRIP) (2007), it was explicitly stated in Article 3 that 'Indigenous peoples have the right to self-determination. By virtue of that right, they freely determine their political status and freely pursue their economic, social, and cultural development'. However, UNDRIP was equally explicit that according to their understandings, this right does not extend to secession: In article 46, it is stated that 'Nothing in this Declaration may be interpreted as implying any action which would dismember or impair, totally or in part, the territorial integrity or political unity of sovereign and independent States'. Hence, under these international frameworks, the content of the collective right to Indigenous self-determination remains unclear, although little doubt is left as to which powers will ultimately administer it (Minton et al., in press). I am greatly indebted to my friend and colleague Dr Hadi Strømmen Lile for this particular argument, which appeared in the afore-referenced co-authored chapter.

25. This declaration was made during the seventy-one-day occupation (27 February–08 May 1973; the so-called Wounded Knee Incident') of the town of Wounded Knee, South Dakota (the significance of which, if not already known, might be recalled from endnote 6), by two hundred Oglala Lakota residents of Pine Ridge reservation, who were joined by activists from the American Indian Movement, and supporters from North America and beyond, in demanding the removal of Oglala Sioux Tribal Chairman Richard 'Dick' Wilson from office (Crow Dog & Erdoes, 2011; Means, 1996; Reinhardt, 2007). Wilson had been accused of corruption, the intimidation and abuse of political opponents, and cronyism (specifically, systematic prejudice against full-blooded Oglala people). Additionally, many in the American Indian Movement, and a not insignificant proportion of Pine Ridge Residents, did not accept the validity of the system of tribal chairs (see Means, 1996). During the occupation, the Wounded Knee site was cordoned off by US Marshals and FBI agents; there were exchanges in gunfire, resulting in the deaths of two Indians, and injuries to thirteen others (see Crow Dog & Erdoes, 2011; Reihardt, 2007).

26. The proposed 'Republic of Lakotah' comprises an area of 77,200 square miles, within the present-day American states of North Dakota, Montana, Nebraska, South Dakota, and Wyoming. Its borders are those which were established at the 1851 Treaty of Fort Laramie between the United States and representatives of the Arapaho, Arikara, Assiniboine, Cheyenne, Crow, Hidatsa, Mandan, and Sioux nations (Republic of Lakotah, 2017).

References

Adams, D.W. (1995). *Education for Extinction: American Indians and the Boarding School Experience 1875–1928*. Lawrence, KS: University Press of Kansas.

Aikio, M. (1989). The Kven and cultural linguistic pluralism. *Acta Borealia: A Nordic Journal of Circumpolar Societies*, 6(1): 86–97.

Altaha, N. & Kraus, S. (2012). *Kill the Indian, Save the Man: Native American Historical Trauma in College Students*. Durango, CO: Psychology Department, Fort Lewis College.

Andersen, A.N. (2014). *The Greenlandic Reconciliation Process: Project Description.* Available online: http://www.martinbreum.dk/wp-content/uploads/2014/12/Carlsbergansøgning-2014-EV.pdf [Accessed April, 2019].

Andersen, S., Idivuoma, A.M. & Somby, L.I. (2016). Norskspråklige lærere var et overgrep fra norske myndigheter. [Norwegian-language teachers were an abuse by the Norwegian authorities]. *NRK Sápmi.* Available online: http://www.nrk.no/sapmi/professor_-_-norske-myndigheter-forbrot-seg-mot-barna-pa-internatskolene.-1.12906901 [Accessed April, 2019].

Armitage, A. (1995). *Comparing the Policy of Aboriginal Assimilation: Australia, Canada, and New Zealand.* Vancouver, Canada: University of British Columbia Press.

Bear, C. (2008). American Indian boarding schools haunt many. *Morning Edition,* May 12.

Bear, T. & Andersen, C. (2017). Three years later, is Canada keeping its truth and reconciliation Commission promises? *Toronto Globe and Mail,* April 21.

Bess, J. (2000). 'Kill the Indian and save the man!' Charles Eastman surveys his past. *Wicazo Sa Review,* 15(1): 7–28.

Black Elk, N. (1972). *Black Elk Speaks: Being the Life Story of a Holy Man of the Oglala Sioux, as Told Through John G. Neihardt (Flaming Rainbow).* New York: Bison Books.

Brown, D. (1970/1991). *Bury my Heart at Wounded Knee: An Indian History of the West.* London: Vintage.

Bruchac, J. & Smelcer, J. (2013). *The Boarding School Experience in American Indian Literature.* Available online: http://www.graphicclassics.com/pgs/American%20Indian%20Boarding%20Schools.pdf [Accessed April, 2019].

CBC News (2015). Residential schools findings point to 'cultural genocide,' commission chair says. Available online: http://www.cbc.ca/news/politics/residential-schools-findings-point-to-cultural-genocide-commission-chair-says-1.3093580 [Accessed April, 2019].

Chrisjohn, R.D. & Wasacase, T. (2009). Half-truths and whole lies: Rhetoric in the 'apology' and the truth and reconciliation commission. In G. Younging, J. Dewar & M. DeGagné (eds.), *Response, Responsibility, and Renewal: Canada's Truth and Reconciliation Journey.* Ottawa, Canada: Aboriginal Healing Foundation.

Chrisjohn, R.D., Wasacase, T., Nussey, L., Smith, A., Legault, M., Loiselle, P. & Bourgeois, M. (2002). Genocide and Indian residential schooling: The past is present. In R.D. Wiggers & A.L. Griffiths (eds.), *Canada and International Law: Peacekeeping and War Crimes in the Modern Era.* (pp. 229–266). Halifax, Canada: Centre for Foreign Policy Studies, Dalhousie University.

Chrisjohn, R.D., Young, S.L. & Maraun, M. (1994). *The Circle Game: Shadows and Substance in the Indian Residential School Experience in Canada: A Report to the Royal Commission on Aboriginal Peoples.* Ottawa, Canada: Royal Commission on Aboriginal Peoples.

Chrisjohn, R.D., Young, S.L. & Maraun, M. (2006). *The Circle Game: Shadows and Substance in the Indian Residential School Experience in Canada.* Penticton, BC: Theytus Books.

Churchill, W. (2004). *Kill the Indian, Save the Man: The Genocidal Impact of American Indian Residential Schools.* San Fransisco, CA: City Lights Books.

Cole, T. (2012). The white saviour industrial complex. *The Atlantic,* March 21.

Corntassel, J. & Holder, C. (2008). Who's sorry now? Government apologies, truth commissions, and indigenous self-determination in Australia, Canada, Guatemala, and Peru. *Human Rights Review,* 9(4): 465–489.

Crow Dog, M. & Erdoes, R. (2011). *Lakota Woman.* New York: Grove Atlantic Inc.

de Costa, R. (2009). Reconciliation and Neoliberalism. Presented at the Canadian Political Science Association Annual Conference 2009, Carleton University, Ottawa, ON, Canada, May 27–29.

DIIS (Dansk Institut for internationale studier) [Danish Institute for International Studies]. (2015). New research project on Greenland's reconciliation process. Available online: http://www.diis.dk/en/node/4791 [Accessed April, 2019].

Fontaine, T. (2010). *Broken Circle: The Dark Legacy of Indian Residential Schools: A Memoir*. Victoria, BC: Heritage House Publishing Co.

Goffman, E. (1961/1991). *Asylums: Essays on the Social Situation of Mental Patients and Other Inmates*. London: Penguin.

Green, J. (1994). The medals of wounded knee. *Nebraska History*, 75: 200–208.

Green, R. (1923). 'Kill the Indian and save the man': Indian education in the United States. In P.F., Molin & M. I., Hultgren (eds.), *To Lead and to Serve: American Indian Education at Hampton Institute 1878–1923* (pp. 9–13). Virginia Beach, VA: Virginia Foundation for the Humanities and Public Policy.

Hagen, R.B. (2015). *De Nordnorske Hekseprosessene* [The Northern Norwegian Witch Trials] 1593–1695. Tromsø, Norway: University of Tromsø: Institute for History and Religion.

Haig-Brown, C. (1989). *Resistance and Renewal: Surviving the Indian Residential School*. Vancouver, Canada: Arsenal Pulp Press.

Hansen, K.L., Melhus, M., Høgmo, A. & Lund, E. (2008). Ethnic discrimination and bullying in the Sami and non-Sami populations in Norway: The SAMINOR study. *International Journal of Circumpolar Health*, 67(1): 97–113.

Hansen, K.L., Minton, S.J., Friborg, O. & Sørlie, T. (2016). Discrimination amongst arctic indigenous Sami and non-Sami populations in Norway: The SAMINOR 2 questionnaire study. *Journal of Northern Studies*, 10(2): 45–84.

Hayner, P. (2010). *Unspeakable Truths: Transitional Justice and the Challenge of Truth Commissions*. London: Routledge.

Hunt, D. (2012). BIA's impact on Indian education is an education in bad education. *Indian Country Today*, January 30.

Jacobs, M.D. (2006). *Indian Boarding Schools in Comparative Perspective: The Removal of Indigenous Children in the United States and Australia, 1880–1940*. Lincoln, NE: University of Nebraska, Lincoln, Faculty Publications.

Jacobsen, S. (2014). Greenland commission will probe Danish colonial abuses. Reuters, May 2. Available online: http://www.reuters.com/article/us-greenland-denmark-primeminister-idUSBREA410J920140502 [Accessed December, 2017].

James, M. (2008). Wrestling with the past: Apologies, quasi-apologies, and non-apologies in Canada. In M. Gibney, R. Howard-Hassman, J-M. Coicaud & N. Steiner (eds.), *The Age of Apology: The West Faces Its Own Past*. Philadelphia PA: University of Pennsylvania Press.

Lakota People's Law Project (2015). *Truth and Reconciliation in the United States of America: A Call for the U.S. to Reconcile with the American Indigenous Community over the Mistreatment of Indian Children in Boarding Schools*. Bismarck, ND: Lakota People's Law Project.

Lewis, P.J. (2018). What does it mean to be an ally? (Part II). *International Review of Qualitative Research*, 11(1): 46–50.

Lightfoot, S. (2015). Settler-state apologies to indigenous peoples: A normative framework and comparative assessment. *Native American and Indigenous Studies*, 2(1): 15–39.

Lile, H.K. (2011). FNs barnekonvensjon artikkel 29 (1) om formålet med opplæring: En rettssosiologisk studie om hva barn lærer om det samiske folk. [The UN's Convention on Children Article 29(1) on the purpose of education: A sociology of law study of what children learn about the Sami people]. PhD thesis: Faculty of Law, University of Oslo (ISSN 1890-2375).

Means, R. (1996). *Where White Men Fear to Tread: The Autobiography of Russell Means.* New York: St. Martin's Press.
Means, R. (2009). Russell Means interview with Dan Skye of High Times. May 20. Available online: http://www.russellmeansfreedom.com/tag/freedom [Accessed April, 2019].
Milloy, J.S. (1999). *A National Crime: The Canadian Government and the Residential School System.* Winnipeg, MB: University of Manitoba Press.
Minde, H. (2005). Assimilation of the Sámi – Implementation and consequences. *Journal of Indigenous Peoples' Rights,* 3: 1–33.
Minton, S.J. (2014). Prejudice and effective anti-bullying intervention: Evidence from the bullying of 'minorities'. *Nordic Psychology,* 66(2): 108–120.
Minton, S.J. (2016). *Marginalisation and Aggression from Bullying to Genocide: Critical Educational and Psychological Perspectives.* Rotterdam, The Netherlands: Brill.
Minton, S.J. (2017). Why aren't we beating bullying? *The Psychologist,* 30: 40–43.
Minton, S.J. & Lile, H.S. (2018). A conversation about the proposed truth commission in Norway for the Sámi and Kven peoples: What can be learnt from truth and reconciliation processes elsewhere? 14th International Congress of Qualitative Inquiry, University of Illinois in Urbana-Champaign, USA, May 16–19.
Minton, S.J. & Lile, H.S. (2019). Considering a truth commission in Norway with respect to the past forcible assimilation of the Sámi people. In S. Wilson, A. Breen & L. DuPré (eds.), *Research Is Reconciliation?* Toronto, ON: Canadian Scholars Press.
Minton, S.J., Wilson, S., Lile, H.S., Hansen, K.L. & Svalastog, A.L. (in press). Research ethics and the Sámi people: Self-governance, collective consent and the importance of historical contexts. In L. Briskman, D. Zion & A. Bagheri (eds.), *Indigenous Bioethics: Local and Global Perspectives.* Singapore: World Scientific Publishing.
National Indian Law Library (2017). *Meriam Report: The Problem of Indian Administration (1928).* Available online: http://www.narf.org/nill/resources/meriam.html [Accessed April, 2019].
Palmater, P.M. (2015a). Canada was killing Indians, not cultures. *Telesur,* June 8.
Palmater, P.M. (2015b). Canadian and church officials must be accountable for genocide. *Telesur,* June 17.
Pratt, W.H. (2004). *Battlefield and Classroom: Four Decades with the American Indian, 1867–1904.* (ed.), R.M. Utley. Norman, OK: University of Oklahoma Press.
Quartz Media (2017). *A Guide on How Not to Act Like a 'White Savior' While Volunteering in Africa.* Available online: https://qz.com/1150047/voluntourism-a-guide-on-how-not-to-act-like-a-white-savior-while-volunteering-in-africa/ [Accessed April, 2019].
Reinhardt, A.D. (2007). *Ruling Pine Ridge.* Lubbock, TX: Texas Tech University Press.
Republic of Lakotah (2017). Home page. Available online: http://www.republicoflakotah.com [Accessed April, 2019].
Sellars, B. (2013). *They Called Me Number One: Secrets and Survival at an Indian Residential School.* Vancouver, Canada: Talon Books.
Smith, A. (2009). *Indigenous Peoples and Boarding Schools: A Comparative Study.* Prepared for the Secretariat of the United Nations Permanent Forum on Indigenous Peoples. Available online: https://www.un.org/esa/socdev/unpfii/documents/E_C_19_2009_crp1.pdf [Accessed April, 2019].
Somby, Á. (2015). *Oral presentation at the Creative Time Summit 2015: The Geography of Learning.* Venice, Italy: Venice Art Biennale.
Stannard, D.E. (1992). *American Holocaust: The Conquest of the New World.* Oxford: Oxford University Press.

Stats N.Z. (2017). Home page. Available online: https://www.stats.govt.nz [Accessed April, 2019].
Truth and Reconciliation Commission of Canada (2015). *Honouring the Truth, Reconciling for the Future: Summary of the Final Report of the Truth and Reconciliation Commission of Canada.* Available online: http://www.trc.ca [Accessed April, 2019].
Tutu, D. (2016). Truth and reconciliation commission South Africa (TRC). *Encyclopædia Britannica.* Available online: http://www.britannica.com/topic/Truth-and-Reconciliation-Commission-South-Africa [Accessed April, 2019].
Urbanczyk, P. (1980). Formation and Structure of Archaeological Multi-Strata Sites: Medieval Arctic Norway. Ph.D. thesis, Polish Academy of Sciences, Warsaw.
Verstad, A.B., Larsson, C-G. & Idivuoma, A.M. (2017). JA til sannhetskommisjonen på Stortinget. [YES to the truth commission in the national parliament). *NRK Sápmi,* June 7. Available online: https://www.nrk.no/sapmi/ja-til-sannhetskommisjonen-pa-stortinget-1.13549426 [Accessed April, 2019].
Wilson, S. (2008). *Research is Ceremony: Indigenous Research Methods.* Halifax & Winnipeg: Fernwood Publishing.
Witmer, L.R. (1993). *The Indian Industrial School: Carlisle, Pennsylvania, 1879–1918.* Carlisle, PA: Cumberland County Historical Society.

Chapter 2

Some theoretical touchstones

Stephen James Minton

Indigenous as 'Other'

First, let us consider what can be meant, in terms of international law, when the word 'Indigenous' is used. A definition of the word 'Indigenous' was put forward by Martínez-Cobo in 1981, in his report as Special Rapporteur to the United Nations on Discrimination against Indigenous Populations:

> Indigenous communities, peoples, and nations are those that, having a historical continuity with pre-invasion and pre-colonial societies that developed on their territories, consider themselves distinct from other sectors of the societies now prevailing in those territories, or parts of them. They form at present non-dominant sectors of society and are determined to preserve, develop, and transmit to future generations their ancestral territories, and their ethnic identity, as the basis of their continued existence as peoples, in accordance with their own cultural patterns, social institutions and legal systems. (p. 10)

There are three UN bodies that are mandated to deal with the concerns of Indigenous peoples: (i) the *Permanent Forum on Indigenous Issues* (UNPFII), which is '… a high-level advisory body to the Economic and Social Council', established on 28 July 2000 by Resolution 2000/22, and meeting yearly (for ten days) since 2002, which is mandated to deal with Indigenous issues related to '… economic and social development, culture, the environment, education, health and human rights' (United Nations, 2017a); (ii) the *Expert Mechanism on the Rights of Indigenous Peoples* (EMRIP), which was established as a subsidiary body of the UN Human Rights Council in 2007 under Resolution 6/36, and consists of seven independent experts, and is mandated to provide the Human Rights Council with '… expertise and advice on the rights of Indigenous peoples', and to provide assistance (on request) to UN member states on the promotion, protection and fulfilment of these rights (United Nations, 2017b); and (iii) the *Special Rapporteur on the Rights of Indigenous Peoples*, appointed for the first time in 2001 by the UN Commission on Human Rights, who reports annually to the UN Human Rights Council and is mandated to promote '... good practices, including new laws, government programmes, and constructive agreements between indigenous peoples and states, to implement international standards concerning the rights of indigenous peoples', to provide country reports and thematic studies on human rights situations of Indigenous peoples in selected countries, and to address '... specific cases of alleged violations of the rights of indigenous peoples through communications with Governments and others' (United Nations, 2017c).

According to United Nations' understandings, the rights of Indigenous peoples (as advised upon by the aforementioned EMRIP; United Nations, 2017b) are set out in the *Declaration on the Rights of Indigenous Peoples* (UNDRIP; United Nations, 2007), which was adopted by General Assembly of the United Nations on 13 September 2007. However, when we consider the overall significance of the three UN-mandated bodies, I believe that it is important to ask ourselves why this mandating (i) was necessary in the first place, (ii) can be dated to no earlier than the first decade of the twenty-first century, and (iii) took so long to establish? The latter of these three inter-connected questions can also be raised regarding the UNDRIP, which took around a quarter of a century to formulate, and whilst it was accepted with a majority (144) of member states in favour, there were eleven abstentions, and four votes against it. (Significantly, these four were Aotearoa/New Zealand, Australia, Canada,[1] and the United States – post-colonial nation states which have lengthy and negative histories regarding the treatment of Indigenous peoples by subsequent settlers of European origin.) And whilst the questions regarding the timing, and time taken, for the mandating of UN bodies might be answered semi-critically with some musings around a lack of prioritisation, I believe that in terms of tracing the roots of today's apparent indifference, it is important to take that critical view one step further. The global inaction and assumed indifference of the late twentieth century cannot be seen in isolation from, or anything other than a predictable outcome, the fifteenth- to nineteenth-century (depending on the region) treatment of Indigenous peoples as *enemy populations* by colonisers. As the United Nations Special Rapporteur on the Rights of Indigenous Peoples (2017c) pointed out:

> Indigenous peoples across the world experience the consequences of historical colonisation and invasion of their territories, and face discrimination because of their distinct cultures, identities and ways of life.

History provides ample documentation (some of which will be referred to in this book) that when the Europeans set out on their 'voyages of discovery', with the grab for land and resources that almost inevitably followed such initial strikings-out, they invariably treated the 'natives' who they found in these 'new worlds' as something *other than human*. Or, in cases where human physical form[2] was acknowledged, certainly as *Other*. In Western philosophy, the concept of 'Other'-ness features strongly in phenomenological and existential thinking, and subsequently became influential in phenomenological and existential psychology, and throughout the subject disciplines of the humanities and social sciences, and the understandings that these fields promote. Conceptually, 'Other'-ness is clearly articulated in the pivotal feminist text *The Second Sex*, where the philosopher Simone de Beauvoir demonstrated that women, in historical and contemporary societies, have been and almost invariably are positioned as 'Other', and outlined the sociopolitical importance of that positioning. She described the category of the 'Other' as being distinct, and inherently oppositional, to the self (the 'One'), and as ontologically and existentially primal (1949):

> The category of the Other is as primordial as consciousness itself. In the most primitive societies, in the most ancient mythologies, one finds the expression of a duality – that of the self and the Other .... No group ever sets itself up as the One without setting up the Other over against itself. (pp. 16–17)

According to this argument, then, human beings inevitably position themselves in relation to 'Others' in these oppositional ways, and this process is, of course, reciprocal. In other words, I (that is to say, my own 'One') am my 'Other's' 'Other', as she or he is her or his own 'One'. Jean-Paul Sartre (1943/1958) provided a description of the inescapable conflict that results in individual terms (in Warnock, 1970):

> While I attempt to free myself of the hold of the Other, the Other is trying to free himself from mine; while I seek to enslave the Other, the Other seeks to enslave me .... Descriptions of concrete behaviour must be seen within the perspective of conflict. (p. 117)

From this (existential) point of view, the same dynamism is evident in relationships between *groups* of people, as what we hold to be true of the I, the me, and the mine extends into our conceptions of those we hold to be the we, the us, and the ours: me and people like me, me and the 'us' to which I feel myself to belong. De Beauvoir continued (1949) as follows:

> In small-town eyes, all persons not belonging to the village are 'strangers' and suspect; to the native of the country all who inhabit other countries are 'foreigners', Jews are 'different' for the anti-Semite, Negroes are inferior for American racists, aborigines are 'natives' for colonists, proletarians are the lower class for the privileged. (p. 17)

De Beauvoir's demonstration of the categorisation of women as 'Other' was an early and brilliantly effective illustration of the fact that such categorisation is not based on the 'Other' being a *numerical minority* (as would be the case, say, in a stranger being left out of a group of people who were on long-standing friendly terms), but rather a deliberately cultivated disadvantage in *power* relationships. After all, there are, and always have been, as many women as there are men. Indeed, as I have argued elsewhere (Minton, 2016), it takes no real effort to call to mind an instance within living memory when a numerical majority has been positioned in as 'Other' – black people, a clear *majority* of the country's population in apartheid-era South Africa, were so positioned in every conceivable way. At the outset of European colonisation and conquest, of course, Indigenous people were inevitably numerical majority populations, yet from those outsets, colonisers appeared to have understood themselves as the 'One', and Indigenous peoples as the 'Other'. It is true to say, of course, that whilst the initial numbers of 'explorers' may have been small, in the cases that the land (or the physical resources that the land contained) that those 'explorers' 'discovered' was deemed valuable, then the location became attractive for further waves of their countrymen. So, initial 'pioneering' parties paved the way for wave after wave of land and resource-hungry would-be colonists, reducing, and in most cases, eventually reversing, the initial numerical advantage of the Indigenous people. However, as we have seen, 'Otherness' and numerical disadvantage are relatively independent. So the question here remains as to how such power got located within the hands of – or rather, was appropriated by – the colonisers. Where did the stranger in a strange land get her or his sense of entitlement from to 'claim' land and resources, *for* herself or himself, or in the name of some foreign power, but actually *from* its native inhabitants (whom, it seems the colonisers might have supposed, had been simply waiting around to be 'discovered' for past few millennia)? How did the settler manage to 'legitimise' the actions of the subjugation, enslavement, and/or massacre of the native population of the land that she or he, or her or his compatriots, 'discovered' in order to effectively expedite the theft of that land and its resources?

Let us return to the aforementioned example of Columbus, and consider in a little more detail just the *immediate* course of *some* of his activities. Here was a Genoese explorer, who arrived on 12 October 1492 on an island which is now known as the Bahamas archipelago (rather than in Japan, where he had been expecting to land). Having received financial support for this journey from the King Ferdinand II and Queen Isabella I of Aragon, Castile and Leon (having tried unsuccessfully to engage such support from the Courts of the Kings of Portugal, and then England), he was subsequently given the rank of Admiral of the Ocean Sea, and appointed Viceroy and Governor of all the new lands he could claim for the Spanish monarchy (Stannard, 1992). Through his colonisation of the island that is now known as Hispaniola, and the attendant unrestrained enslavement, rape, torture, and murder committed by his soldiers, and decimation wrought by the diseases they carried, the native Taíno people's population reduced from an estimated 300,000 before his arrival, to less than 500 fifty-six years later (Crosby, 2003). Bartolomé de las Casas, who travelled to the Spanish colonies numerous times between 1516 and 1540, recorded that (see de las Casas, 1992)

> From 1494 to 1508, over three million people had perished from war, slavery, and the mines. Who in future generations will believe this? I myself, writing it as a knowledgeable eyewitness, can hardly believe it.

As members of one of those 'future generations' that de las Casas spoke of, we might again ask ourselves: What power on Earth could have authorised such audacious, avaricious, and murderous actions? It is in the very phrasing of this question that we may find something instructive: What power *on Earth* ...? Given the Christian religion of Columbus and the various conquistadors and other European colonists who succeeded him in the so-called 'New World', and elsewhere around the globe, it was held by the colonists, and the countries which grew rich and aggrandised on their plunder, that a *power beyond the Earth* was both guiding and supporting such actions. Amongst other provisions, the still-controversial (and still significant) *Inter Caetera* Papal Bull issued by Pope Alexander VI on 4 May 1493, granted to the Castilian monarchs all lands one hundred leagues west and south of the Azores and Cape Verde islands. Whilst the final edict of the Bull explicitly referred to the spreading the Roman Catholic faith in these lands (Verzijl, Heere & Offerhaus, 1979), it was generally (and conveniently) interpreted by the Castilian monarchs, and the conquistadors and colonists, as having divinely ordained their respective absolute sovereignty, and their rights of conquest, in these areas (Stannard, 1992). Some forty-four years would elapse before the issuing of the *Sublimus Deus* Papal Bull by Pope Paul III (on 2 June 1537), which declared the Indigenous peoples of the Americas to be rational beings, with souls, and therefore condemned and forbade their enslavement. (What might have been expected to be an interim period, of course, was characterised by the actions described by Stannard (1992) and de las Casas (1992) above.) However, whilst *Sublimus Deus* eventually became the official position of Charles V of Spain (although he opposed the excommunication of Christians who enslaved Indigenous people), it was usually ignored by the conquistadors and colonists (Maxwell, 1975). Hence, the mass enslavement and slaughter of the Indigenous peoples of what is now the South American continent continued, either as a matter of 'divine right', or 'right of conquest' (under *Inter Caetera*), or with no fear of earthly retribution (as the provisions of *Sublimus Deus* were not put into practice).[3]

Influential though these arguments were at the time, on the decline in religious fervour in Europe that followed the Reformation and the seventeenth century European religious wars, other currents in European thought emerged that have, conveniently for European colonists, enabled the continued and seemingly intractable 'Othering' of Indigenous peoples. Social Darwinism, which as I have opined elsewhere, is better thought of as a bastardisation, rather than a 'logical' extension of Darwin's own thinking (Minton, 2016), provided Europeans with a (pseudo-) 'scientific', rather than theological, basis to their assumptions of inherent superiority (the justified, colonising 'One') over Indigenous peoples (the colonised, native, 'Other'). As we shall see time and again in the following chapters, the emergence, development, and general implementation of such intellectual ideas at the very time (the late nineteenth and early twentieth centuries) when residential school systems for Indigenous peoples were emerging, being developed, and implemented, is surely no coincidence. In a still-pervasive, and yet entirely erroneous understanding of evolution as leading to progression, rather than natural selection acting on random patterns of diversity (which perhaps began with Sir Francis Galton's reading of his cousin Charles Darwin's work in the 1870s as being supportive of his own ideas of eugenics), Social Darwinism is characterised by the attempt to apply these (misunderstood) concepts to social theory (see Claeys, 2000, for a review). An idea of a continuous progressive chain of animal forms, from beast to man, and especially from ape to modern man, was asserted, with the European races invariably occupying the higher strata, and non-European races occupying the lower strata. Hence, cultural, historical, and economic differences were falsely 'biologised' (see Gould, 1997). In the twentieth century, such ideas reached their repulsive extremes in the 'racial hygiene' laws and practices of National Socialist Germany, where those categorised *Lebensunwertes Leben* ('life unworthy of life'; a designation which was first attached to mentally ill people, and those with disabilities, but subsequently to all 'enemies' of the Reich, including enemy 'races'), were legally 'euthanised' (see Rees, 2017, for a contemporary review).

Prior to the horrors of the Third Reich, however, and as we shall see in the following chapters, Social Darwinist ideas became rather mainstream in many areas of European and North American thought. In *Framing the Moron: The Social Construction of Feeble-Mindedness in the American Eugenic Era*,[4] O' Brien (2013) referred to the use of metaphor in the simultaneous processes of labelling those affected, and appealing to the general public for their support of legal frameworks of social control. O' Brien (2013) held that the 'feeble-minded' 'Other' was variously cast as (i) a diseased entity, (ii) an atavistic subhuman, (iii) an enemy force, and (iv) a poorly functioning human. Similar ideas, then, were clearly and firmly influential in the way in which Indigenous peoples of lands colonised by Europeans were treated.[5] In this respect, then, – that is to say, in the 'legitimisation' of colonisation and genocide perpetrated by Europeans against Indigenous peoples – Western 'scientific' and 'religious' value systems were, for once, in agreement. It must, of course, be acknowledged that the outward manifestation of this 'One' and 'Other' understanding took, and still takes, a variety of (inevitably, 'Other'-destructive) forms.

As has previously been acknowledged, the scope of this book is deliberately confined to the institution and operation of systems of residential schooling. In the sections that follow, the view will be advanced that in these residential schooling systems, the instructional and self-formational aspects that one might associate with systems of education was either minimal, obscure, or entirely absent. In their stead, a deliberate (but in some cases, deliberately disavowed) function of 'Other'-destructiveness was served – and the correct term for this total Other-destructiveness is *genocide*.

Educational systems as agents of (cultural) genocide

Although examples of genocidal actions, certainly in the context of conquest and colonisation, appear throughout history, the term 'genocide' itself belongs to the mid-twentieth century, and was originally coined by the Polish lawyer Raphael Lemkin (b. 1900, d. 1959). In an article of April 1945, Lemkin wrote (emphasis mine):

> The crime of the [German] Reich in wantonly and deliberately wiping out whole peoples is not utterly new in the world. It is only new in the civilised world as we have come to think of it. It is so new in the traditions of civilised man that he has no name for it. *It is for this reason that I took[6] the liberty of inventing the word, 'genocide'.* The term is from the Greek word 'genos' meaning tribe or race and the Latin 'cide' meaning killing. Genocide tragically enough must take its place in the dictionary of the future beside other tragic words like 'homicide' and 'infanticide'… the term does not necessarily signify mass killings although it may mean that. More often it refers to a coordinated plan aimed at destruction of the essential foundations of the life of national groups so that these groups wither and die like plants that have suffered a blight.

Subsequently, Lemkin lobbied (successfully) for the adoption of the concept of 'genocide' into international law (Davidson, 2012). Hence, although a legal definition of the crime of genocide was not provided at that time, the first session of the UN General Assembly in 1946 adopted a resolution that affirmed that genocide was a crime under international law. This resolution was succeeded in 1948, by the Convention on the Prevention and Punishment of the Crime of Genocide[7], Article II of which *did* define genocide, thus

> … any of the following acts committed with intent to destroy, in whole or in part, a national, ethnical, racial or religious group, such as:
>
> a   Killing members of the group;
> b   Causing serious bodily harm, or harm to mental health, to members of the group;

    c   Deliberately inflicting on the group conditions of life calculated to bring about its physical destruction in whole or in part;
    d   Imposing measures intended to prevent births within the group;
    e   Forcibly transferring children of the group to another group.

Whereas only one of these five categories of genocide involves directly murdering people (which reflects Lemkin's (1944, 1945) 'non-restricted' view of typologies [see above]), a view of genocide as being perpetrated solely in this way informs many people's understandings of the term. This is perhaps due to those understandings being shaped by the infamy of the most notorious methods and mechanisms of the Nazi Holocaust (Minton, 2016).[8] However, it is possible to trace a 'broader' understanding of genocide directly in Lemkin's original conceptions of the term. Lemkin described the general process of genocide as having '... two phases; one, destruction of the national pattern of the oppressed group; the other, the imposition of the national pattern of the oppressor' (1944, p. 79), and stated that the ends of genocide may be accomplished by

> ... the forced disintegration of political and social institutions, of the culture of the people, of their language, their national feelings and their religion. It may be accomplished by wiping out all basis of personal security, liberty, health and dignity. When these means fail the machine gun can always be utilised as a last resort.

Lawrence Davidson (2012) noted that whilst the term 'cultural genocide' was considered in the drafting of the UN 1948 Convention, it was ultimately dropped; nevertheless, it has been used quite broadly since.[9] In the context of the current book, the most significant use of the term 'cultural genocide' has been by the Truth and Reconciliation Commission of Canada, whose final report opens with the following statement (2015):

> For over a century, the central goals of Canada's Aboriginal policy were to eliminate Aboriginal governments; ignore Aboriginal rights; terminate the Treaties; and, through a process of assimilation, cause Aboriginal peoples to cease to exist as distinct legal, social, cultural, religious, and racial entities in Canada. The establishment and operation of residential schools were a central element of this policy, which can best be described as 'cultural genocide'. (p. 1)

In its report, the Truth and Reconciliation Commission of Canada (2015) argued that cultural genocide was distinct from physical genocide (which it defined as '... the mass killing of the members of a targeted group' – hence, identical with the first of the five categories specified in the 1948 UN Convention) and biological genocide (which it defined as '... the destruction of the group's reproductive capacity' – perhaps closest to the third and fourth of the five categories specified in the 1948 UN Convention). It defined cultural genocide as '… the destruction of those structures and practices that allow the group to continue as a group', occurring when States

> … set out to destroy the political and social institutions of the targeted group, and exemplified when, '… land is seized, and populations are forcibly transferred and their movement is restricted. Languages are banned. Spiritual leaders are persecuted, spiritual practices are forbidden, and objects of spiritual value are confiscated and destroyed. And, most significantly to the issue at hand, families are disrupted to prevent the transmission of cultural values and identity from one generation to the next. (p. 1)

Rinehart (2018, p. 34) noted that many non-Indigenous Americans continue to resist the label of genocide to describe the mass murder of a people, citing Strickland's (1985–1986) example of 'supposed "lawful" extermination':

> There were, of course, great and tragic Indian massacres and bitter exiles and exoduses … but I am not talking about those cold-blooded atrocities but about law and the ways in which genocidal objectives have been carried out under colour of law …. These were legally enacted policies whereby a way of life, a culture, was deliberately obliterated.

Rinehart (2018) described the results of these 'legally enacted policies' in '… imperialist policies that corrode ways of being in the world', which are based on the insistence that '… whatever views I have are somehow superior to the views that you have. It can mean that a dominant group can insist on children attending schools where their native language is forbidden' (p. 34). This he described as '… genocide at its purest, where the "velvet noose" of assimilation eventually makes physical extermination a given' (pp. 34–35).

My own previously published view has been that making a distinction between physical genocide and cultural genocide can be useful (see Minton, 2016). In the first place, and as I have indicated above, the recognition that genocide can be perpetrated by other than direct means of physical killing can contribute to the restoration of Lemkin's original understandings for the term he had invented. Secondly, I have argued that when genocide is waged by cultural means, it is more insidiously covert than the physical extermination of peoples (c.f. Rinehart's description of assimilation as a 'velvet noose', above). It has therefore been easier for perpetrators of cultural genocide, through processes of self- and other-deception, mystification and denial, to position their activities as helpful acts of charity, civilisation, or other form of public service to the people whose culture is, through those 'helpful' acts, systematically destroyed (Minton, 2016). Nevertheless, views on this point other than what mine has been do, of course, exist, and given their content and impressive articulation, I am bound to say I find some of them increasingly persuasive.

Whilst acknowledging that a good start in terms of Canada stopping '… trying to eliminate Indians and [starting to] work together in peace … would be to implement the recommendations in the TRC report', Dr Pamela D. Palmater[10] has been sharply critical of the term 'cultural genocide', especially as it has been used in the Canadian Truth and Reconciliation Commission. In a 2015 newspaper article, which was unequivocally entitled, *Canada Was Killing Indians, Not Cultures*, Palmater (2015a) argued that Canada's record is not indicative of a '… desire to rid Indians of their cultures' but rather, '… about eliminating Indians'. She noted that 'Canada didn't forcibly sterilise indigenous women and girls without their consent to stop them from speaking their languages – they did it to eliminate the population. By the UN definition – that is genocide'. Hence, in the residential schools, she further noted that

> Instead of receiving an education (most never received more than a grade 6 education), most were starved, beaten, tortured, raped, and medically experimented on. In some schools, upwards of 40 percent of indigenous children never made it out alive. Nationally, the death rate for these children was 1:25 – higher than the 1:26 death rate for WWII enlistees – and that was war.

In a newspaper article published nine days later, Palmater (2015b) asserted that

> What happened in residential schools were criminal acts back then, just as they are now. If there is to be true reconciliation, there must be justice. What happened in residential schools was not 'cultural genocide'. It wasn't 'language genocide'. And it wasn't 'almost genocide'. What happened in residential schools was genocide.

Significantly, Palmater raised the importance of the term 'cultural genocide', and why an admission to this charge might not be the acknowledgement of responsibility that at the time I (see Minton, 2016) and others took it (seemingly, uncritically and at face value) to represent, but rather, serve as a cynical obviation of fact:

> It is too easy for politicians to claim 'cultural genocide' now, when they are well aware that cultural genocide was specifically left out of the United Nations Convention on the Prevention and Punishment of the Crime of Genocide …. The mass murder or manslaughter of our people requires criminal prosecution – just like it would anywhere else in the world. Canada doesn't receive a 'Get out of Jail free' card simply because it said 'sorry'. Real reconciliation requires justice.

The individual chapter authors in this book have their own, and differing, views on whether 'cultural genocide' is a useful, or an obviating, term – or maybe, if such a thing is possible, some shade in between. As I have hopefully demonstrated, I feel that I have moved some distance from my earlier published views (Minton, 2016), and this has been a result of informing myself better regarding critical standpoints, and particularly those critical standpoints offered by Indigenous authors.[11] Hence, in deference to the possibility of diverging and critical views on the very real social and legal importance of this point, I have left the term 'cultural' in parentheses in the heading of this section. On completion, the reader of this book will either be able to make up her or his own mind on this issue or, at the very least, can expect to be better informed on it.

The residential school as a 'total institution'

Within the social sciences, the term 'total institution' is most associated with the sociologist Erving Goffman, who provided an influential account of how power relationships are constructed and conducted in mental hospitals in his *Asylums: Essays on the Social Situation of Mental Patients and Other Inmates* (1961/1991). Although in this text Goffman was mostly concerned with the provision of an in-depth consideration of one type of total institution[12] (mental hospitals), he also described boarding schools as an example of a total institution.[13] According to Goffman (1961/1991), a total institution is

> 'A social hybrid, part residential community, part formal organisation; therein lies its special sociological interest. There are other reasons for being interested in these establishments, too. In our society, they are the forcing houses for changing persons; each is a natural experiment of what can be done to the self'. (p. 12)

Chrisjohn, Young and Maraun (2006) characterised what can be done by total institutions thus

> Whether it was preparing prisoners for their eventual release into society, novitiates for service to a religious order, inductees to follow without question the orders of their superior officers, or victims of genocide to submit with minimal resistance to their destruction, the point of total institutions was the total war on the inner world ... and the reconstitution of what was left along lines desired, or at least tolerated, by those in power. (p. 62)

As we shall see in Chapter 8, residential schools have not only been used as key strategy in the forcible assimilation of Indigenous people but as also as a 'moral hospitalisation' measure in the supposed 'reformation' of 'potential adult criminals' (MacLellan & Mauger, 2013). Those interred in such institutions, almost inevitably, were the children of the poor (Lynch & Minton, 2016).[14] In the context of the present discussion, it is important to note that the children who were detained in the industrial schools (some 105,000 between 1868 and 1969), had been directly committed there by the courts. Section 58(1) of the Children Act (1908) (as amended by the Children Acts, 1929 and 1941) allowed for the detention of a child or young person under three broad categories: 'lack of proper guardianship', 'non-attendance at school', and 'indictable offences' (Raftery & O'Sullivan, 1999, p. 20), and, from 1966, being 'uncontrollable' (Tuairim, 1966). Prior to the passing of Children Act (2001), which raised the age of criminal responsibility in Ireland to twelve years, it had been just five years; hence, children who had committed these offences were brought before the courts, just like adults. Whereas a parent was required by law to be present at the hearing, the Commission to Inquire into Child Abuse (2009) found that practice was often very different. In the majority of cases, the children were almost always (legally) unrepresented, and neither they, nor their parents, were questioned or consulted with in any way before the order for detention was made (Commission to Inquire into Child Abuse, 2009).

Margaret Jacobs (2006) provided accounts from Rose Mitchell, or Tall Woman, a Navajo woman in the United States, and Iris Burgoyne, a Mirning-Kokatha woman in Australia, of the kidnapping of children by the authorities, and the (usually, ultimately unsuccessful) attempts made by those Indigenous communities to prevent it.[15] Jacobs noted that whilst these women's accounts were '... remarkably and disturbingly similar'

> ... they took place in almost opposite corners of the world in the early twentieth century.... Rose and Iris, as well as their Indigenous communities, shared a common experience at the hands of white governmental authorities and the missionaries and local police forces that carried out their bidding. (p. 203)

In such cases, then, the 'enrolment' of the child in the industrial or residential schools was not only forcible, and made against the will of the child and her or his family, but also (appallingly) absolutely legal. Szasz (1961/2010) argued that the involuntary commission of mental patients in hospitals is made possible by the 'skewed' relationship that exists between the law and the field of medicine that is made manifest in the practice of psychiatry. In the case of Indigenous children, their involuntary enrolment in residential schools was made possible by a similarly skewed relationship between the law and the providers of the 'education' that these children were to go on to receive.

Goffman (1961/1991) further argued that once the patient has been committed, the closed system of the mental hospital means that she or he is not permitted to exert any agency. As Szasz (1961/2010) noted, the aforementioned skewed relationship ensures that on involuntary commission, the psychiatric patient has no legal right to choose where she or he lives, nor even the right to refuse medical treatments; effectively, she or he is deprived of the most basic of human rights. Procedurally, Goffman (1961/1991) showed that following admission, the patient's former life (her or his social context, and eventually her or his sense of self) is literally stripped away, terming this process 'disculturation'. Whilst head shaving and the issuing of compulsory hospital pyjamas, the effect of which was the deindividuated and uniform physical appearance of the patients in the hospital, were mentioned by Goffman, the physical means of the stripping away of the pre-institutional identity of Indigenous children on their enrolment in residential schools was often more extreme. Having being shorn of their long hair (a particularly undignified and traumatic experience for Indigenous children)[16]; deprived of their jewellery and clothing; forbidden to use their native languages, to or follow their traditional religious practices; and their given (tribal) names being replaced by convenient Christian/English-language substitutes,[17] the Indigenous children in boarding schools were ready to be 'civilised', and to learn white, Christian culture. Primo Levi provided a description of the psychological impact of the process of being interred in his account of his personal survival of Auschwitz, *If This is a Man* (Levi, 1979):

> Then for the first time we became aware that our language lacks words to express this offence, the demolition of a man. In a moment, with almost prophetic intuition, the reality was revealed to us: we had reached the bottom. It is not possible to sink lower than this; no human condition is more miserable than this, nor could it be conceivably so. Nothing belongs to us any more; they have taken away our clothes, our shoes, even our hair; if we speak, they will not listen to us, and if they listen, they will not understand. They will even take away our name: and if we want to keep it, we will have to find ourselves the strength to do so, to manage somehow so that behind the name, something of us, us as we were, still remains. (pp. 32–33)

There are some points of parallel and interest here. It is instructive that Levi, a writer of consummate skill and (having been born an Italian Jew in Turin, which is close to the French border, and through the necessity of his wartime experiences) being something of a polyglot, felt himself – as an *adult* – to have come up against the limits of language in describing this experience. How, then, might an Indigenous *child*, on her or his forcible enrolment in a residential school, have been expected to understand similar experiences? In an interview he gave for the PBS television documentary *We Shall Remain* (Mattau & Nelson, 2009), Dennis Banks, who co-founded the American Indian Movement (AIM) in 1968, and continued as a prominent representative and activist until his death (in October 2017) at eighty years of age, described his own struggle to find the strength to keep his name, so that behind it (to paraphrase from Levi's account, above), something of himself remained. He said that on arrival at the boarding school:

> You couldn't sing any Indian songs, or tribal songs. They just started using English, you could only – you could not use any other language …. It's like I had to be two people. I had to be Nowa Cumig, and Dennis Banks. Nowa Cumig is my real name, my Ojibwa name. Dennis Banks had to be very protective of Nowa Cumig. So I learnt who the presidents were, and I learned the math, and I learned the social studies, and I learned the English. And Nowa Cumig was still there.

According to Goffman (1961/1991), interment in the total institution inevitably leads to the individual's demoralisation, and the controlled and controlling nature of the institution results in the deterioration of her or his pre-interment life skills. Eventually, that individual's abilities to manage her or his life in the 'outside' world are diminished, and with the passage of (interred) time, extinguished altogether – in other words, she or he is thereby 'institutionalised'. Whilst it is important to recognise the effects on individuals of their experiences of total institutions, what often happens is that these *effects* come to be seen as *causes* located *within* individuals. In other words, Goffman's descriptions of how these effects are produced by the individual's experience of the total institution is overlooked; the true agency of causality (i.e. powerful agents in society, through the medium of institutions) is rendered invisible, and the individual (or affected population) is held to responsible for the effects that have been located within them. Chrisjohn, McKay and Smith (2017, p. vii) have described the way in which they have experienced people (including suicidologists) typically thinking and talking about the problem of Indigenous suicide in Canada:

> Science or not, suicidology has chosen to reformulate the question: 'Why are Indians killing themselves at such high rates?' as 'What's wrong with Indians that makes them want to kill themselves at such high rates?' The tendency to cast the 'Indian suicide problem' as some function of our own peculiarities is so common (we are tempted to characterise it as *universal*) that here we will call it the *Broken Indian Model*. Simply, the model presumes that deficiencies or defects or shortcomings *in us* are responsible for our acts of suicide. The basic task of 'suicide science', then, is to discover the responsible defect(s).

If we are to avoid the type of victim blaming that Chrisjohn, McKay and Smith (2017) are describing ('What's wrong with Indians ...?'), and truly discover, or perhaps clearly articulate, some of the 'responsible defect(s)', the effects of total institutions on individuals must be seen as exactly that – *effects*. To me, this is one advantage of a sociological understanding such as Goffman's over, say, an individualised post-trauma model that one might expect to appeal to a psychologist such as myself. A further advantage offered by Goffman's work in *Asylums* is that it highlights the deceptive way in which social control can be manifested in not only the operation of the total institution but also through the positioning of the total institution, and the public service it supposedly provides, as benign, or more often, *helpful*. The mental hospital or asylum is one location where the public service of psychiatry is provided; ostensibly, what happens is that 'sick' people, who are diagnosed as suffering some sort of 'illness' or 'infirmity of mind', are 'treated' by specialised medical practitioners. This is, at least, what is outwardly avowed. However, what actually happens in the mental hospital, according to Goffman (1961/1991), is the forcible socialisation of individuals into the 'dull, harmless, and inconspicuous' role of the 'good patient'. Hence, not only does the total institution render those involuntarily detained as powerless, it also allows those who detain them to morally disengage from and deny their roles as gaolers, and to feel professionally and personally good about their detention of others (or, perhaps, 'Others'). Abuse (or at least certain categories of abuse)[18] and the deprivation of liberty can therefore be 'justified', and even championed, under the various guises of 'treatment', 'education', or serving the broader 'social good'. Indeed, all over the globe, genocidal actions against Indigenous people were committed, systematised, legalised, and otherwise legitimised, through the seemingly benign practice of 'education', permitting those individuals, organisations and nation states who planned, perpetrated, subsequently concealed, and eventually disavowed such actions to position themselves throughout as progressive, benevolent, and physical saviours and 'friends' of Indigenous peoples.

Assimilation and nation state identity

Adams (1995, p. 5) stated that the policy issue facing the new national government of the United States in the late eighteenth century could, in the main, '... be reduced to this fact: Indians possessed the land, and whites wanted the land'. Further,

> According to prevailing Lockean theory, only a society built upon the broad foundation of private property could guarantee public morality, political independence, and social stability. It followed that the fate of the republic was inextricably linked to an almost endless supply of free or cheap land; and if the nation possessed anything, it possessed an

inexhaustible supply of land. Or rather, Indians possessed it. For early policy makers, then, a major priority was the creation of a mechanism and rationale for divesting Indians of their real estate.

The nineteenth century saw (in Adams' words), '... one tribe after another crushed on the battlefield' (p. 7), the appropriation of vast tracts of Indigenous peoples' territory, and the establishment of the reservation system, under which Indigenous people were deemed as wards of the government, by the act of Congress in 1871 (see Brown, 1970/1991; Stannard, 1992). In the following years, the means by which this 'Manifest Destiny'[19] had been fulfilled, and the government's subsequent treatment of its Indigenous wards on the reservations, had incurred critical commentary from at least some white observers. And it was in this context that Pratt established the Carlisle school – as a key measure in philanthropic 'reform' (Adams, 1995). Under the prevailing Social Darwinist understandings of 'savage' societies inevitably giving way to 'civilised' societies, a philanthropic position could be asserted (with the additional understanding of 'savage' culture not necessarily being 'in the blood', but rather 'in the upbringing') that hitherto 'uncivilised' people could, and even should, be given a chance to adapt to 'civilised' culture, and thereby to take their places in the new society. This 'generosity' on the part of 'civilised' white cultures was bolstered by an idea of 'best interests' – that there were some groups of people, including Indigenous peoples, who thrived under strict and responsible supervision. O' Brien (2013, p. 118) quotes the assertion of an 'eminent judge from Pennsylvania', John Broomhall in 1895:

> The Indian, the lunatic, the imbecile, the public enemy, submits to the law of kindness. The wayward child obeys those who love it. Even wild beasts are subject to this law. The successful lion-tamer is the man who loves the lion, and his first lesson is to teach the pupil that he loves it.[20]

Furthermore, the 'chance' to have one's 'best interests' served by the 'loving kindness' of the institution was deemed to be (at least for native peoples in the United States) time-limited – as a school superintendent in Kansas put it (in Adams, 1995):

> Gradually have their possessions dwindled, reservation after reservation disappearing before the invisible march of civilisation, till now their domain is reckoned in acres instead of continents .... The only alternative left is civilisation or annihilation, absorption or extermination. (p. 16)

And the highest hopes that reformers had for bringing 'civilisation' to the remaining Indigenous people – which was inevitably involve their eventual assimilation into white American society – became firmly located within the sphere of the education of Indigenous children. Adams (1995) outlined the aims for 'Indian' schooling: Children must be taught to read, write, and speak the English language, and at least be introduced to the other branches of knowledge; they must be individualised, through being taught how to work (i.e. to learn to perform white trades), and to value private property, and the accumulation of wealth; they must be Christianised; and they must be trained in American citizenship. The chasm that existed between these educational aims, and the traditional patterns of the various Indigenous cultures, was and is vast. 'Kill the Indian, save the man', indeed.

On the other side of the Atlantic, territorial disputes in the Arctic also led to the forcible assimilation of Indigenous peoples in attempts to secure national boundaries, and to assert unified nationhood. The traditional lands of the Indigenous Sámi people cross four modern-day nation states – Finland, Norway, Russia, and Sweden. In the mid-nineteenth century, however, Finland was a Grand Duchy of Tsarist Russia (1809–1917), and Norway, although having declared independence (from Denmark) in 1814, had been ceded to Sweden at the end of Napoleonic wars, and remained in this involuntary union until 1905.[21] By the 1850s, Norway, with its ambitions towards full national independence, and given the might of Russia, was keen to secure its northern borders. In *Den finske fare* ('The Finnish Danger'), Norwegian historians Knut Einar Eriksen and Einar Niemi (1981) argued that due to concerns in some sections of the Norwegian government that there were too many 'Finnish' (meaning Kven; see Chapter 1, endnote 1) people in the northernmost Norwegian region of Finnmark, who might be expected to advance or comply with possible Finnish territorial claims, it was necessary to 'Norwegianise' the people living there, and thus consolidate the Norwegian claim. As is the case today, Finnmark's population then consisted of ethnic Norwegians, and also the Kven and Indigenous Sámi populations. As we have already seen (Chapter 1, the section 'Some initial thoughts on the possibilities for processes of truth, restitution, reconciliation, and reclamation'), this 'Norwegianisation' (which was operational between 1850 and 1980) was carried out through the compulsory education of children at residential schools.

Hence, for those in many nation states, the expansion (or in the consolidation) of 'their' lands, a sense of a national security has seemed to lie in the idea of the state as a 'homeland' for a single, homogenous people – effectively, a 'tribe'. Whilst this aspiration was (in)famously made explicit in Hitler's *Ein Reich, Fin Volk …* ('One realm, one people … '), and in many slogans of the nationalist right, we see less contentious, but no less definite, echoes of the same in the very names of some modern nation states – to give some European examples, in England (the land of the Angles), France (land of the Franks), Magyarország (Hungary) (land of the Magyars), Scotland (land of the Scots),[22] and Sverige (Sweden) (the land of the Svear). Once consolidation (or colonisation) was underway, which in the case of the countries featured in this book was by the nineteenth century at the latest, these nation states appear to have conceived (or come to conceive) of education not as a right of its citizens (as we might do today), but rather as a responsibility, or even duty, that the state had towards its citizens (and sometimes, its wards). In every case, the education that was provided exclusively reflected the concerns and ambitions of the dominant (colonising) population; and in every case, education and schooling systems were used in the deliberate assimilation of Indigenous populations. As we have already seen, Reverend J.A. Lippincott told a graduating class at the Carlisle Indian School (Chapter 1, endnote 7; from Adams, 1995, p. 274), 'The Indian is dead in you. Let all that is Indian within you die! You cannot become truly American citizens, industrious, intelligent, cultured, civilised until the Indian within you is dead.' Such were the aims of the 'enlightened', 'philanthropic' educational reformers of the day. But as Dame Iritanga Tāwhiwhirangi said (see Chapter 3, section 'Historical Contexts'):

> 'We [Māori] are not supposed to be here …. They [the European Colonists] used government policy in the 1800s to try to 'smooth the pillow of a dying race'. Dying out, however, was not a fate our ancestors saw for us. They saw a vibrant, positive future for our people. A future in which we would stand tall and strong. That is the future that Māori in Aotearoa strive for. That is the future that we are determined to give to our children. That is the future that our ancestors require us to walk towards each day of our lives.

A substantial portion of the rest of the book is devoted to accounts of how Indigenous peoples, given the specific experience of residential schooling systems in processes of colonisation, have attempted to walk towards a future such as that described by Tāwhiwhirangi. In closing this chapter, I am distinctly privileged to be able to turn over by far the greater part of the task of the provision of such accounts to those who are, in every sense of the word, in a far better position than I am to provide them.

Notes

1. It is to be acknowledged that Canada formally removed its objector status in 2016.
2. I emphasise the recognition of 'human physical form' because, as we shall see, for forty-four years (between 1493 and 1537), the official Roman Catholic position on the Indigenous peoples of what is now South America (who at that time were being slaughtered and enslaved in huge numbers, as part and parcel of their lands being colonised by the Iberians) was that they were beings without souls.
3. Stannard (1992) advanced a compelling argument regarding the differences in patterns of genocidal colonisation observable north and south of the Rio Grande being attributable to Christian denominational differences between the colonisers. In Central and South America, the Roman Catholic Spanish and Portuguese, who brought with them their histories of *contemptus mundi*-rooted corporal mortification and the Inquisition, were more than willing to apply these beliefs and practices in

their treatment of the apparently uncivilised, non-Christian/non-European 'wild man' races, whom they saw as an inexhaustible slave-labour force provided by God for their precious metal mines. In North America, the Calvinist and Puritanical British settlers reasoned that, '... those without a sense of private property were, by definition, not putting their land to "good or profitable use", and therefore deserved to be dispossessed of it' (Stannard, 1992, p. 234). As the British and Americans were hungry for the land itself, and unlike their Iberian counterparts had no need of a slave-labour force to extract its resources, given that the Indigenous peoples of North America had '... shown themselves to be beyond conversion to Christian and civil life ... [the] straightforward mass killing of the Indians was deemed the only thing to do' (Stannard, 1992, p. 247).
4. O' Brien (2013) positioned the 'Eugenics Era' as 1900–1930; and, on the reverse cover of this work noted that, 'Many people are shocked upon discovering that tens of thousands of innocent persons in the United States were involuntarily sterilised, forced into institutions, and otherwise maltreated within the course of the eugenic movement .... The book will be of interest not only to disability and eugenic scholars and historians, but to *anyone who wants to explore the means by which pejorative metaphors are used to support social control efforts against vulnerable community groups*' [italics mine]. I count myself as one amongst that 'anyone', and I can confirm the book was indeed of interest; and I would like to express my gratitude to my friend and colleague, Dr Jeremiah J. Lynch, for seeing its relevance of, and drawing my attention to, O' Brien's book during the writing of this chapter.
5. In the foreword to his novel, *The History of Danish Dreams*, Danish author Peter Høeg (1996) wrote that 'I believe that, encapsulated within many everyday events ... lies the essence of an entire century' (p. 2). Although repellant to modern-day sensibilities, it is a fact that from the late nineteenth century until the 1950s, 'ethnological exhibitions', or *human zoos*, were a feature of many public amusement parks and fairs (Bancel, Blanchard & Lemaire, 2000; Coos, 2002). For me, a single image that similarly encapsulates the Social Darwinist-'legitimised' 'Othering' of Indigenous people is a photograph in my possession of a group of South Sámi people who were exhibited, along with their tents, sledges, weapons and (to my eyes, at least) some rather confused-looking reindeer, at the Tierpark Hagenbeck in Hamburg, Germany, in 1928 – apparently in the next enclosure to a group of Sāmoan natives (Bancel et al., 2000). I have not been able to find any record of what either the Sāmoan or the South Sámi people so exhibited thought about their situation, nor about one another.
6. Lemkin wrote in the past tense here (i.e. about having already invented the term 'genocide') as the 1945 article referred to here was intended as a popularisation, for a more general audience, of the concepts he had developed in a chapter published the previous year (see Lemkin, 1944).
7. Having been adopted on 9 December 1948, the *Convention on the Prevention and Punishment of the Crime of Genocide* came into effect on 12 January 1951 (Resolution 260 [III]).
8. Although inextricably linked in most people's minds, the Nazi defendants at the 1946 Nuremberg Trials were not charged with genocide, but rather on the four counts of (i) conspiracy to commit crimes against peace, war crimes, and crimes against humanity; (ii) crimes against peace; (iii) war crimes; and (iv) crimes against humanity (see Gellately, 2007). This is because, as we have seen (see endnote 7, above), whilst Lemkin coined the phrase 'genocide' in 1944, it was not formally adopted into international law until the UN Convention of 1948.
9. Famously, including the description by the Dalai Lama of the deliberate and systematic destruction of Tibetan culture under the Chinese annexation of Tibet as 'cultural genocide' (see BBC News, 2008).

10. Dr Palmater is a Mi'kmaw citizen, and member of the Eel River Bar First Nation in northern New Brunswick. She is a practicing lawyer, and an associate professor and the chair in Indigenous Governance at Ryerson University, Toronto, Canada.
11. On this point, I am greatly indebted to Professor Roland Chrisjohn, who in a Skype conversation in July 2017, took the time to explain, in a kind and patient manner, why he felt that I had been wrong to render the two distinct ('physical genocide' and 'cultural genocide') in my then-recent book (Minton, 2016). My memory of the views that he expressed to me in that conversation was that they were not dissimilar to the views of Pamela D. Palmater, which I have quoted above. It is to be acknowledged, of course, that Roland Chrisjohn has been making such points consistently (see especially Chrisjohn, McKay & Smith, 2014; Chrisjohn & Wasacase, 2009; Chrisjohn et al., 2002) and for rather a long time (see Chrisjohn, Young & Maraun, 1994).
12. What is 'total' in 'total institutions' is the directionality of power relationships. In his *Discipline and Punish: The Birth of the Prison*, Michel Foucault (1975/1991) discussed such institutions as 'complete and austere institutions'.
13. Along with concentration camps, leprosariums, mansions (at least from the servants' points of view), nursing homes, orphanages, penitentiaries and prisons, poor houses, prisoner-of-war camps, sanitariums, religious retreats (including abbeys, convents, monasteries and other cloisters), ships and work camps (Goldstein & Goldstein, 1984). Chrisjohn et al. (2006) stated that whilst Goffman '... developed his account with no apparent knowledge of [Indian] residential schools ... the relevance of his analysis to Indian Residential Schools has not been overlooked' (p. 62) and provide previous examples of applications of Goffman's ideas.
14. Historically, the development of the industrial schools system in Ireland owed much to the workhouse model established in Ireland during the 1840s as a response to the poverty caused by the Irish Famine, and the establishment of 'ragged schools' for destitute children in England by Mary Carpenter from the 1840s (Lynch & Minton, 2016). The workhouse system had been developed in England from the seventeenth century, although it (and its ethos) can be seen as being rooted in the Poor Law Act of 1388, and successive 'poor laws' that criminalised vagrancy, poverty, and destitution. Conditions in workhouses were deliberately austere; poor diet, poor or non-existent education (for children), harsh discipline, mismanagement, and the separation of families were general features (see Higginbottom, 2012, for review). Workhouses in the United Kingdom were finally abolished under the National Assistance Act of 1948. A number of my own paternal ancestors, including my grandparents, spent time in workhouses.
15. Rose Mitchell reported that 'The agents were sending out police on horseback to locate children to enrol [in school]. The stories we heard frightened us; I guess some children were snatched up and hauled over there because the policemen came across them while they were out herding, hauling water, or doing other things for the family. So we started to hide ourselves in different places whenever we saw strangers coming toward where we were living' (pp. 202–203). Iris Burgoyne reported that '[A Sister] would visit the mission every month or so in a shiny black car with two other officials and always leave with one or two of the fairer-skinned children .... [We] wised up! Each time that car pulled into the mission, our aunties, uncles and grandparents would warn the older children and they grabbed the little ones and ran into the scrub .... I shed tears when I remember how those children were ripped from their families, shoved into that car and driven away .... The distraught mothers would be powerless and screaming, "Don't take my baby!"' (in Jacobs, 2006, p. 203).

16. Jacobs (2006) cited a Lakota woman, Zitkala-Sa's, account: 'I remember being dragged out, though I resisted by kicking and scratching wildly. In spite of myself; I was carried downstairs and tied fast in a chair. I cried aloud, shaking my head all the while until I felt the cold blades of the scissors against my neck, and heard them gnaw off one of my thick braids. Then I lost my spirit .... Our mother had taught us that only unskilled warriors who were captured had their hair shingled by the enemy. Among our people, short hair was worn by mourners, and shingled hair by cowards'! (p. 216).
17. This was seemingly approached by the 'educators' at the boarding schools as a random, and certainly meaning-devoid process. Jacobs (2006) cited an account from Daklugie, a Chiricahua Apache who had been taken to the aforementioned Carlisle Indian School: 'They marched us into a room and our interpreter ordered us to line up with our backs to a wall .... Then a man went down it. Starting with me he began: "Asa, Benjamin, Charles, Daniel, Eli, Frank ...". I became Asa Daklugie. We didn't know till later that they'd even imposed meaningless new names on us .... I've always hated that name. It was forced on me as though I had been an animal' (pp. 217–218).
18. Szasz articulated throughout his life that the physical bases of what are commonly assumed to be, and are treated as, 'mental diseases' are often obscure, at best. He argued that in his experience, what prospective patients present with to psychiatric and psychological services are more often 'problems of living', rather than *bona fide* biological 'diseases'. What happens, though, in psychiatry is that *metaphorical* diseases are treated as if they are *physically* located within the individual. That is to say, these 'diseases' are 'treated' via the physical means that are familiar to medically trained practitioners (as psychiatrists are), such as drugs, surgery, and electroconvulsive therapy. Szasz (1961/2010) argued that the fact that these sometimes permanent physical procedures may be performed upon people who have been involuntarily detained means that, correctly considered, they are *tortures* rather than treatments.
19. Dee Brown (1970/1991) notes that by the time of the US Civil war, '... to justify these breaches of the "permanent Indian frontier", the policy makers in Washington invented "Manifest Destiny", a term which lifted land hunger to a lofty plane. The Europeans and their descendants were ordained by destiny to rule all of America. They were the dominant race and therefore responsible for the Indians – along with their lands, their forests and their mineral wealth' (p. 8).
20. In a further parallel between the 'philanthropic'/eugenic treatments of native peoples and other peoples of colour, and those with intellectual disabilities, and which also illustrates the confidence that policy-makers had in the humanity of such treatments, O' Brien also cites M.W. Barr, who in a paper addressed to the 1902 National Conference on Charities and Correction, asked why '... a reservation was not set aside for the feeble-minded, since they were "as deserving" of one as were "the Indian or the Negro"' (Barr, 1902 in O' Brien, 2013, p. 118).
21. Having been attacked by Britain in 1807, Denmark–Norway entered into alliance with Napoleon. In 1814, under the Treaty of Kiel, Denmark was forced to cede Norway to Sweden. Although declaring independence that year, Norway was neither strong nor rich enough for a prolonged war with Sweden. The Norwegian king Christian Frederik abdicated, and the Swedish king Charles XIII was elected king of Norway in his place, which established the union of Sweden–Norway.
22. Interestingly, the late-Latin term *Scotia* (the land of the Gaels) originally referred to Ireland, and the Angles were, of course, just one of several tribes that arrived in Britain from the European continent prior to the Norman Conquest.

References

Adams, D.W. (1995). *Education for Extinction: American Indians and the Boarding School Experience 1875–1928*. Lawrence, KS: University Press of Kansas.

Bancel, N., Blanchard, P., & Lemaire, S. (2000). Ces zoos humains de la République coloniale. [The human zoos of the colonial Republic]. Le Monde Diplomatique [The Diplomatic World], August.

BBC News (2008). 'Eighty killed' in Tibetan unrest. Available online: http://news.bbc.co.uk/1/hi/world/asia-pacific/7299212.stm [Accessed December, 2017].

Brown, D. (1970/1991). *Bury my Heart at Wounded Knee: An Indian History of the West*. London: Vintage.

Chrisjohn, R.D., McKay, S.M. & Smith, A.O. (2017). *Dying to Please You: Indigenous Suicide in Contemporary Canada*. Penticton, BC: Theytus Books.

Chrisjohn, R.D. & Wasacase, T. (2009). Half-Truths and whole lies: Rhetoric in the 'apology' and the Truth and Reconciliation Commission. In G. Younging, J. Dewar & M. DeGagné (eds.), *Response, Responsibility, and Renewal: Canada's Truth and Reconciliation Journey*. Ottawa, Canada: Aboriginal Healing Foundation.

Chrisjohn, R.D., Wasacase, T., Nussey, L., Smith, A., Legault, M., Loiselle, P. & Bourgeois, M. (2002). Genocide and Indian residential schooling: The past is present. In R.D. Wiggers & A.L. Griffiths (eds.), *Canada and International Law: Peacekeeping and War Crimes in the Modern Era*. (pp. 229–266). Halifax, Canada: Centre for Foreign Policy Studies, Dalhousie University.

Chrisjohn, R.D., Young, S.L. & Maraun, M. (1994). *The Circle Game: Shadows and Substance in the Indian Residential School Experience in Canada: A Report to the Royal Commission on Aboriginal Peoples*. Ottawa, Canada: Royal Commission on Aboriginal Peoples.

Chrisjohn, R.D., Young, S.L. & Maraun, M. (2006). *The Circle Game: Shadows and Substance in the Indian Residential School Experience in Canada*. Penticton, BC: Theytus Books.

Claeys, G. (2000). The 'survival of the fittest' and the origins of social Darwinism. *Journal of the History of Ideas*, 61(2): 223–240.

Commission to Inquire into Child Abuse (2009). *Report of the Commission to Inquire into Child Abuse* (Vols. 1–5). Dublin, Ireland: Stationery Office.

Coos, P. (2000). Zoo humain en Belgique. [Human zoo in Belgium]. Le Soir, July 27.

Crosby, A.W. (2003). *The Columbian Exchange: Biological and Cultural Consequences of 1492* (30th anniversary edn.). Westport, CT: Praeger.

Davidson, L. (2012). *Cultural Genocide: Genocide, Political Violence and Human Rights*. New Brunswick, NJ: Rutgers University Press.

De Beauvoir, S. (1949). *The Second Sex*. Harmondsworth, London: Penguin.

de las Casas, B. (1992). *A shot account of the Destruction of the Indies*. Harmondsworth: Penguin Classics.

Eriksen, K.E. & Niemi, E. (1981). *Den finske fare. Sikkerhetsproblemer og minoritetspolitikk i nord 1860–1940* [The Finnish Danger: Security Problems and Minority Politics in the North 1860–1940]. Oslo, Norway: University of Oslo Press.

Foucault, M. (1975/1991). *Discipline and Punish: The Birth of the Prison*. Transl. A. Sheridan. London: Penguin Social Sciences.

Gellately, R. (2007). Introduction: Nuremberg – voices from the past. In L.N. Goldensohn, *The Nuremberg Interviews: Conversations with the Defendants and Witnesses*. London: Pimlico.

Goffman, E. (1961/1991). *Asylums: Essays on the Social Situation of Mental Patients and Other Inmates*. London: Penguin.

Goldstein, M. & Goldstein, I. (1984). *The Experience of Science: An Interdisciplinary Approach.* New York: Plenum.

Gould, S.J. (1997). *The Mismeasure of Man* (Revised edn.). Harmondsworth, London: Penguin.

Higginbottom, P. (2012). *The Workhouse Encyclopedia.* Stroud, Gloucestershire: The History Press.

Høeg, P. (1996). *The History of Danish Dreams.* London: Harvill Press.

Jacobs, M.D. (2006). *Indian Boarding Schools in Comparative Perspective: The Removal of Indigenous Children in the United States and Australia, 1880–1940.* Lincoln, NE: University of Nebraska, Lincoln, Faculty Publications.

Lemkin, R. (1944). *Axis Rule in Occupied Europe.* Washington DC: Carnegie Institution.

Lemkin, R. (1945). Genocide – A modern crime. *Free World: A Non-Partisan Magazine Devoted to the United Nations and Democracy,* 4, April, 39–43. Available online: http://www.preventgenocide.org/lemkin/freeworld1945.htm [Accessed April, 2019].

Levi, P. (1979). *If This is a Man and The Truce.* London: Abacus.

Lynch, J.J. & Minton, S.J. (2016). Peer abuse and its contexts in industrial schools in Ireland. *Journal of Aggression, Conflict and Peace Research,* 8 (2): 76–85.

MacLellan, A. & Mauger, A. (eds.) (2013). *Growing Pains: Childhood illness in Ireland* (pp. 1750–1950). Dublin, Ireland: Irish Academic Press.

Martínez-Cobo, J.R. (1981). Study of the Problem of Discrimination Against Indigenous Populations. UNESCO. Available online: https://www.un.org/esa/socdev/unpfii/documents/MCS_intro_1981_en.pdf [Accessed April, 2019].

Mattau, S. (Series Co-Ordinating Producer) & Nelson, S. (Director). (2009, May 11th). *We Shall Remain. Episode Five: Wounded Knee.* [Television broadcast]. Arlington Co., VA: PBS.

Maxwell, J. (1975). *Slavery and the Catholic Church: The History of Catholic Teaching Concerning the Moral Legitimacy of the Institution of Slavery.* Chichester, England: Rose.

Minton, S.J. (2016). *Marginalisation and Aggression from Bullying to Genocide: Critical Educational and Psychological Perspectives.* Rotterdam, The Netherlands: Brill.

O' Brien, G.V. (2013). *Framing the Moron: The Social Construction of Feeble-Mindedness in the American Eugenic Era.* Manchester, England: Manchester University Press.

Palmater, P.D. (2015a). Canada was killing Indians, not cultures. *Telesur,* June 8.

Palmater, P.D. (2015b). Canadian and church officials must be accountable for genocide. *Telesur,* June 17.

Raftery, M. & O'Sullivan, E. (1999). *Suffer the Little Children: The Inside Story of Ireland's Industrial Schools.* Dublin, Ireland: New Island.

Rees, L. (2017). *The Holocaust: A New History.* London: Penguin.

Rinehart, R.E. (2018). New critical pan-pacific qualitative inquiry: Reciprocal respect in aotearoan and pacifica research methodologies. *International Review of Qualitative Research,* 11(1): 28–38.

Sartre, J-P. (1943/1958). *Being and Nothingness: An Essay on Phenomenological Ontology.* Transl. H.E. Barnes. London: Routledge.

Stannard, D.E. (1992). *American Holocaust: The Conquest of the New World.* Oxford: Oxford University Press.

Szasz, T.S. (1961/2010). *The Myth of Mental Illness: Foundations of a Theory of Personal Conduct* (Revised edn.). New York: Harper Perennial.

Truth and Reconciliation Commission of Canada (2015). *Honouring the Truth, Reconciling for the Future: Summary of the Final Report of the Truth and Reconciliation Commission of Canada.* Available online: http://www.trc.ca [Accessed April, 2019].

Tuairim (1966). *Some of our Children: A Report on the Residential Care of the Deprived Child in Ireland.* Dublin, Ireland: Irish Printers.

United Nations (2007). *United Nations Declaration on the Rights of Indigenous Peoples.* Available online: http://www.un.org/esa/socdev/unpfii/documents/DRIPS_en.pdf [Accessed April, 2019].

United Nations (2017a). *United Nations Permanent Forum on Indigenous Issues (UNPFII).* Available online: https://www.un.org/development/desa/indigenouspeoples/unpfii-sessions-2.html [Accessed April, 2019].

United Nations (2017b). *United Nations Expert Mechanism on the Rights of Indigenous Peoples.* Available online: http://www.ohchr.org/EN/Issues/IPeoples/EMRIP/Pages/EMRIPIndex.aspx [Accessed April, 2019].

United Nations (2017c). *United Nations Special Rapporteur on the Rights of Indigenous Peoples.* Available online: http://www.ohchr.org/EN/Issues/IPeoples/EMRIP/Pages/EMRIPIndex.aspx [Accessed April, 2019].

Verzijl, J.H.W., Heere, W.P. & Offerhaus, J.P.S. (1979). *International Law in Historical Perspective.* The Hague, The Netherlands: Kluwer Law International.

Warnock, M. (1970). *Existentialism* (Revised edn.). Oxford, Oxford University Press.

Chapter 3

Aotearoa/New Zealand

Tania Ka'ai

Historical contexts

The establishment of residential schools for the Māori, as the Indigenous people of Aotearoa/New Zealand, can only be understood in the wider context of the establishment of education in Aotearoa/New Zealand by British colonials, and the underlying philosophy of using assimilation of Māori children in education: a philosophy emanating from a Western world-view. A policy of assimilation was introduced in 1847 by Sir George Grey,[1] only seven years after the signing of *Te Tiriti o Waitangi* (The Treaty of Waitangi; see below) in 1840, to civilise Māori from barbaric practices and pagan beliefs to Christianity (Ka'ai-Oldman, 1988; Walker, 1990). Māori tribalism and communal land ownership were viewed by the colonisers as a 'mark of primitive and barbaric people' (Walker, 2017, p. 19). This 'civilising' agenda of the nineteenth-century state in Aotearoa/New Zealand was employed specifically to facilitate the 'Europeanising' of Māori (Simon & Smith, 2001). The struggle for the survival of Māori as the Indigenous people of Aotearoa/New Zealand is set against a backdrop of colonisation:

> We [Māori] are not supposed to be here. Not as a people. Not as a language. Not as a unique indigenous culture. Our fate, in the eyes of some, was that we would die out. Their actions were driven by this view. They used government policy in the 1800s to try to 'smooth the pillow of a dying race'. Dying out, however, was not a fate our ancestors saw for us. They saw a vibrant, positive future for our people. A future in which we would stand tall and strong. That is the future that Māori in Aotearoa strive for. That is the future that we are determined to give to our children. That is the future that our ancestors require us to walk towards each day of our lives. (Tāwhiwhirangi,[2] n.d.)

Te Tiriti o Waitangi

The first mission school was established in 1816 in Rangihoua, in the Bay of Islands, by Thomas Kendall,[3] twenty-four years before the signing of

Te Tiriti o Waitangi. Te Tiriti o Waitangi was signed on 6 February 1840. Te Tiriti was meant to establish a partnership between the British Crown and Māori as the Indigenous people of Aotearoa/New Zealand. Since its signing, Te Tiriti has been the focus of controversy and scrutiny due mostly to the fact that two versions of Te Tiriti were produced (Kaʻai-Mahuta, 2010, p. 134). Te Tiriti, that is, the Māori text, was signed by both Māori and the Crown. It was later translated into English text by the European missionary Henry Williams.[4] However, the translation was not at all a correct interpretation. It is the English text, however, that has been used by the Crown as the definitive version, and this is the cause of contention to this day between Māori and the Crown (Kaʻai-Mahuta, 2010, p. 134).

Māori have always regarded Te Tiriti o Waitangi as a solemn agreement that was presumed to be the basis of a national dual planning system, incorporating both Māori and Pākehā[5] values into every aspect of decision-making in Aotearoa/New Zealand (Glynn, 1998). Furthermore, this agreement was also signed under the pretence that it would serve to protect Māori rights. However, only four years after the signing of Te Tiriti o Waitangi and the promise of a national dual planning system, the 1847 Education Ordinance was introduced and activated a strategy of using the state education system to erode the status of the Māori language and achieve cultural assimilation and language domination. Language domination occurs when members of the dominant culture silence an Indigenous language (Darder, 1991, p. 36). This often takes place in the classroom, when the dominant language is viewed as superior to the Indigenous language as a result of the values and beliefs instilled in the school system (Darder, 1991, p. 36). It was intended that Māori would become absorbed by European culture through education and would have to adjust to this change. Although legislation such as the 1847 Education Ordinance was a common practice at that time, today it is seen as a policy that was in violation of the rights of Indigenous peoples, as outlined by the World Council of Indigenous Peoples in the Declaration of Principles of Indigenous Rights (Kaʻai-Mahuta, 2010, p. 139). According to Anaya (1996), Principle 14 of this Declaration states that 'Indigenous peoples have the right to receive education in their own language' (p. 189). History shows that this right was not upheld for Māori.

Mission schools

As we have seen, mission schools were established as far back as 1816; missionaries saw themselves as the instrument by which the Māori people would be brought from the state of barbarism to civilised life (Kaʻai-Oldman, 1988, p. 22). Missionaries sought to interrupt the inter-generational transmission of language and culture, thereby invalidating the Māori world view. By the 1850s, the European settler population exceeded that of Māori, and the decline in Māori numbers was compounded by deaths from introduced diseases and from the Land Wars (between certain tribes and the British Crown) of the 1860s (Moorfield, 2006, p. 109). The Land Wars, later known as the New Zealand Wars, were a series of armed conflicts that took place in New Zealand from 1845 to 1872 between the New Zealand government and Māori. Large areas of land were confiscated from Māori by the government, legitimised by the New Zealand Settlements Act 1863, as punishment for Māori rebellion against the state (Walker, 1990). The confiscations had a lasting impact on the social and economic development of the affected tribes. The New Zealand Wars were also responsible for the closure of many mission schools and, subsequently, the end of the missionary period in Aotearoa/New Zealand: 'War closed the schools, and their closing can be taken to symbolise the break in relations which had occurred between the two races' (Barrington & Beaglehole, 1974, p. 95).

Native schools

The 1867 Native Schools Act was introduced to establish native schools under the administration of the government, thus providing the government with more control over the content of the curriculum (Walker, 1990). The Act replaced mission schools by establishing native schools for Māori children. The curriculum reflected the values of the state and the new settler government, and neglected the needs of the Indigenous people. The New Zealand settler government was to claim part responsibility for the provision of teachers and school buildings, provided that Māori gifted land for the school to be built and covered the remaining costs for teachers, buildings, and books (Barrington, 2008).

The Native Schools Code of 1880 outlined the expectation that teachers have knowledge of the Māori language, but only in the context of teaching English to the junior classes (Walker, 1990). Therefore, the 1880 Native Schools Code aided the process of assimilation by placing restrictions on the Māori language in schools (Ka'ai-Oldman, 1988). The legislation and regulation of the state education system, such as the 1880 Native Schools Code, is an example of institutional racism against Māori. Another example of institutional racism is making attendance at school compulsory (from 1894 when the School Attendance Act was enacted). For European children, it was compulsory for them to attend school from seven years of age to thirteen years of age, yet for Māori, it was only compulsory for them to attend school up until the age of ten. The state clearly had different educational assumptions and expectations for Māori (Simon & Smith, 2001). Māori language continued to be a focus of the state. According to Walker (1990), the Revised Native Schools Code that was introduced in 1897 allowed for the Māori language to be spoken in junior classes for the express purpose of teaching English. However, it was argued that the use of the Māori language should cease, and that English should become the sole language in the classroom (Barrington & Beaglehole, 1974).

The impact of Māori language loss

By 1903, the use of Māori as a medium of instruction and communication within schools was officially discouraged by educational authorities (Bell, 1991). In 1905, teachers in native schools were strongly advised by the Inspector of native schools to encourage Māori children to speak only English in the playground (Walker, 1990). This led to widespread prohibition, and eventually children in native schools were forbidden to speak the Māori language in the classroom, or in the playground, and in many cases, corporal punishment was used freely as an oppressive tool against children who disobeyed (Ka'ai-Oldman, 1988). According to Walker (1990), 'the damaging aspect of this practice lay not in corporal punishment *per se*, but in the psychological effect on an individual's sense of identity and personal worth' (p. 147).

Pere (1997) argued that language is not only a form of communication, but that it helps transmit the values and beliefs of people. The language is the life-line and sustenance of a culture as it provides the tentacles that can enable a child to link up with everything in his or her world. It is one of the most important forms of empowerment that a child can have. Therefore, it follows that suppressing language as a form of 'psychological violence' (Darder, 1991). McCarthy (1997) also illustrates the psychological effect of language prohibition:

> Native Māori speakers who were graduates of the 1900s schooling era have in the majority of cases deliberately not taught their children to speak Māori. Responses of this kind are directly linked to the belief, firmly inculcated, that to speak Māori was of no practical use. (p. 33)

Effectively, if speakers of the Māori language did not have positive attitudes towards their native tongue, they were reluctant to transmit their knowledge to new generations, regardless of how proficient their language skills were. Moreover, many Māori who had been physically punished for speaking Māori language during their schooling were subsequently reluctant to submit their own children to this experience, and therefore chose to speak only English to their children. Thus, Māori people are victims of inter-generational historical and cultural trauma. This is exacerbated by the exclusion of the Māori language from the primary school curriculum and negative attitudes of many teachers towards the language, which negatively affected the attitude of Māori people themselves towards their own language (Ka'ai-Oldman, 1988). Māori often felt embarrassed by, and ashamed of, the Māori language, due to the European attitude that the English language was superior.

In 1930, there was an attempt by the New Zealand Federation of Teachers to have the Māori language introduced as part of the curriculum. Unfortunately, this was rejected by T. B. Strong, who was Director of Education at that time. Strong advocated that 'the natural abandonment of the native tongue involves no loss to the Māori' (Ka'ai-Oldman 1988, p. 24; Moorfield, 2006, p. 109). Ka'ai-Mahuta (2010) argues that this attitude politically fuelled the continued opposition by the dominant European culture towards the Māori language (p. 146).

1907 Tohunga[6] Suppression Act

The introduction of the Tohunga Suppression Act in 1907 affectively eroded traditional Māori communities in that Māori were restricted from accessing their traditional spiritual healers and practitioners (McCarthy, 1997). The Act essentially made criminals out of tohunga and forced them 'underground' which disrupted the transmission of the traditional esoteric knowledge associated with tohunga (Ka'ai-Mahuta, 2010).

The World Wars

Both World War I and II had a huge impact on Māori society because many Māori men were killed and never returned home to Aotearoa/New Zealand.[7] The majority of the Māori population at this time were native speakers of the Māori language, so the inter-generational transmission of the Māori language and cultural knowledge changed dramatically as a result of massive social, political, and economic changes within Māori society at that time.

Migration

In the 1950s, there was a migration of Māori from rural areas to the urban centres seeking employment. The steady urban drift led to the disintegration of rural Māori language-speaking communities (Benton, 1981). At this time, there was a policy of 'integrating' urban Māori families into the wider dominant population. This policy (known as 'pepper-potting') placed Māori families in predominantly European suburbs, in the hope that they would 'integrate' into mainstream society (Walker, 1990). The policy had been created in order to prevent the development of urban Māori communities and had the follow-on effect of preventing the formation of Māori language-speaking groups, because Māori speakers were physically isolated from other Māori speakers. Therefore, English was firmly established as the language of not only the workplace but also of the local neighbourhood (Ka'ai-Mahuta, 2010). Consequently, English became the primary language through which daily social interactions were undertaken (Te Taura Whiri i te Reo Māori, 2018). This policy had far-reaching repercussions, of which the most severe was that for the first time, Māori children were being raised as monolingual speakers of English. These conditions led to a rapid language shift amongst the Māori population, especially amongst the first generations of Māori who were born and raised in the city (Kingi, 2005).

Biculturalism and the Māori language

In 1960, the Hunn[8] Report was released. The significance of this report is that it proposed 'a society that should embrace and respect Māori as a minority group in Aotearoa/New Zealand' (Ka'ai-Mahuta, 2010, p. 148). Whilst this sounds impressive, Ka'ai-Oldman (1988) argued that Hunn's vision for a pluralistic society 'never came to fruition, as people involved in State education across the country were resistant to changing their attitudes' (p. 24). Walker (2017) argued that whilst Hunn's findings were useful, he did not question the moral integrity of an education system that tracked Māori away from the professions and into manual work. Nor did he see structural inequality in the distribution of power as the root cause (p. 30).

Some recognition of biculturalism within the classroom emerged by the late 1960s. In 1967, the Report on Māori [sic] education was released by the New Zealand Educational Institute. This report recognised the value of biculturalism by stating that '… it must be remembered that the Māori is both a New Zealander and Māori. He has an inalienable right to be both, and to be consciously both, and he is likely to be a better citizen for being both' (Ka'ai-Oldman, 1988, p. 25). However, the reality is that this being embraced widely in education contexts and adopted in curricula did not occur. The state continued to ignore the benefits of the relationship between Māori children's self-esteem and educational success by understanding the intersections of language, culture, and identity. Instead the state, in 1973, tried to address the issue of disparity by introducing Māori studies courses in all seven teachers colleges around the country. Following this, in 1974, the Department of Education created six new posts for Māori Education Advisers (Ka'ai-Oldman, 1988).

Whilst in 1900, over 90 per cent of Māori children started school with the Māori language as their first language, by 1960, this had fallen to 25 per cent (Ka'ai-Oldman, 1988). By 1979, the loss of the Māori language was so great it was predicted that it would become extinct if nothing was done to save it (Walker, 1990). By 1984, the number of children entering primary school with Māori as their first language was most likely less than 2 per cent (Ka'ai-Oldman, 1988, p. 24). Further evidence of the success of colonial tools, such as language domination, can be found in the fact that Aotearoa/New Zealand is amongst the most monolingual countries in the world. It is estimated that between 90 and 95 per cent of New Zealanders cannot speak any other language apart from English (Bell, 1991).

The faces of colonisation have had significant impact on the health and well-being of Māori and Māori society as the Indigenous people of Aotearoa/New Zealand. Efforts by Māori people themselves have challenged the state to address issues of educational disparities with the establishment of Māori educational initiatives in the 1970s, such as *Te Kōhanga Reo* (Māori language immersion early childhood centres, referred to as 'Language Nests'), *Kura Kaupapa Māori* (Māori language immersion primary schools), *Wharekura* (Māori language immersion secondary schools), and *Wānanga* (pan-tribal or tribal-based tertiary education with curricula, often delivered in the Māori language). These have helped to offset the impact of the closure of residential secondary schools for Māori, increase Māori educational options for Māori families, and cushion the impact of Māori language loss amongst our Māori population.

The operation of the residential schools system

A network of church-operated boarding schools was established in 1844 across several different denominations and continued up until 1948 (Calman, 2012). These schools provided the main post-primary education option for Māori up to the 1940s. The oldest of these schools started as mission schools, and were initially for Māori boys. They included St. Stephen's School, Bombay, in South Auckland, which was founded by the Anglican Church in 1844; Wesley College, also in South Auckland, which was founded by the Methodist Church in 1844; and Te Aute College in southern Hawkes Bay, which was founded by the Anglican Church in 1854.

Subsequent to this was the establishment of similar schools for Māori girls by the Anglican Church. These were Hukarere Māori [sic] Girls' School in Napier in 1875, followed by Queen Victoria School in Auckland in 1901. These two schools were sister schools to Te Aute and St. Stephen's. Hukarere school closed between 1970 and 1992, but the hostel remained open, and so the girls could attend Napier Girls' High School. In 1993, the school was re-established, and relocated to Eskdale, on the outskirts of Napier, in 2003. Queen Victoria School closed at the end of 2001, after the closure of its brother school, St Stephen's, in 2000.

Essentially, the girls' schools were set up to domesticate the girls for their future role as mothers and housewives (Walker, 1990). The boys' schools, such as Te Aute, did provide an academic curriculum in the late 1800s, where a few boys each year passed the matriculation exam, enabling them to go on to university. However, this changed with the appointment of subsequent Directors of Education, who refocussed the curriculum on agricultural and manual training, thus creating a two-tiered system of education that affirmed European dominance and Māori subordination (Walker, 1990).

Other Māori church boarding schools included Waerenga-a-Hika College, Poverty Bay (Anglican, 1856–1937); St. Joseph's Māori Girls' School, Napier (Catholic, 1867–current); Hikurangi College, Clareville, Wairarapa (Anglican, 1903–1932); Turakina Māori Girls' College, Marton (Presbyterian, 1905–2016); Otaki Māori College (Anglican, 1908–1938); Te Waipounamu

Māori Girls' College, Christchurch (Anglican, 1909–1990); Hato Petera College, Auckland (Catholic, 1928–2018); and Hato Paora College, Feilding (Catholic, 1948–current). There are only five residential schools operating today, two of which were founded by the Catholic Church, which are St. Joseph's Māori Girls' School and Hato Paora College Church. The three remaining schools are Hukarere Girls College, Wesley College, and Te Aute College. The St. Stephen's Old Boys Association was successful in rallying support to have the school reopened, which will occur in 2020.

One of the biggest challenges for Māori boarding schools is that they really have two operations: first, the educational arm of the school, which is governed by a board of trustees and funded by the government; and second, the residence or hostel, which is normally governed and funded by the Church. Too often, they are like two distant cousins, and more often than not they are not even on speaking terms (Maniapoto, 2015). This has caused huge problems for families and students navigating their health and well-being at school. Another issue which has emerged from the rift between the two operations is that Māori boarding schools have sometimes become a dumping ground for 'problem kids', and referrals from the child, youth, and family service (now known as *Oranga Tamariki*). This has impacted on the traditional chemistry and camaraderie amongst the students, where social issues became more pronounced, including the proliferation of smoking and abuse, including bullying and humiliation. This has triggered parents to review the education of their children, and many withdrew their children from these Māori residential schools (Maniapoto, 2015).

Reviews of Māori church boarding schools have often resulted in a dramatic change, where the hostel and school have come under the control of the school principal, thus resolving the historical rift between the church and the school. This was certainly the case regarding the review of Te Aute in 2011 by Elizabeth Ellis who was appointed as a Commissioner by the Minister of Education. The closure of several of the Māori boarding schools were either related to natural disasters, such as fires (as was the case with Hikurangi College in Clareville, Wairarapa and Waerenga-a-Hika College in Poverty Bay), financial reasons (as was the case with Otaki Māori College), or performance issues (as was the case with Hato Petera in Auckland), despite many of these boarding schools becoming integrated into the state system, which was a necessity for their survival.

The legacy of the residential schools system

Many of the Māori boarding/residential schools boast an impressive alumnus of sports stars, politicians, community leaders, educationalists, and leaders in the commercial world. For example, when the former co-leader of the Māori Party and politician Te Ururoa Flavell talked about his experience at St. Stephen's in the 1970s, he said '… it was a great experience … it pretty much set me up for life – sure it didn't have everything that other schools had – but what we did have was a brotherhood and bond' (Boynton, 2018).

Ms. Elizabeth Ellis, when employed by the Education Review Office (ERO), had had a hand in the reviews of Hato Tipene (St. Stephen's), Queen Victoria, Wesley College, Hato Petera, Hato Paora, Hato Hohepa (St. Josephs Māori Girls College), Turakina, and Hukarere (on the old site), as well as other integrated church boarding schools around the country. It did not take her long to recognise that Māori boarding schools were being seriously short-changed by the Church – all she had to do was compare their facilities, resources, and activities with those of more affluent boarding schools (Maniapoto, 2015). Ms. Ellis sees Te Aute College as an important icon for Māori. She said (in Maniapoto, 2015) that it is growing proud Māori men:

> They arrive in February as timid, apprehensive, new boys and, by December, they are confident, strong Māori. By the time they leave school, they are able to conduct themselves well on *marae*[9] and at Māori gatherings, know the traditional performing arts, have immense pride in the history of the college, as well as a devotion and loyalty to the school and to each other that endures for life.

Moana Maniapoto (2015) said about her own time at St. Joseph's Māori Girls College as

> I loved my years at Hato Hohepa (St. Joseph's Māori Girls College). Lazy Sundays learning to play guitar on the Marian steps, composing a song, practising *poi*,[10] or writing a letter home. I credit St Joe's for teaching me how to harmonise, speak in public, debate and be independent. The college gave me friends for life and engendered pride in me as a Māori woman. And I became part of a club. There's no secret handshake, but there is a bond. Every time I drive past Bombay, I look wistfully towards the orange rooftops of St Stephen's. And, in my mind, I can still see the lemon sweaters of the Queen Victoria girls from Parnell.

It is reasonable to suggest that the strength of these Māori boarding schools can be attributed to the Māori student population, especially as many of them came from families whose parents were alumni of their schools. The experiences of these Māori students shared many common features, for example:

- Students were likely to have been native speakers of the Māori language, especially those students from rural areas where the Māori language was still spoken in homes and practiced *tikanga Māori* (Māori customary practices and behaviours).

- Students were likely to communicate in the Māori language amongst themselves, such as in the hostels, on the sports-fields, and in other social contexts.
- The curriculum in residential schools often included the Māori language; church schools were known to be the first to teach the Māori language.
- The Māori performing arts were fostered by the students, especially as they were sorted into school houses where they would compete against each other in various activities, such as the performing arts and Māori speech competitions.
- Students also identified themselves using their tribal areas, which provided another common bond between them and a sense of pride and unity.
- Students implemented values from the Māori world, and observed *tikanga Māori*: thus the school environment operated within a Māori-centric framework.

Many of the 'old boys' and 'old girls' from these schools returned as teachers to the boarding schools to impart their knowledge and exact their influence over the schools including improving various features of the school, expanding the curriculum to keep it relevant, and finally, to serve as a bridge between the school, the families, and the tribal communities. They also created a legacy of educational success. Some of these old boys and girls returned to their alma mater to take up the Principal's position. Such is the case with Te Aute, St. Joseph's, St. Stephen's, and Hato Paora. Alumni of Māori boarding schools often speak of the camaraderie formed, alliances made, and a strong code of ethics in supporting each other through school, and beyond school. This is evident from the many alumni who have returned to teach at their old schools, alumni sending their children to their alma mater, the support they offer their respective alumni associations, and the continued loyalty to their old schools, sustained well into their old age. Such is the legacy of these schools.

Processes of truth, restitution, reconciliation, and reclamation

The Waitangi Tribunal

In 1975, the Waitangi Tribunal was established by the Labour Government under the Treaty of Waitangi Act. It was set up to deliberate and rule on alleged breaches of Te Tiriti o Waitangi. It serves, in a way, as a process of truth, restitution, reconciliation, and reclamation for Māori issues of injustice, and has become the focus of Māori resource claims against the Crown, and the source of major settlements that have invigorated Māori tribal activity across Aotearoa/New Zealand (Walker, 1990). The Waitangi Tribunal is a standing commission of inquiry. It makes recommendations on claims brought by Māori relating to legislation, policies, actions, or omissions of the Crown that are alleged to breach the promises made in the Treaty of Waitangi. Under the Treaty of Waitangi Act 1975, any Māori can take a claim to the Tribunal that they have been disadvantaged by any legislation, policy, or practice of the Crown since 1840. The Tribunal does not enforce the law, but has the power to make recommendations to the government (Waitangi Tribunal, 2018a).

There are historical claims and contemporary claims. Historical claims are those that relate to matters that occurred before 21 September 1992. Since 1 September 2008, no new historical claims are able to be filed. Most historical claims have been addressed in district inquiries. Contemporary claims are those that relate to matters that occurred on or after 21 September 1992, and commonly focus on specific issues and local areas. After 2020, the Tribunal will focus on contemporary claims. Some claims may be left over from previous Tribunal inquiries and from settlements restricted to historical grievances. Others may be addressed in the *kaupapa* inquiry programme.[11] A dedicated inquiry process will be required to address them efficiently.

Several Waitangi Tribunal claims have cited injustices regarding Māori language loss, assimilation, and colonisation. Examples of two historical claims relating to language and cultural loss are the *WAI11 Report of the Waitangi Tribunal on the Te Reo Māori Claim,* and the *WAI262 Indigenous Flora and Fauna and Cultural Intellectual Property Claim,* which are discussed in the following section.

The WAI11 report of the Waitangi Tribunal on the te reo Māori claim

The basis of the WAI 11 claim was a treaty breach by the Crown (Waikerepuru & Nga Kaiwhakapumau I Te Reo Incorporated Society, 1986 (Waitangi Tribunal, 1986):

> The Crown did promise to recognise and protect the language and that that promise has not been kept. The 'guarantee' in the Treaty requires affirmative action to protect and sustain the language, not a passive obligation to tolerate its existence and certainly not a right to deny its use in any place. It is, after all, the first language of the country, the language of the original inhabitants and the language in which the first signed copy of the Treaty was written. But educational policy over many years and the effect of the media in using almost nothing but english has swamped the Māori [*sic*] language and done it great harm. (p. 1)

The claimants recommended that (Waikerepuru & Nga Kaiwhakapumau I Te Reo Incorporated Society, 1986)

Te reo[12] Māori [sic] should be restored to its proper place by making it an official language of New Zealand with the right to use it on any public occasion, in the Courts, in dealing with government departments, with local authorities and with all public bodies. We say that it should be widely taught from an early stage in the educational process. We think instruction in Māori should be available as of right to the children of parents who seek it. We do not recommend that it should be a compulsory subject in the schools, nor do we support the publication of all official documents in both English and Māori, at least at this stage in our development, for we think it more profitable to promote the language than to impose it. For that reason we favour instead the appointment of a Māori language Commission to foster it, watch over its progress and set standards for its use. (p. 1)

Sir James Hēnare, when giving evidence in 1986 to the Waitangi Tribunal relating to the WAI11 claim lodged about the Māori language, said (Waikerepuru & Nga Kaiwhakapumau I Te Reo Incorporated Society, 1986):

The language is the core of our Māori [sic] culture and mana[13]. *Ko te reo te mauri o te mana Māori.* [The language is the life force of the mana Māori]. If the language dies, as some predict, what do we have left to us? Then, I ask our own people who we are? (pp. 40–41)

And furthermore,

'Language' according to Oliver Wendell Holmes, 'is a solemn thing, it grows out of life, out of its agonies and ecstasies, its wants and its weariness. Every language is a temple in which the soul of those who speak it is enshrined.' Therefore, the *taonga* [tongue], our Māori language, as far as our people are concerned, is the very soul of the Māori people. What does it profit a man to gain the whole world but suffer the loss of his own soul? What profit to the Māori if we lose our language and lose our soul? Even if we gain the world. To be mono-lingual, a Japanese once said, is to know only one universe'.

WAI262 Indigenous flora and fauna and cultural intellectual property claim

In 2010, the Waitangi Tribunal described the health of the Māori language as approaching a crisis point (Waitangi Tribunal, 2011). The late Dr Darrell Posey, Special Rapporteur to the United Nations and an expert on Indigenous people's rights, described the Tribunal findings on the health of te reo Māori contained in the WAI 262 claim on Indigenous flora and fauna and cultural intellectual property, as one of the most significant claims of its kind anywhere in the world particularly (in this case) to the status of te reo Māori and the lack

Table 3.1 The Waitangi Tribunal assessment of te reo Māori 2010

We have not seen evidence of true partnership between Māori and the Crown. The 2003 Māori Language Strategy, we believe, is a well-meaning but essentially standard and pre-consulted Crown policy that does nothing to motivate Māori at the grassroots.

Not enough has been done to implement the 1986 Tribunal recommendation that speakers be enabled to use te reo in any dealings with the courts, government departments, and other public bodies. Even in the courts, the use of the language remains heavily circumscribed.

There have been repeated failures of policy. The most profound was the failure to train enough teachers to meet the predictable demand for Māori-medium education demonstrated by the surge in Te Kōhanga Reo enrolments in the 1980s. So strong was this demand that, in the early 1990s, it had no apparent ceiling. But it soon became choked by the lack of teacher supply, and the language suffers the consequences to this day.

The Māori Language Strategy is another failure of policy. It is too abstract and was constructed within the parameters of a bureaucratic comfort zone. There have also been genuine problems with its implementation due to a lack of leadership and commitment amongst the responsible Crown agencies.

Given the failures of policy, so must it follow that the resources made available to te reo have been inadequate. The level of resources should follow directly from the identification of the right policies.

of government support to ensure its survival. The Tribunal's assessment of the Crown's contribution to te reo Māori over the last twenty-five years (cited in Anaru, 2018, pp. 4–5) are identified in Table 3.1.

The Waitangi Tribunal (2011) report states that the revitalisation efforts of the Māori language since the 1970s have been predominantly due to Māori community efforts, and makes no apology for its far-reaching proposals. In Table 3.2 four fundamental recommendations that were proposed in the Waitangi Tribunal (2011 cited in Anaru, 2018, pp. 4–5) are outlined.

Table 3.2 Recommendations of the Waitangi Tribunal (2011)

Te Taura Whiri [the Māori Language Commission] should become the lead Māori language sector agency. This will address the problems caused by the lack of ownership and leadership.

Te Taura Whiri should function as a Crown-Māori partnership through the equal appointment of Crown and Māori appointees to its board. This reflects our concern that te reo revival will not work if responsibility for setting the direction is not shared with Māori.

Te Taura Whiri will also need increased powers. This will ensure that public bodies are compelled to contribute to te reo's revival and key agencies are held properly accountable for the strategies they adopt. For instance, targets for the training of te reo teachers must be met, education curricula involving te reo must be approved, and public bodies in districts with a sufficient number and/or proportion of te reo speakers and schools with a certain proportion of Māori students must submit Māori language plans for approval.

These regional public bodies and schools must also consult iwi in the preparation of their plans. In this way, iwi will come to have a central role in the revitalisation of te reo in their own areas. This should encourage efforts to promote the language at the grassroots.

The Tribunal recognised that implementing the entirety of its report on the Māori language would bring Aotearoa/New Zealand in line with language policies in similar countries worldwide (Waitangi Tribunal, 2011).

An example of a contemporary claim relating to language and cultural loss and education is the WAI2336 *Matua Rautia: Report on the Kōhanga Reo Claim*. The WAI2336 claimants from the Te Kōhanga Reo National Trust raised wide-ranging allegations of a treaty breach concerning the Crown's treatment of kōhanga reo (Māori language early childhood centres) over the past two decades. In particular, they said (Waitangi Tribunal, 2013):

> The Crown had effectively assimilated the kōhanga reo movement into its early childhood education regime under the Ministry of Education, stifling its vital role in saving and promoting the Māori language and leading to a long decline in the number of Māori children participating in early childhood immersion in te reo me ngā tikanga Māori, (p. 99)

The Tribunal concluded that

> ... significant prejudice to the claimants had occurred as a result of the Crown's breaches of Treaty principles. It considered that as a result the claimants had suffered, and were likely to continue to suffer, significant prejudice. The Tribunal accordingly adjudged the claim to be well founded. (p. 239)

Whilst the WAI2336 claim has not reached its final conclusion in terms of the negotiations with the Crown for the implementation of the recommendations, the Te Kōhanga Reo movement has survived thirty-seven years, and continues to provide Māori families with a vehicle for the education of their children – zero to five years within an immersion Māori context, and a curriculum based on a Māori world-view, delivered using Māori pedagogical practices. In summary, whilst the Waitangi Tribunal is still a Crown-initiated system and it has its limitations, it is acknowledged that it is a system where Māori grievances can be heard through a process of truth, restitution, *reconciliation*, and reclamation.

A final note

The re-opening of St. Stephen's School in 2020 signals hope for a new area of Māori boarding schools providing Māori boys with state of the art education, and associated resources located and embedded in a Māori-centric framework. There is a raft of possibilities that this new school can offer, including a curriculum being delivered in the Māori language. But 203 years since the inception of education in Aotearoa/New Zealand in 1816, the reality for some Māori (and Pasifika[14]) students in mainstream schools is that the New Zealand education system has still got it all wrong; they remain sites of resistance. According to a Year 13 Tongan student at a secondary school in Ōtara, Auckland, speaking at a conference of the Association for Research in Education (in Collins, 2018):

> Education initiatives should aim not to 'fix' Māori and Pasifika students who are seen as 'failures', but to fix 'the whiteness of our education system' … that their success should be measured in their strength in their own cultures, as well as in their knowledge of English or maths.

Furthermore, she issued a plea to educators not to make her a 'brown *Palangi*' (a brown-skinned person with European values):

> The young woman has challenged schools to reject the racist view that Māori and Pasifika students are 'dumb' … that a transformed education system would actively reject that stereotype and stop expecting that we should change into some brown version of Palangi to be seen as 'successful'.

Thus, the establishment of Māori boarding schools has made a significant contribution historically to the education of young Māori men and women in Aotearoa/New Zealand because they have sought to educate students through the mainstream curriculum, and the students themselves have held on to their language and cultural values, resulting in graduates who can walk securely and with strength in both the European and the Māori worlds.

Notes

1. Sir George Grey (b. 1812, d. 1898) was a British colonial administrator, serving twice as the governor of New Zealand (1845–1853 and 1861–1868), and was the eleventh premier of New Zealand (1877–1879). He was arguably the most influential single individual in the European colonisation of Aotearoa/New Zealand.
2. Dame Iritana Te Rangi Tāwhiwhirangi DNZM MBE (b. 21 March 1929) is an Aotearoa/New Zealand advocate of Māori language education.
3. Thomas Kendall (b. 1778, d. 1832) was a British schoolmaster and Anglican minister, who having learnt the Māori language, wrote the first book that was published in Māori (*A korao no New Zealand; or the New Zealander's First Book; Being an Attempt to Compose some Lessons for the Instruction of the Natives*) in 1815 (Kendall, 1815). He was a missionary in New Zealand from 1813–1825.
4. Henry Williams (11 February 1792 to 16 July 1867) was a British former Royal Navy man, who was the leader of the Church Missionary Society between 1823 until his dismissal in 1849. Williams, with the help of his son Edward, is reputed to have made the translation referred to above in a single overnight sitting (King, 2003). The issue of the (mis)translation of Te Tiriti o Waitangi has been the subject of scholarly, political, and cultural debate in Aotearoa/New Zealand for generations (see Bell, 2009; Ka'ai-Mahuta, 2010).

5. *Pākehā* is the Māori language term for New Zealanders of European ancestry. Recent research demonstrates that whilst the term is not often self-applied, it is not considered to be a pejorative or derogatory term by the majority of New Zealanders of European ancestry (New Zealand Attitudes and Values Study, 2017).
6. A tohunga is an expert practitioner, spiritual or otherwise. Traditionally, these included *tohunga ahurewa and tohunga kiato* (priests), *tohunga whakairo* (carvers), *tohunga tātai arorangi* (experts at reading the stars), *tohunga tārai waka* (canoe builders), *tohunga wetereo* (experts in the language), *tohunga tā moko* (tattooists), *tohunga mahi toi* (artists), and *tohunga o tumatauenga* (experts in weapons or war), amongst others (Shortland, 1882).
7. During the First World War, 2,227 Māori and 458 Pacific Islanders served in the New Zealand (Māori) Pioneer Battalion of the New Zealand Expeditionary Force, at Gallipoli and on the Western Front. Of these, 336 were killed on active service, and 734 were wounded (New Zealand History, 2017). During the Second World War, around 3,600 served in the twenty-eighth (Māori) Battalion (also known as the Māori Battalion), in the Greek, Crete, North African, and Italian campaigns. Of these, 649 were killed on active service, and 1,712 were wounded (28th Māori Battalion, 2018).
8. This report was named for Sir Jack Kent Hunn (b. 1906, d. 1997), the civil servant who, whilst Secretary of Māori Affairs, was engaged by then-New Zealand Prime Minister Walter Nash to conduct a review of the Māori Affairs Department.
9. *Marae* are courtyards; they are the open area in front of a *wharenui* (traditional Māori meeting house), where formal greetings and discussions take place; it also includes the complex of buildings around the marae. Many Māori people see their *marae as tūrangawaewae* – their place to stand and belong.
10. *Poi* are the Māori performing arts; the word can refer to the physical objects used by the dancers, the choreography, or the accompanying music (see Huata & Papesch, 2000).
11. A memorandum concerning the Kaupapa Inquiry Programme was issued in 2015 by the Waitangi Tribunal's Chairperson, Chief Judge Wilson Isaac. Kaupapa (thematic) inquiries are not specific to any district, but rather deal with nationally significant issues affecting Māori as a whole. The kaupapa inquiries topics are military veterans; constitution, self-government and electoral system; health services and outcomes; mana tane and mana wahine (approaches that explicitly examine the intersection of being Māori and male, and Māori female, respectively); education services and outcomes; identity and culture; natural resources and environmental management; social services, social development and housing; economic development; justice system; and citizenship rights and equality (Waitangi Tribunal, 2018b).
12. *Te reo Māori,* or *te reo,* are the Māori language terms for 'the Māori language', or 'the language'.
13. *Mana* has been translated into English as 'pride', 'power', or 'effectiveness'; however, such single-word translations does not do the concept justice, as mana reflects a Māori/Polynesian, rather than Western, world-view. Mutu (2011, p. 13) characterises mana as 'Power, authority, ownership, status, influence, dignity, respect derived from the god/atua' (atua are the gods and spirits of the Māori); and in terms of terms of leadership and the reciprocal relationships thereby conferred; Jones (2014) characterises it as 'authority… the central concept that underlies Māori leadership and accountability' (p. 194), noting that '… the powers and authority of leaders can be seen to reflect the autonomy and self-determination of the community itself, rather than the absolute authority of an individual leader' (p. 196).
14. *Pasifika* is a term used to refer to New Zealanders of Pacific Island heritage (chiefly Samoan, Cook Islands Māori, Tongan, and Niuean), who are distinct from the Indigenous Māori.

References

Anaru, N.A. (2018). *A critical analysis of indigenous Māori language revitalisation and the development of an ontological data base*. Ph.D. thesis, University of Technology, Auckland, New Zealand.

Anaya, S.J. (1996). *Indigenous Peoples in International Law*. New York: Oxford University Press.

Barrington, J. (2008). *Separate but Equal? Māori Schools and the Crown 1867–1969*. Wellington, New Zealand: Victoria University Press.

Barrington, J.M. & Beaglehole, T.H. (1974). *Maori Schools in a Changing Society: An Historical Review*. Wellington, New Zealand: New Zealand Council for Educational Review.

Bell, A. (1991). The politics of English in New Zealand. In G. McGregor & M. Williams (eds.), *Dirty Silence: Aspects of Language and Literature in New Zealand* (pp. 65–75). University of Waikato Winter Lecture Series of 1990. Auckland, New Zealand: Oxford University Press.

Bell, R. (2009). 'Texts and translations': Ruth Ross and the treaty of Waitangi. *New Zealand Journal of History*, 43(1): 39–58.

Benton, R.A. (1981). *The Flight of the Amokura: Oceanic Languages and Formal Education in the South Pacific*. Wellington, New Zealand: New Zealand Council for Educational Research.

Boynton, J. (2018). Old boys to announce Māori boarding school reopening plans. *Radio New Zealand*. Available online: https://www.radionz.co.nz/news/te-manu-korihi/348929/oid-boys-to-announce-maori-boarding-school-reopening-plans [Accessed April, 2019].

Calman, R. (2012) Māori education – mātauranga: Māori church boarding schools. *Te Ara – The Encyclopedia of New Zealand*. Available online: https://teara.govt.nz/en/maori-education-matauranga/page-4 [Accessed April, 2019].

Collins, S. (2018). Tongan student pleads: Don't make me a brown Palagi. *New Zealand Herald*, November 27.

Darder, A. (1991). *Culture and Power in the Classroom: A Critical Foundation for Bicultural Education*. Westport, CT: Bergin & Garvey.

Glynn, T. (1998). Bicultural challenges for educational professionals in aotearoa. *Waikato Journal of Education*, 4: 3–16.

Huata, N. & Papesch, T.R. (eds.). (2000). *The Rhythm and Life of Poi*. Auckland, New Zealand: Harper Collins.

Jones, C. (2014). A Māori constitutional tradition. *New Zealand Journal of Public and International Law*. 11(3): 187–204.

Ka'ai-Mahuta, R. Te A. (2010). *He kupu tuku iho mō tēnei reanga: A critical analysis of waiata and haka as commentaries and archives of Māori political history*. Ph.D. thesis, Auckland University of Technology.

Ka'ai-Oldman, T. (1988). A history of New Zealand education from a Māori perspective. In W. Hirsch & R. Scott, *Getting it Right: Aspects of Ethnicity and Equity in New Zealand Education*. Auckland, New Zealand: Office of the Race Relations Conciliator.

Kendall, T. (1815). *A korao no New Zealand; or, The New Zealander's First Book; Being an Attempt to Compose Some Lessons for the Instruction of the Natives*. Sydney, NSW: G. Howe.

King, M. (2003). *The Penguin History of New Zealand*. London: Penguin Books.

Kingi, T.K. (2005). Indigeneity and Māori mental health. Paper presented at *Te Pūmanawa Hauora/Te Mata o te Tau Research Centre for Māori Health and Development*. Copthorne Resort, Waitangi, New Zealand.

Maniapoto, M. (2015). *The Joys (and Trials) of Boarding School*. Available online: https://e-tangata.co.nz/comment-and-analysis/the-joys-and-trials-of-boarding-school [Accessed April, 2019].

McCarthy, M. (1997). Raising a Māori child under a new right state. In P. Te Whāiti, M. McCarthy & A. Durie (eds.), *Mai I Rangiātea Māori Wellbeing and Development* (pp. 25–38). Auckland, New Zealand: Auckland University Press with Bridget Williams Books.

Moorfield, J.C. (2006). Teaching and learning an Indigenous language through its narratives: Māori in Aotearoa/New Zealand. *Junctures: The Journal for Thematic Dialogue*, 6: 107–116.

Mutu, M. (2011). *State of Māori Rights*. Wellington, New Zealand: Huia.

New Zealand History (2017). Māori in the NZEF. Available online: https://nzhistory.govt.nz/war/maori-units-nzef [Accessed April, 2019].

The New Zealand Attitudes and Values Study (2017). New Zealand: University of Auckland. Available on-line: https://www.psych.auckland.ac.nz/en/about/our-research/research-groups/new-zealand-attitudes-and-values-study.html [Accessed April, 2019].

Pere, R.T. (1997). *Te Wheke: A Celebration of Infinite Wisdom* (2nd edn.). Whakatāne, New Zealand: Ao Ako Global Learning New Zealand Ltd. (with the assistance of Awareness Book Company Ltd.).

Shortland, E. (1882). *Māori Religion and Mythology*. London: Upland & Co.

Simon, J. & Smith, L.T. (eds.) (2001). *A Civilising Mission? Perceptions and Representations of the New Zealand Native Schools System*. Auckland, New Zealand: Auckland University Press.

Tāwhiwhirangi, I. (n.d.). *The Fate of Māori as a Race*. [Unpublished paper].

Te Taura Whiri i te Reo Māori – Māori Language Commission. (2018). *History of the Māori Language*. Available online: https://nzhistory.govt.nz/culture/maori-language-week/history-of-the-maori-language [Accessed April, 2019].

28th Māori Battalion (2018). *School Resources*. Available online: https://28maoribattalion.org.nz/school-resources [Accessed April, 2019].

Waitangi Tribunal (1986). *Report of the Waitangi Tribunal on the Te Reo Māori Claim: A claim lodged by Huirangi Waikerepuru and nga Kaiwhakapumau i te Reo Incorporated Society Waitangi Tribunal Report 11*. Wellington, New Zealand: Waitangi Tribunal.

Waitangi Tribunal (2011) Indigenous Flora and Fauna and Cultural Intellectual Property Claim: *Waitangi Tribunal Report 262*. Wellington, New Zealand: Waitangi Tribunal.

Waitangi Tribunal (2013) *Matua Rautia: Report on the Kōhanga Reo Claim. Waitangi Tribunal 2336*. Wellington, New Zealand: Waitangi Tribunal. Available online: https://www.waitangitribunal.govt.nz/news/wai-2336-matua-rautia-report-on-the-kohanga-reo-claim-2/ [Accessed April, 2019].

Waitangi Tribunal (2018a). *About the Waitangi Tribunal*. Available online: https://www.waitangitribunal.govt.nz/about-waitangi-tribunal/ [Accessed April, 2019].

Waitangi Tribunal (2018b). Kaupapa inquiries. Available online: https://www.waitangitribunal.govt.nz/inquiries/kaupapa-inquiries/ [Accessed April, 2019].

Walker, R. (1990). *Ka Whawhai Tonu Matou, Struggle Without End*. Auckland, New Zealand: Penguin Books (NZ) Ltd.

Walker, R. (2017). Reclaiming Māori education. In J. Hutchings & J. Morgan (eds.), *Decolonisation in Aotearoa: Education, Research and Practice*. Wellington, New Zealand: NZCER Press.

Chapter 4

Australia's native residential schools

Rosemary Norman-Hill

Introduction

From the early days of colonisation, missionaries saw the civilisation of the 'savage heathens' as a priority in Australia. Those from the northern hemisphere, with their seafaring spirit and sense of superiority, were relative newcomers to these ancient lands. The Australia that greeted the British in 1788 was a continent of many landscapes, cared for by Aboriginal peoples for thousands of generations. At the time of writing my PhD thesis (2018), Europeans had only been in Australia for 230 years. However, within forty years of first contact, missions had sprung up in New South Wales (NSW), followed soon after in other settler states. Telling the story of my ancestors, my PhD research explores the first Aboriginal peoples impacted by colonisation. In particular, I focus on the story of my great, great, great grandmother, 'Black Kitty' as she was known, from the Cannemegal/Warmuli clan of the Darug. As a young five-year-old, Black Kitty was in the first cohort of children placed in the Parramatta Native Institution (1814–1822), the first native residential school in this country.

What began as a 'great feast' for local Aboriginal clans, on a hot summer's day late in December 1814, opened the door to a chain of events which over the next 150 years would result in thousands of native children being forcibly removed from their families across Australia. Eighteen days earlier, Governor Lachlan Macquarie had proclaimed, under Government and General Orders, fourteen rules and regulations for the establishment of the native school which he described as an 'Asylum for the Native Children of both sexes'.[1] The intention was to 'educate, Christianise, and civilise' local Aboriginal children. When the institution officially opened on 18 January 1815, the systematic removal and redemption of the most vulnerable of the native population had begun. Separation ensured the students would be 'dispossessed of their family, culture, language, land and general freedom' (Das, 2013, p. 5). Rule 14 of those orders stipulated that once placed, the children were not to be taken away from the school. Announced in the *Sydney Gazette* on 10 December 1814, those General Orders formalised the first Aboriginal child removal policy in Australia.

From those first years, Aboriginal children were taken to live with Europeans. Some were removed when their families were murdered, others were cared for after surviving the smallpox epidemic of 1789 (Collins 1798; Tench 1793). It was not long before missionaries saw the value in taking children into their homes. The younger children were to be inculcated with European beliefs, the older ones trained as servants (Kidd, 2002):

> As European exploration increased around the globe, the colonisation of Indigenous peoples varied considerably in the 'new' territories. In their treatment of Indigenous children, colonists often drew on established models of child 'rescue' and labour, adapting these to local needs and circumstances, and reflecting race attitudes of the time. (p. 148)

Before coming to Australia, missionaries across the colonised world had 200 years of experience in removing native children to residential schools, particularly in Canada and America (Cassidy, 2009). They believed the way to salvation was civilisation, and the most effective way to do this was by taking the children away from the care of their parents and tribal influences. The first missionary to use this method in Australia was William Shelley. He believed that placing Aboriginal children under the care of missionaries, would break familial attachments; those removals destroying important relationships and connections, which had sustained Aboriginal families for over 60,000 years (Berndt & Berndt, 1999). The removals also broke their connection to Country,[2] to the ancestors, and to the Dreaming.[3] For the Europeans, the separation of Aboriginal children and indoctrination into the European way of life through education and Christian teachings was seen to be far more productive. The logic was to 'civilise the savage', then make them useful to settler society. Many thousands of Aboriginal and Torres Strait Islander children forced to grow up apart from family, community, and culture have come to be known across Australia as the 'Stolen Generations' (Wilson, 1997).

This chapter on the Australian experience begins with the historical context that led to the formation of the Parramatta Native Institution (1814–1822). Then, I discuss details of other types of native residential schools established during the nineteenth century, culminating in Aboriginal child removals becoming an accepted part of government policy in all states and territories in Australia. Following this is the legacy of continuing policies of child removals through the stages of separation, assimilation, integration, and 'self-determination'. The chapter concludes with a discussion of the current status of the processes of truth telling, restitution, reconciliation, and reclamation in native and European relations.

Historical contexts

Australia's European history began on 26 January 1788, when over 1,000 boat people arrived unannounced and uninvited to the shores of what the new arrivals called 'Botany Bay'. The eleven ships, making up the First Fleet, carried the flotsam of British human life (Bennett, 2009; Ritchie, 1986), mainly unwanted prisoners clogging up the jails and hulks of Britain. This cargo of human misery, 'the scraps, the junk, the waste from a new age' (Elder, 1998, p. 2), did not settler farmers or tradesmen, but convicted criminals, over 750 of them. In the heat of summer, the local inhabitants watched in awe and bewilderment as the strange vessels entered their place and space. Warrior men, armed and prepared to defend their Country, challenged the British as they tried to set foot on Australian soil. Taken aback, the newcomers were led to believe '… the great south land was scarcely inhabited or at most inhabited by savages' (Fletcher, 1989a, p. 13). They were very mistaken.

Although no war was ever declared by the British against the native peoples of Australia, the frontier war of native[4] resistance against the British began from the first landing of the First Fleet in Sydney, the fighting persisting '… well into the twentieth century' (Bottoms, 2013 cited in Hunter & Carmody, 2015, p. 112). Aboriginal men were fighting to keep their traditional lands, to feed their families, and to protect sacred places. These sites held the memory of the dreaming where for thousands of generations, Aboriginal clan groups gathered together for feasting, celebration, rituals, and ceremonies. Whilst they continued to defend what was rightfully theirs, more settlers arrived and conflicts escalated. Murders and massacres against Aboriginal peoples were perpetrated overtly and covertly across the country (Elder, 1998). More often than not, the deaths were disregarded by colonial authorities.

Whilst this is part of the black history of this nation, it has largely been accepted as the progression towards 'civilisation'. Fighting for their very existence, it is estimated that 30,000 Aboriginal people may have died during those early years of conflict (Reynolds, 2013, p. 134). Great fighters such as Pemulwuy (Willmot, 1987), Windradyne (Coe, 1999), Jandamarra, and Yagan (Newbury, 1999), along with many others, gave their lives fighting for Country, whilst it was systematically taken from them by government grants and the settler economy. The myth that Aboriginal peoples did not fight for their lands 'needed to be put to rest' (Smith, 2001, p. 23). Noted historian Geoffrey Blainey (2015) added:

> Europeans too had their own blindness. They could not understand that the Aborigines, though not gardeners and not inclined to remain long in one place, loved their own ancestral land intensely and depended on it. How could they sell it or rent it out to sheep-owners when, in their eyes, it was inalienable, having been presented to them for all time by their divine ancestors? (p. 322)

Whilst their lands were being misappropriated, Aboriginal peoples' health suffered. Diseases, to which they had no immunity, further impacted on their physical, mental, emotional, and spiritual health. Australia, now part of the expanding British Empire, claimed Aboriginal peoples as citizens under British law. Aboriginal societies, developed over many thousands of years, were now set up for extinction. Considered heathens in need of saving, their traditional lifestyles were believed to be wild and savage. Over the coming years, more settlers arrived to build new lives, thus sealing the fate of Aboriginal peoples, who in time were believed to be a 'dying race' (Reynolds, 2001, p. 139).

Killings were accepted in the spirit of European assumptions about 'progress', as in all parts of the country Aboriginal people struggled to keep what was rightfully theirs. During violent clashes, men were killed, women and girls were raped, and children were kidnapped. Many were taken as slaves, or were exploited as cheap labour (Ramsland, 1986; Reynolds, 2001; Wilson, 1997). Whilst the killings continued, the settlement of this nation brought the 'enlightened' to our shores. Missionaries and salvationists, imbued with evangelical Protestant humanitarianism, came to eradicate 'savage' Indigenous cultures, and save the 'un-enlightened' natives (Barry, 2008; Brook & Kohen, 1991; Cruickshank, 2008; Gladwin, 2012; O'Brien, 2008). Recounting the attitudes of European people, Cruickshank (2008) expounded:

> Among missionaries and administrators concerned about the fate of Aborigines in early colonial Australia, many concluded that boarding schools or orphanages for young Aboriginal children would be the most effective tool for Christianisation and civilisation. (p. 115)

Not recognised by the Europeans, the assumed 'savage and heathen' ways of Aboriginal families were, in reality, healthy and productive; incorporating a way of 'doing and being' that had sustained them for many thousands of years. This way of life not only promoted good physical health through their hunter-gatherer lifestyle but also produced strong social, emotional, physical, mental, cultural, and spiritual well-being. Children, who represented 'the future of the Dreamtime' (Parbury, 1988, p. 25), began their education at birth. They grew up, generation after generation, safe within their clan of families. Being part of a well-structured community meant living within a solid kinship system, providing a mental map of relationships (Parbury, 2008). Through hearing, seeing, and doing, everyday life became a totality of learning, and the surrounding environment was their classroom. Learning through interaction rather than reaction, children were immersed in Culture[5] from the time they were born, which at a deep ontological level defined their nature of reality (Sheehan et al., 2009). This successful system of relationships and connections was not acknowledged or understood by the imperious Europeans.

The establishment of the residential schools system in Australia

The Parramatta Native Institution (1814–1822)

The Parramatta Native Institution opened on 18 December 1815, under the management of Missionary William Shelley, a member of the London Missionary Society. Whilst the Aboriginal students were to be educated, civilised, and Christianised, there was an expectation that at the appropriate time, they would then be married off, to each other. The Governor of the colony, Lachlan Macquarie, although seeing value in the school, was more concerned with the confronting problems of drought and frontier violence across the region. However, by taking local Aboriginal children into this residential school, he had a chip with which to bargain. William Shelley, who had been providing schooling to Aboriginal children in the area, proposed the idea in a letter sent to Macquarie in 1814, suggesting the school to begin with six girls and six boys. He explained that he found the children '… remarkably teachable with a peculiar aptness in learning the English language … they are as capable of instruction as any other untutored Savages' (Brook & Kohen, 1991, p. 57). Macquarie agreed to this proposal, possibly considering this an opportunity to quell the Aboriginal hostilities, whilst William Shelley wrote that he wanted to learn the local Aboriginal language.

For the civilisation of these children to be effective, they needed to live away from the influence of both their parents and tribe (Melville, 2006); however, the adults were not attracted to most aspects of European civilisation (Rowley, 1970). William Shelley was aware that Aboriginal young people returned back to the bush after spending years living in European households. This, he believed, was due to them not fitting into colonial society, rather than having the 'bush in their blood'. He saw human development as environmental, refusing to consider native peoples as being racially determined. Shelley believed behaviours '… could be refashioned by altering their environment' (Fletcher, 1989b, p. 19). He had a vision to create a special 'civilised' class of Aborigine. Through influencing the children in the institution to marry, he envisaged they would provide a level of support to each other, independent of their tribal connections (Brook & Kohen, 1991; Read, 2006).

Whilst around sixty Aboriginal people tentatively gathered around the market place on the aforementioned feast day in 1814, to hear about this school, many more stayed on the periphery, full of doubt about Macquarie's intentions (Brook & Kohen, 1991). Walking amongst the group, Macquarie spoke of the benefits of following the ways of white people 'by applying themselves to "moderate industry", and having their children educated at the new school' (Brook & Kohen, 1991, p. 66). Aboriginal parents were offered plots of land to farm if they allowed their children to receive the 'white man's education'. The Aboriginal families listened as they ate a generous meal of roasted beef and bread, washed down with ale. They listened as William Shelley and the Institution Committee explained a number of rules they would need to adhere to if their children were to be educated. They were informed that once placed, their children could not be removed, and visitation rights would be limited to once a year, on the anniversary of the feast. They listened, and they walked away.

On 31 December 1814, the *Sydney Gazette and New South Wales Advertiser* reported the day of the 'great feast' to be a success (Sydney Gazette and New South Wales Advertiser, 1814). The newspaper article claimed four children had been given up freely to William Shelley, without 'solicitation or persuasion', due to families feeling the beneficence of the idea. This number was far less than the required twelve pupils originally proposed by Shelley, and needed by Macquarie, for the sustainability of the institution. These children were not orphans, and Shelley believed the 'chief difficulty' of his plan was removing them from their parents; however, he ominously told the governor – 'I am informed that in many Cases this could be easily done' (Read, 2007, p. 33). The first four children who entered were most likely to those previously schooled by Shelley. When William Shelley passed away six months after the Parramatta Native Institution opened, his wife Elizabeth and daughter (also named Elizabeth) took over the roles of manager and teacher.

With Aboriginal parents being reluctant to hand over their children, over the next eighteen months there was only one new admission. Desperate to fill the quota needed to sustain the institution, Macquarie ordered the removal of Aboriginal children during frontier conflicts. Several children were sent in from the Appin Massacre of 1816, when their families were slaughtered and pushed over the cliff. By 1819, Yarramundi of the Burraberongal Tribe feared the 'men dressed in black' (Brook & Kohen, 1991, p. 70) taking children from the Richmond area. They came from as far away as Newcastle, some mere babies. The residential school did not appeal to the majority of the boys with many absconding, some within days of placement. There were also parents who ignored rule 14 of Macquarie's regulations, and took their children back from the care of Elizabeth Shelley.

As William Shelley had predicted, Aboriginal children had the ability to learn as well as European children did. During an examination in 1819, a fourteen-year-old student from the Parramatta Native Institution took out the main educational prize in the colony. Twenty young people from the native school sat the exam, along with a hundred European children (Brook & Kohen, 1991; Fletcher, 1989a). Being a major achievement for the institution, it received a mention in the *Sydney Gazette and New South Wales Advertiser* on 17 April 1819 (Sydney Gazette and New South Wales Advertiser, 1819). However, although receiving a good education, the Aboriginal children were also at risk from 'demoralising influences', as expressed by the Reverend Robert Cartwright to Governor Macquarie (Rowley, 1970, p. 90). Cartwright proposed moving the institution away from Parramatta, and Macquarie had to agree.

A plan was put in place to formally shut down the Parramatta Native Institution and move the children to a country location on Richmond Road at Blacktown, where a dormitory was being constructed. This native school was located alongside a number of small farm lots given to the girls from the institution when they married. By the time the institution finally closed its doors on 31 December 1822, sadness and sickness had fallen on the school with a number of children falling sick and dying from an unknown complaint. The surviving children left for Blacktown on New Year's Day 1823, to join their married friends. One of those couples was my ancestor, Black Kitty, and her husband Colebee, a black constable. Colebee, the son of Yarramundi, had become the first Aboriginal person granted land in the colony in 1819. Having married Black Kitty on 12 June 1822, they had their first and the only child Samuel at their Blacktown property the following year. It was sensible to build the Blacktown Native Institution close to where the married girls were living. They could assist the missionaries at the school, and already had established relationships with the surviving Parramatta students.

The Blacktown Residential Institution (1823–1833)

Whilst the Parramatta and Blacktown Native Institutions were both managed by missionaries, there was a difference. At Parramatta, the children were kept completely segregated from their families and could only see them once a year, whereas at Blacktown, families were encouraged to settle close to the school. The experiences of the children in both institutions were mixed. Both schools provided children with a rudimentary education and conversion to Christianity (Fletcher, 1989a). The boys gained skills in carpentry, farming, and agriculture, whilst the girls learnt domestic duties, at both locations. The days were regimented from morning till night, with study and scripture, and a minimal play period before going back to work (Brook & Kohen, 1991). Both institutions ensured the children were indoctrinated into the European way of life, always under the watchful eye of missionaries – evangelicals, who were driven to both 'civilise the savage child', and save their souls. By changing their 'heathen ways', and teaching them employable skills, missionaries believed that the children could become productive in colonial society.

When the Blacktown Native Institution was unable to provide care due to lack of missionary staff, the children went to other orphan schools. The boys were sent to Liverpool, from where they quickly absconded, running back to the bush (Fletcher, 1989a), and the girls went to the Female Orphan School at Parramatta, where they were put into service to European families. When the girls returned to Blacktown in 1826, those families demanded their return. One such demand came from Francis Oakes of Parramatta who requested 'Nelly, a half-caste girl … to be apprenticed to him' (Brook & Kohen, 1991, p. 205). Nelly's fate was then sealed.

By the end of 1828, the Blacktown Native Institution was short of pupils, and described as 'chronically ill with malnutrition'. Young girls were also afflicted with 'internal hereditary disease' (Fletcher, 1989a, p. 223), which was later identified as venereal disease. Children, who had previously led happy, healthy lives under the watchful care of their kin, were now exposed to deadly diseases and the exploitation of Europeans. Not all of the children were Aboriginal, as some Māori children were also placed there (Brook & Kohen, 1991). Over the years that it operated, the Blacktown Native Institution was thwarted by drought, disease, and death. It died its own lingering death in 1833, with surviving students sent back to orphan schools at Parramatta and Liverpool, whilst three older girls were taken to the emerging Wellington Valley Mission.

It is unknown exactly how many children passed through the doors of those first two institutions. I suggest it would be unlikely that the children would remember, or have retained any teachings, from their kin, nor did the missionaries understand the importance of those learnings. Rather, they '… entailed a wholesale attack on Indigenous oral tradition, culture and law' (Kociumbas, 1997, p. 11). Even so, once their education was complete, many of the young people returned once again to their cultural roots, rejoining their sacred lifestyle which had existed for thousands of generations (Fletcher, 1989a).

Mission schools and orphanages in the 1830s and 1840s

Whilst both native institutions were considered failures in their mission to civilise the students, they paved the way for the systematic removal of Aboriginal children and young people in every state and territory in Australia. Over the next four decades, charities and churches continued to monopolise the education system in NSW. Throughout the 1830s and 1840s, mission schools rose up in western NSW, Victoria, and Queensland. It was not until 1848 when the NSW government formally took on the responsibility for education (Burridge & Chodkiewicz, 2012). Whilst policies of the day excluded Aboriginal children from attending any government schools, in 1840, a school in Adelaide South Australia (SA) reported Aboriginal children as having 'a capacity for learning and [are] not at all inferior to the best class of European children' (Barry, 2008, p. 41.4).

Some evangelicals set up institutions in their homes, whilst others procured huge parcels of land, calling them 'missions'. The first bill for the Protection of Aborigines was drafted in 1838, after the massacre of thirty unarmed Aboriginal men, women, and children at Myall Creek, NSW in June of that year (New South Wales Government Office of Environment and Heritage, 2019). This was followed years later by protectorates, which were set up across Australia (Parbury, 1988, p. 65). When native schools opened on Aboriginal missions, families could reside nearby. However, the day-to-day care of those children usually fell under the watchful eye of the missionaries, and families were kept at a distance. States and territories, that had smaller Aboriginal populations such as Victoria and Tasmania, removed Aboriginal children and placed them in orphanages and child welfare institutions (Clark, 2002).

Aboriginal parents, whilst wanting their children educated, were not considered worthy of raising their progeny. The attitudes of the clergy and officials continued to keep Aboriginal peoples as a class below Europeans. Bishop Broughton reported that 'after an intercourse of nearly half a century with a Christian people, these hapless human beings continue to this day in their original benighted and degraded state' (Barry, 2008, p. 41.7). Removing children from their families continued to be thought of as being in their best interest. Regarded as a race of people with no hope, no ability, and no destiny in the modernity that characterised the new nation, dislocation, separation, and then assimilation became the order of the day.

The Camfield School in Western Australia

Whilst native residential schools in Australia often differed in their set-up, operations, and purpose, the ideological belief in the necessity to 'civilise' Aboriginal children underpinned every single one. In Western Australia (WA), an Englishwoman with a passion for education set up a school at her home in Albany in November 1852. Anne Camfield and her husband Henry were devout evangelicals, and had taken some Aboriginal children into their home. Anne, like Elizabeth Shelley from the Parramatta Institution (but unaware of her existence), also took on the role of primary teacher and carer. Within six months, Anne was caring for ten children with the help of two Aboriginal assistants, Ellen Wells and Ellen Trimme (Cruickshank, 2008). Henry Camfield, in support of his wife's endeavours, wrote in a letter, 'Anne is very much interested in the sable race. There is plenty to work upon if their presently dark minds were duly cultivated' (Cruickshank, 2008, p. 119). Later erecting accommodation next to their home, the institution was known as 'Annesfield' or 'the Camfield' (p. 119). In 1865, Florence Nightingale used Annesfield '... as evidence of Aboriginal ability in a lecture given to the National Association for the Foundation of Social Service in England' (p. 121).The success of the school was measured by the high level of education (then marriage) of the young women, and the failure was that even educated Aboriginal women could not take their rightful place amongst European society.

The Poonindie Native Training Institution (1850–1894)

In SA, the Poonindie Native Training Institution opened fifteen kilometres north of Port Lincoln, using a different model, as it focused on an older group of young people, and had a training arm. This saw many young Aboriginal men gain expert training in agriculture. Established under the Anglican Church, the institution was managed until 1856 by Archdeacon Matthew Hale (later, Bishop of Perth and Brisbane). According to Peggy Brock (1987), Poonindie was founded fourteen years after the arrival of Europeans in SA. Much like the other native schools, Hale wanted to 'experiment by isolating his prospective Aboriginal charges from the influence of their own people and from the corrupting influence of many of the settlers in Adelaide' (Brock, 1987, p. 119). Arguing that people were not forced to go to Poonindie, nor held against their will, Brock (1987, p. 120) described that 'Hale's intention was to save Aborigines so they could become "civilised" and Christianised, not to incarcerate them and kill them'. However, many did die whilst living there, as over the first few years, 'fifty per cent of the residents died' (Brock, 1987, p. 120).

Marrying the young people to suitable partners was high on the agenda at Poonindie, as it was at Parramatta and Annesfield. It was not long before half-caste children from Adelaide arrived at the institution and when Hale returned to Perth in 1856, he also sent across half-caste children from Annesfield in Albany, WA. According to Brock (1987), Aboriginal people who lived at the institution developed a strong connection to the place, regardless of where their traditional lands were. Most of the people who lived there retained their Aboriginal identity, many continuing to have a strong relationship and sense of belonging to the site.

The second wave of missions and schools

During the colonisation and settling of Australia, whole communities were pushed off, or forcibly removed, from traditional lands. Safe within their family unit, home for many Aboriginal children '… was a camp on the fringe of town, a pastoral station, or far out in the bush' (Allam, 2002, p. 37). They survived as they had done for thousands of generations, 'happily unaware that they were considered "poor and deprived"', by a 'do-gooder' society, the children enjoyed life 'hunting, fishing and inventing games' (p. 38). By the middle of the nineteenth century, Australian states began to formally act against native families. They appointed boards for their 'protection', and protectors to enact the laws (Read, 2007):

> The second wave of missions and schools established from the 1870s onwards, were mostly run by state governments. The power of the state to disrupt Aboriginal life was a far greater force to be reckoned with than the power of the missionaries. (p. 36)

Whilst placement on missions, or reserves, provided some security from the influence and racism of European settlers, it also took away Aboriginal people's right to live traditional lives, eat traditional foods, and raise their children in a cultural way. Initially set up under the control of missionaries, these places were to provide a 'humane environment while their race supposedly died out' (Grant, 2014, p. 47). Forced to live in substandard accommodation, families became dependent on their caregivers. With poverty knocking at the door, and the system wrapped in a shrouded cloak waiting around the corner, removal of their children became a daily reality. Children and young people were forced to flee if strangers came too near. By 1883, the NSW government instigated managed reserves through the NSW Aborigines Protection (later Welfare) Board (Read, 2015). With the number of half-caste children growing exponentially, assimilation was deemed necessary. Children then became 'segregated, biologically assimilated and vigorously integrated into the mainstream White culture' (Das, 2013, p. 5). This was effectively a social engineering programme designed to breed out 'the colour of both body and mind' (van Krieken, 2004, p. 127).

Not all Indigenous children suffered removal from families, and not all families were moved off their traditional lands. However, very few escaped the trauma of dislocation, separation, and assimilation. Children from mixed descent were at greater risk of removal. Much depended on the location and intent of the Aboriginal protector. Nevertheless, between 1870 and 1950, part-descent children were separated from full-descent children in the hope 'that the latter would disappear as quickly as possible' (Read, 2006, p. 35). Early in the twentieth century, authorities gained more powers to remove Aboriginal children and place them in reformatory schools and children's homes, the enactment of those laws systematically taking away the rights of Aboriginal parents to raise their children (Rowley, 1970). Whilst the states differed in the way they wrote these laws, the intent and end result was the same: forced removals of native children. The State became the legal guardian, and child welfare institutions their home. Mixed race children were most at risk: The lighter the skin, the higher the chance of being taken and absorbed into 'white Australia' (Jacobs, 2006, p. 203).

The missionaries continued to play a role, and by the beginning of the twentieth century, New South Wales Aborigines' Mission (NSWAM) (later, the Australian Aboriginal Mission and United Aborigines Mission) set up multiple sites across the country based on the basic principle of 'trusting God to provide'. The organisation became 'an effort of evangelical Christians of all denominations to give the Gospel to the aborigines of Australia – a real union of Christian fellowship and activity' (Clark, 2002, p. 167). The Australian Inland Mission and the Uniting Church Frontier Services were set up in more remote areas across the continent. The United Aborigines Mission was responsible for setting up the first Aboriginal Children's Home in the twentieth century: the Bomaderry Aboriginal Children's Home for babies and young children. Situated south of Sydney, it started taking children from 1908, and was in operation longer than any other Aboriginal children's home in NSW (New South Wales Government Office of Environment and Heritage, 2019).

In 1910, the Northern Territory Aboriginals Department was established through the Northern Territory Aboriginals Act 1906, appointing a chief protector (the position created under the law) as the 'legal guardian of every Aboriginal and every half-caste child up to the age of 18 years' Australian Human Rights Commission (2019). In 1915, an iron shed named the Bungalow became the Alice Springs Half-Caste Institution or Half-Caste Home. Conditions there were appalling, and the children were subjected to sexual abuse. A letter sent to the minister outlined the horrific living standards (Find and Connect, 2019) as

> The accommodation provided for them exhausts my power to paint adequately. A rough floor of burnt lime and sand to make a form of cement has been laid down. A very rough framework of wood was put up, and some dilapidated sheets of corrugated iron roughly thrown over it. There are no doors or windows …. The children are issued with two blankets and lie on the floor. One small stove has to cook bread for over fifty people. They apparently have never had fruit or vegetables …. The only lighting is two hurricane lamps. The children have no games or amusements of any description. Cooking utensils are practically nil. There are six bowls and twenty towels to serve everybody.

The Moore River Native Settlement in WA was a government institution opened in 1918, under the supervision of the protector of Aborigines, A.O. Neville. His policy of biological absorption '… was based on the assumption that Aboriginal culture was inherently inferior, and a threat to the successful inculcation of white ways' (McHugh, 2002, p. 128). Known for its poor sanitation, overcrowded facilities, and dilapidated buildings, the settlement posed a serious health risk to the children forced to live there. Research completed by the Aboriginal History WA unit indicates that the majority of the 374 people who died at Moore River were children who succumbed to treatable respiratory and infectious diseases (Perpitch, 2018). Their daily routine was regulated and controlled by 'rules, timetables and regimens, and in nearly all institutions, children's lives were governed by the ringing of bells' (Clark, 2002, p. 169). These were not isolated cases, with Wilson (1997) finding that when children were removed:

> The physical infrastructure of missions, government institutions and children's homes was often very poor and resources were insufficient to improve them or to keep the children adequately clothed, fed and sheltered. (p. 137)

Native children were removed by the State because it was deemed 'in their best interest'. They were not just separated from their families and communities but also dislocated from Country and Culture. Many were forced to live in substandard conditions, many suffered from neglect, and most were abused and used as free labour. All suffered ongoing trauma, perpetrated by the very system set up to protect them – and this was done 'for their own good'?

The legacy of the residential schools system in Australia

Native residential schools were not a new phenomenon in the Western world, having been established in colonised countries for almost 200 years (Cassidy, 2009; Claes & Clifton, 1998; Prochner, 2004). Whilst the civilising and christianising of native children has been the impetus for all native residential schools, Australia has differed from those in other parts of the world in the ways in which the institutions were set up. Whilst the American Indian Boarding School system fell under education clauses contained in treaties signed by Indian Nations between 1780 and 1870 (Cassidy, 2009), no such accords existed in Australia. The education of native children at residential schools was placed largely in the hands of 'voluntary religious organisations' (Prochner, 2004, p. 9). In Canada, the majority of native children receiving an education were also placed in boarding schools; however, Carney (1995) found that most 'went unwillingly, without the consent of their parents' (p. 14). Many were forcibly kept there for years.

When Australia implemented laws to remove children from their parents and place them under the guardianship of the State, most if not all of them also went unwillingly, usually without parental consent. However, education, although seen as important, was not the sole purpose of these Australian native residential schools. Christian teachings underpinned the educational process, as only a few hours each day were set aside for reading and writing (Buti, 2002). With the colour of their skin denoting inferiority, and their nakedness degradation (Harris, 1994), 'civilising' the children was deemed to be the only way (Rowley, 1970). Read argues that '... children's minds were like a kind of blackboard on which the European secrets could be written' (Read, 2006, p. 10).

Children were also sent out from the institutions during school holidays, to work on farms where many were subjected to physical and sexual abuse. When they reported their treatment, it was they who were castigated and made to feel it was their fault, disbelieved and punished again by the system (Mellor & Haebich, 2002).

In this section, I discuss two main legacies of native residential schools in Australia. First, the pretexts, practices, and policies that have justified a system of forced Aboriginal child removals that continues to this day; and second, the debates about whether such policies and practices constitute a form of genocide.

Pretexts, practices, and policies

From the colonisers' point of view, they did everything they thought necessary to 'help' native peoples from the earliest days of the colony. They set up residential schools to educate Aboriginal children. Cared for by missionaries, the children had a 'good Christian upbringing', which in turn would save their souls. Taught employable skills, the children were given every chance to become part of European society. With settlement expanding on every front, state governments introduced protection policies to keep native peoples safe. Removing them from traditional lands and placing them on missions and reserves could be viewed as a humanitarian act of ensuring native peoples' rights, whilst protecting them from molestation by white settlers. The government appointment of protectors ensured '… their mission would be a civilising one – rounding up Aborigines and showing them the benefits of Christianity' (Barta, 1987, p. 246).

The opening of the Native Institution at Parramatta set the precedent and laid the foundation for all native schools across Australia. The practice of removing Aboriginal children became 'official government policy until 1969' (Grant, 2014, p. 49). With removals often crossing states, many children and young people grew up far from home, many never knowing their roots, or from whence they came. As we have seen, when the laws across Australia took away the rights of Aboriginal parents, removals effectively became a social engineering programme designed to breed out 'the colour of both body and mind' (van Krieken, 2004). Just as states and territories became the legal guardian of native children; child welfare institutions and reformatory schools became their homes. Apart from being forcibly separated from their families, many suffered horrendous cruelty and ill-treatment, including sexual abuse and exploitation (Wilson, 1997). Whilst the most vulnerable and impressionable in native society were being exposed to unimaginable abuses by a 'do-gooder' system removals were considered to be in the children's best interest.

By the middle of the 1930s, the policy of assimilation became the main focus of dealing with 'the Aboriginal problem'. During the 1937 Aboriginal Welfare Conference, assimilation policy was endorsed as the preferred method of control over native peoples' lives. According to Das (2013, p. 7), the policy's intentions were twofold: first, assimilation of Aboriginal people into the dominant white Australian culture; and second, '… an idea of biological-genetic assimilation, which in turn depended on the premise of human genetics and bias against the dark skin colour'. By 1940, assimilation had replaced protection and become official policy in all Australian mainland states and the territories. With the large number of mixed-race children continuing to appear, assimilation policies were enforced, and over time thousands of Aboriginal children were removed from their families. Absorbing them into white society sat well during the age of the 'White Australia' policy, which began in 1901, and was not abolished until 1973 (Moses, 2004). After all, this was the nature of 'progress', the advancement into a new age, the age of 'whiteness' where heathen days and heathen ways would be easily forgotten. Progress would naturally follow. In reality, it represented policies that destroyed native families, communities, and cultures. In the 2006 reprint of his book, *The Stolen Generations* (which he first wrote in 1981), noted historian Peter Read reflected somewhat sombrely on the issue of child separation:

> It was scarcely talked about. Non-Aborigines said it couldn't have happened. The victims of separation thought it shameful to talk about their removal. They believed that maybe their parents hadn't been able to care for them properly, or worse still, didn't want them.

Forced child removals: Genocide, or an inevitable result of 'progress'?

The Polish lawyer Raphäel Lemkin first coined the phrase 'genocide' in 1944 (Lemkin, 1944). Lemkin went on to lobby for the act of genocide to be accepted as a crime under international law. In 1946, the United Nations codified genocide as an independent crime, adopted by Resolution 260 (III) A of the United Nations General Assembly, on 9 December 1948. Article II of the Convention states:

> In the present Convention, genocide means any of the following acts committed with intent to destroy, in whole or in part, a national, ethnical, racial or religious group, as such:
>
> - Killing members of the group
> - Causing serious bodily or mental harm to members of the group
> - Deliberately inflicting on the group conditions of life calculated to bring about its physical destruction in whole or in part
> - Imposing measures intended to prevent births within the group
> - Forcibly transferring children of the group to another group.

During the UN debates on the Genocide Convention, removing children from one group to another was taken very seriously (Reynolds, 2001), with the Greek delegate, Pierre Vallindas, arguing that '... the forced transfer of children could be as effective a means of destroying a human group' (Reynolds, 2001, p. 173). However, Reynolds revealed that Lemkin himself did not regard assimilation as a major issue, as 'cultural genocide related to drastic methods aimed at the rapid and complete disappearance of the cultural, moral, and religious life of a group of human beings', which Lemkin considered to be much more serious than '... a policy of forced assimilation by moderate coercion' (Reynolds, 2001, p. 175).

The Australian parliamentary debate about the Genocide Convention in 1949 strongly refuted the notion that Australia's treatment of Aboriginal peoples could be seen as genocide. For example, Archie Cameron, Liberal member for Barker, claimed (in Tatz, 1999):

> No one in his right senses believes that the Commonwealth of Australia will be called before the bar of public opinion, if there is such a thing, and asked to answer for any of the things which are enumerated in this Convention. (p. 315)

In the same session, Leslie Haylen, Labour Member of Parliament for Parkes, remarked (in Tatz, 1999):

> The horrible crime of genocide is unthinkable in Australia. That we detest all forms of genocide ... arises from the fact that we are moral people. (p. 315)

However, in the aforementioned book *The Stolen Generations*, Peter Read (1981) argued that

> Genocide does not simply mean the extermination of people by violence, but may include any means at all. At the height of the policy of separating Aboriginal people from their parents the Aborigines Welfare Board meant to do just that. The 1921 Report of the Board stated that, 'the continuation of this policy of dissociating the children from camp life must eventually solve the Aboriginal problem'.... Some were taken so young that they did not remember where they had come from or even who their parents were .... Many of these children did not, and could not, return to their families. (p. 3)

To highlight this attitude, Read (1981) quoted from a letter from the Aboriginal Welfare Board to a police sergeant at a mid-western town in NSW in 1958:

> In view of the inadequate provision as regards housing, food and care of the children of __ on the Aboriginal reserve at __ would you kindly charge the children as neglected and commit them to the care of this Board. (p. 3)

Today, any notion of genocide against Australia's native peoples continues to sit uneasily in this country. The mainstream view in Australia today is not that far from the views held by politicians debating the issue seventy years ago: namely, that Australia is a nation 'built on the backbones of pioneers'. This is particularly demonstrated on days of national significance, such as Anzac and Remembrance Days, when we come out in force to remember and honour our fallen soldiers. Genocide is viewed as something that was committed elsewhere: the Holocaust in Germany, in Stalin's Russia, Pol Pot's Cambodia, Bosnia, Rwanda, or in Turkey/Armenia. Genocide represents man's inhumanity to man, and challenges man's inherent right to exist. Suggesting that genocide may have been committed against the original inhabitants of Australia is to admit the unthinkable. It goes against everything this country stands for, which is 'a fair go for all'. For many in the wider population, incidents involving the death of Aboriginal peoples during the early days of Australia's history are seen as a natural part of 'progress'. Tragic as they may have been, the prevailing argument is that they happened at another time – a time when this 'great nation' was being colonised and civilised, when 'pioneers' struggled to eke out a living in a strange and hostile environment, 'creating civilisation out of a wilderness' (Attwood, 2005, p. 14). This was a time of opportunity, of commercialism, capitalism, and advancement.

Many non-Indigenous people fail to realise or acknowledge that 'the battle for Australia was the same kind of war of dispossession which was fought by Europeans anywhere in the world' (Read, 2006, p. 17). Aboriginal people were seen as mere collateral damage on the path to 'inevitable' advancement. To accuse the colonising nation, Great Britain, of any form of genocide, would be to admit wrongdoing during the founding of this country. However, what those who hold such attitudes fail to recognise is, the devastating effect on the native population: with civilisation came dislocation from Country, separation from families, then assimilation into the European way of life. With Christianity came missionaries; and with education came native residential schools, spreading like 'tiny islands scattered across the continent' (Clark, 2002, p. 165). According to Read (2006):

> Children were to be educated as if they were cultureless orphans. Separating children from their extended families created a vacuum in their own cultural knowledge, and a subsequent ignorance of how to parent their own children. The long-term effects were, for some, madness and death, and for others, many generations of desolation and misery. (p. 34)

As I discuss in the next section, it was not until the 1990s that some steps were taken in Australia to acknowledge and recognise the irreparable damage to the peoples whose lives and cultural connections have been devastated by the policies of forced child removals in the name of 'civilisation' and 'progress'.

Processes of truth, restitution, reconciliation, and reclamation

Whilst Australia has a long way to go in acknowledging the damage done through the legacy initiated by the establishment of the first native residential school in Parramatta in 1814, several more recent events have triggered a significant movement towards truth telling and reconciliation between native and non-native Australians: Prime Minister Paul Keating's 'Redfern Speech' in 1992; the report of the *National Inquiry into the Separation of Aboriginal and Torres Strait Islander Children from Their Families* (known as the *Bringing Them Home* report) in 1997; and the *National Apology to Australia's Stolen Generations* by Prime Minister Kevin Rudd in 2008. Before turning to those events, it is worth noting that the first British acknowledgement of disruption to the lives of Aboriginal peoples came on 10 December 1814, when Governor Lachlan Macquarie announced the opening of the Parramatta Native Institution and promises of land to parents, with a purpose to 'effect the civilisation of the Aborigines of NSW and to render their habits more domesticated and industrious'. Describing Aboriginal peoples as '… innocent, destitute, and unoffending race', this experiment was intended to '… not only make them happy in themselves but also in some degree useful to the community'. In the General Orders, Macquarie acknowledged the impact of British Settlement, and the exclusion of '… the natives from many of the natural advantages they had previously derived from the animal and other productions of this part of the territory'.

The Redfern Speech (1992)

One hundred and seventy-eight years after the establishment of the Parramatta Native Institution, the then-Prime Minister of Australia, Paul Keating, delivered a resounding speech in Redfern, Sydney, when launching the 1993 *Year of the World's Indigenous Peoples*. Known as the *Redfern Speech*, it was delivered on 10 December 1992, and marked the first instance of an Australian prime minister admitting the impact of colonisation on the native peoples of this country. Prime Minister Keating spoke the 'unspeakable', and broke the 'great Australian silence' on the national stage. During this address, he named the failure of the Europeans to bring much more than devastation and demoralisation to Aboriginal Australia, an injustice not to be swept aside (Keating, 1992):

> It begins, I think, with that act of recognition. Recognition that it was we who did the dispossessing. We took the traditional lands and smashed the traditional way of life. We brought the diseases. The alcohol. We committed the murders. We took the children from their mothers. We practiced discrimination and exclusion. It was our ignorance and our prejudice. And our failure to imagine these things being done to us. With some noble exceptions, we failed to make the most basic human response and enter into their hearts and minds.

Bringing Them Home report (1997)

Four-and-a-half years later, on 26 May 1997, two events occurred that would both challenge and confront the wider Australian population. The first was the tabling in the Australian Parliament of the *Bringing Them Home* report of the *National Inquiry into the Separation of Aboriginal and Torres Strait Islander Children from Their Families* (Wilson, 1997). Led by Sir Ronald Wilson, the enquiry heard testimony from hundreds of survivors of these policies. The *Bringing Them Home* report clearly demonstrated how Aboriginal and Torres Strait Islander children were systematically taken under the pretexts of education, protection, and assimilation (Wilson, 1997). It highlighted the trauma, loss, and grief that affect most Aboriginal and Torres Strait Islander families across Australia. Importantly, in the light of the earlier discussion about genocide, it noted (Wilson, 1997) that

> The policy of forcible removal of children from Indigenous Australians to other groups for the purpose of raising them separately from and ignorant of their culture and people could properly be labelled 'genocidal' in breach of binding international law from at least 11 December 1946. (p. 239)

The submission to the enquiry from the Sydney Aboriginal Mental Health Unit went further (Wilson, 1997):

> This tragic experience, across several generations, has resulted in incalculable trauma, depression and major mental health problems for Aboriginal people …. This process has been tantamount to a continuing cultural and spiritual genocide both as an individual and a community experience and we believe that it has been the single most significant factor in emotional and mental health problems which in turn have impacted on physical health. (p. 170)

And finally, the enquiry concluded (Wilson, 1997):

> When a child was forcibly removed that child's entire community lost, often permanently, its chance to perpetuate itself in that child. The Inquiry has concluded that this was a primary objective of forcible removals and is the reason they amount to genocide.

The second event on that day was the opening of the Australian Reconciliation Convention in Melbourne, by the then-Prime Minister of Australia, John Howard. In his opening address Howard, referring to the treatment of native Australians since European settlement, called it '… a blemished chapter in our history'. His response is in stark contrast to the speeches of both Paul Keating and later Kevin Rudd, as well as the spirit of the *Bringing Them Home* report (Howard, 1997):

> Personally, I feel deep sorrow for those of my fellow Australians who suffered injustices under the practices of past generations towards indigenous people. Equally, I am sorry for the hurt and trauma many people

here today may continue to feel as a consequence of those practices. In facing the realities of the past, however, we must not join those who would portray Australia's history since 1788 as little more than a disgraceful record of imperialism, exploitation and racism. Such a portrayal is a gross distortion and deliberately neglects the overall story of great Australian achievement that is there in our history to be told, and such an approach will be repudiated by the overwhelming majority of Australians who are proud of what this country has achieved although inevitably acknowledging the blemishes in its past history. Australians of this generation should not be required to accept guilt and blame for past actions and policies over which they had no control.

When the *Bringing Them Home* report was tabled in Parliament that day, it was recommended that the Prime Minister issue a public apology to the Stolen Generations. That apology was not forthcoming from John Howard, who would not subscribe to what he called 'the black armband view of history', and opposed the use of the word 'genocide' in relation to Australia's history (Reynolds, 2001). In lieu of any formal apology, a *National Sorry Day* was established to raise awareness of all native children and young people who were forcibly removed from their families. It stands as a reminder to the wider Australian population that those removals happened, and of the ongoing suffering and pain that still endures, and that this history must never be forgotten. The *Inquiry into the Stolen Generation* submission from the Howard government to the Senate Legal and Constitutional References Committee for the *Bringing Them Home* report stated there was '… never a "generation" of stolen children' (Jonas, 2000). With the Howard Government denying those atrocities ever occurred, it was easy to understand why the majority of Australians felt the same way, preferring to look at those decades of removals as being 'in the best interests of those children'.

National apology to Australia's Stolen Generations

On 13 February 2008, then-Prime Minister Kevin Rudd addressed the Australian people from Parliament to rectify '… this blemished chapter in our national history'. What follows are a few excerpts from that speech (in Hempenstall, 2018):

> Today we honour the Indigenous peoples of this land, the oldest continuing cultures in human history. We reflect on their past mistreatment. We reflect in particular on the mistreatment of those who were Stolen Generations – this blemished chapter in our nation's history …. We apologise for the laws and policies of successive Parliaments and governments that have inflicted profound grief, suffering and loss on these our fellow Australians. We apologise especially for the removal of Aboriginal

and Torres Strait Islander children from their families, their communities and their country. For the pain, suffering and hurt of these Stolen Generations, their descendants and for their families left behind, we say sorry. To the mothers and the fathers, the brothers and the sisters, for the breaking up of families and communities, we say sorry. And for the indignity and degradation thus inflicted on a proud people and a proud culture, we say sorry …. We embrace with pride, admiration and awe these great and ancient cultures we are truly blessed to have among us cultures that provide a unique, uninterrupted human thread linking our Australian continent to the most ancient prehistory of our planet.

Ten years on from the National Apology, the physical, mental, cultural, spiritual, social, and emotional well-being of Australia's Aboriginal peoples is still a matter of concern. Whilst there is no national reparation scheme, NSW, Tasmania, WA, and SA have introduced some form of reparation for members of the Stolen Generations. The Northern Territory, Queensland, and Victoria are still yet to do so. Whilst saying 'sorry' does go a long way in healing the hurt, there are still those in the wider community who continue to believe it was in the best interest of those children to be removed from their parents. However, no words of apology or well meaning attitudes can make up for the loss of family, community, and culture. No words, however well intentioned, can undo the legacy of those destructive government policies and practices.

A final note

Before the arrival of the First Fleet and missionaries, Australia had no jails; no state welfare systems; no drug, alcohol, or mental health facilities; no out-of-home care; and no residential care homes. The effects of colonisation were so catastrophic that they have become embedded in the psyche of Aboriginal and Torres Strait Islander peoples, passing down the genetic line. As a woman of Aboriginal heritage, with experience of working in Aboriginal affairs, I can confidently say that the history of colonisation does not lie dead and forgotten. It lives within us every day, a phenomenon that has come to be recognised as inter-generational trauma.

It is also vital to acknowledge the history of Aboriginal resistance and struggle. In the 1930s, Aboriginal peoples began to fight for their basic human rights to live as equals and raise their children. During the 1970s, voices grew louder and louder, like thunder booming across the landscape. Pitched higher and higher, they screamed, 'This decimation of our families – it has to stop'! Aboriginal organisations began to operate across the country, providing services to Indigenous communities, including Aboriginal legal services and medical centres, along with Aboriginal and Islander child care agencies (AICCAs). The role of the AICCA was to place Indigenous children within their extended family unit or with Indigenous carers, when they needed out-of-home care. Advocating for the best interests of the child and the abolishment of the previous harsh policies and practices, the AICCAs lobbied for national welfare legislation and policies to reduce the over-representation of Indigenous children in the care and protection system. This has resulted in the Aboriginal and Torres Strait Islander Child Placement Principle, which is now enshrined in legislation across the country. The fundamental goal of the Principle is 'to enhance and preserve Aboriginal children's connection to family and community and sense of identity and culture'.

The notion that removing native children from their parents is in the 'best interests of the child' echoes the attitudes and beliefs of missionaries like William Shelley in 1814. Whilst the Principle is definitely a way forward, it is still open to interpretation, with statutory agencies continuing to make the call as to whether they involve Aboriginal welfare agencies or what they consider to be in the 'child's best interests'. These attitudes continue to reverberate across Australia, despite the fact that the Principle has been adopted in every jurisdiction to ensure the 'Stolen Generations' do not happen again (SNAICC, 2017):

> The Aboriginal and Torres Strait Islander Child Placement Principle (ATSICPP) recognises the importance of connections to family, community, culture and country in child and family welfare legislation, policy, and practice, and asserts that self-determining communities are central to supporting and maintaining those connections.

Where native schools operated across Australia, now foster homes and residential care facilities take their place. Children no longer live under the care of missionaries, but under the watchful eye of state welfare systems. Often, workers on shift provide their day-to-day care. Like other colonised nations, Indigenous children (in Australia's case, Aboriginal and Torres Strait Islander children) are over-represented in the care and protection and juvenile justice systems, across every jurisdiction. In 2017, the Australian Bureau of Statistics found that Aboriginal and Torres Strait Islander children made up 36.9 per cent of children placed in care 2016/2017, yet they made up only 5.5 per cent of the population aged–zero to seventeen years. Rates per 1,000 are ten times that of non-Indigenous children (AIHW, 2018).

In an Aboriginal understanding of time, 230 odd years is but a mere moment. Despite all attempts by the colonisers and missionaries to destroy the oldest living cultures on earth, our cultures continue to thrive, languages are being revived, and young people are becoming proud of being First Nations youth. They are the best hope for our future.

88 Rosemary Norman-Hill

Native residential schools across Australia

School/Home/Institute name	State
Bomaderry Children's Home	NSW
Brewarrina Mission	NSW
Blacktown Native Institution	NSW
Cootamundra Domestic Training Home for Aboriginal Girls	NSW
Cowra Mission	NSW
Dubbo Mission	NSW
Farm Home for Boys	NSW
Fingal Mission	NSW
Kinchela Aboriginal Boys' Home	NSW
Mittagong Home	NSW
Mount Penang Boys' Training School	NSW
Parramatta Girls' Home	NSW
Parramatta Native Institute	NSW
Royleston Depot, Glebe	NSW
Turner Cottage	NSW
Wellington Mission	NSW
Amoonguna	NT
Borroloola Mission	NT
Croker Island Mission	NT
Daly River Roman Catholic Mission (Nauiyu Nambiyu)	NT
Darwin 'Half-Caste' Home	NT
Garden Point Mission	NT
Hermannsburg (Finke River Lutheran Mission)	NT
Jay Creek Settlement	NT
Milingimbi Mission	NT
Phillip Creek Settlement	NT
Retta Dixon Home	NT
St. Mary's Anglican Hostel	NT
The Bungalow	NT
Roper River Mission	NT
Aboriginal School on Stradbroke Island	QLD
Archer River Mission (Aurukun)	QLD
Cape Bedford Mission	QLD
Cherbourg Mission	QLD
Daintree River Mission	QLD
Doomadgee Mission	QLD
Good Shepard Sisters Home for Girls	QLD
Horton Village Home	QLD
Mona Mona Mission	QLD
Mornington Island Mission	QLD
Palm Island Settlement	QLD
Salvation Army Home for Boys	QLD
St. Gabriel's Anglican School	QLD
St. George's Parkes Catholic Home	QLD
Woorabinda	QLD
Campbell House Training Farm for Boys	SA
Colebrook Home (Adelaide)	SA
Colebrook Home (Quorn)	SA
Ernabella Mission	SA

Gerard Mission	SA
Kate Cocks Home	SA
Kent Town Salvation Army Boys' Home	SA
Koonibba Lutheran Children's Home	SA
Morialta Children's Home	SA
Point McLeay Mission (Raukkan)	SA
Point Pearce Mission Settlement	SA
Poonindie Native Training Institution/Mission	SA
Salvation Army Home for Boys	SA
Umeewarra Mission	SA
United Aborigines Mission (Oodnadatta)	SA
Ashley Home for Boys	TAS
Cape Barren Island Reserve	TAS
Glenara Children's Home	TAS
Oyster Cove Settlement	TAS
Wybalenna Settlement	TAS
Bacchus Marsh Orphanage	VIC
Ballarat Orphanage/Ballarat Children's Home	VIC
Coranderrk Aboriginal Mission	VIC
Framlingham	VIC
Lake Tyers Aboriginal Settlement	VIC
St. Luke's Toddlers' Home	VIC
Warrawee Children's Reception Centre	VIC
Beagle Bay Mission	WA
Dulhi Gunyah Orphanage	WA
Carrolup Native Settlement	WA
Christian Brothers Clontarf Boys' town	WA
Church of Christ Mission	WA
Fitzroy Crossing Depot (UAM)	WA
Forest River Mission	WA
Gnowangerup Aboriginal Mission	WA
Greenbushes Institute	WA
Hillston Anglican Farm School	WA
Holy Child Orphanage	WA
Home of the Good Shepard Leederville	WA
Katanning Aboriginal Mission School	WA
Mogumber Methodist Children's Home	WA
Moola Bulla Native Settlement	WA
Moore River Native Settlement	WA
Mount Margaret Mission	WA
Nazareth Home	WA
New Norcia Mission	WA
Norseman Mission	WA
Parkerville Children's Home	WA
Roelands Mission	WA
Sister Kate's Home	WA
St. Joseph's Farm	WA
St. Mary's Orphanage New Norcia	WA
Sunday Island Mission	WA
Tardun Children's Home	WA
United Aborigines Mission	WA
Warburton Mission (UAM)	WA
Wotjulum Mission	WA

Other Institutions in which Aboriginal children lived

School/Home/Institute Name	State
Burnside	NSW
Mount Penang Training School for Boys	NSW
Parramatta Girls Home	NSW
Westmead Boys Home	NSW
Methodist Children's Home	WA

Please refer to *Many Voices* (Mellor & Haebich, 2002) and *Bringing Them Home* (Wilson, 1997).

Notes

1. NRS 1046 Colonial Secretary: Copies of Government and General Orders and Notices 1810–1819 [SZ759, pp. 11–14; Reel 6038].
2. The word Country/Countries is capitalised to denote traditional lands of a nation or language group. In Australia, there were thought to be between 500 and 600 different nations, each with their own language at the time of colonisation (Kociumbas, 1997; Kohen, 1993; Parbury, 1988). Many of those languages are now lost.
3. The 'Dreaming' or 'Dreamtime' are English words used to describe the time of creation for Aboriginal peoples (Cowan, 1992; Edwards, 2004; Keneally, 1987; King, 2009; Kohen, 2006; Laidlaw, 1990; Parbury, 1988; Stanner, 1987).
4. The term 'native' is used to describe Aboriginal and Torres Strait Islander peoples as the original inhabitants of Australia.
5. Culture, with a capital 'C', is used to describe the many different cultures of Australia's native peoples.

References

Allam, L. (2002). Memories of home: This beautiful sense of freedom. In D. Mellor & A. Haebich (eds.), *Many Voices: Reflections on Experiences of Indigenous Child Separation* (p. 324). Canberra, Australia: National Library of Australia.

Attwood, B. (2005). *Telling the Truth About Aboriginal History*. Crows Nest, NSW: Allen & Unwin.

Australian Human Rights Commission. (2019). *Bringing Them Home: 8. History – Northern Territory*. Available online: https://www.humanrights.gov.au/publications/bringing-them-home-8-history-northern-territory [Accessed April, 2019].

Australian Institute of Health and Welfare (AIHW). (2018). *Child Protection Australia 2016–17*. Available online: https://www.aihw.gov.au/getmedia/66c7c364-592a-458c-9ab0-f90022e25368/aihw-cws-63.pdf.aspx?inline=true [Accessed April, 2019].

Barry, A. (2008). 'Equal to children of European origin': Educability and the civilising mission in early colonial Australia. *History Australia*, 5(2): 41.41–41.16.

Barta, T. (1987). Relations of genocide: Land and lives in the colonization of Australia. *Genocide and the Modern Age: Etiology and Case Studies of Mass Death*, 2: 237–253.

Bennett, M. (2009). Smallpox and cowpox under the Southern Cross: The smallpox epidemic of 1789 and the advent of vaccination in colonial Australia. *Bulletin of the History of Medicine*, 83(1): 37–62.

Berndt, R.M. & Berndt, C.H. (1999). *The World of the First Australians: Aboriginal Traditional Life, Past and Present* (5th edn). Canberra: Aboriginal Studies Press for the Australian Institute of Aboriginal and Torres Strait Islander Studies.

Blainey, G. (2015). *The Story of Australia's People: The Rise and Fall of Ancient Australia*. Scoresby, Australia: Penguin Random House Australia.

Brock, P. (1987). Writing Aboriginal collective biography: Pooninide, South Australia, 1850-1894. History of an Aboriginal mission. *Aboriginal History*, 11: 116–128.

Brook, J. & Kohen, J. (1991). *The Parramatta Native Institution and the Black Town: A History*. Kensington, NSW: NSW University Press.

Burridge, N. & Chodkiewicz, A. (2012). An historical overview of Aboriginal education policies in the Australian context. In N. Burridge, F. Whalan & K. Vaughan (eds.), *Indigenous Education* (pp. 11–21). Rotterdam, The Netherlands: Sense Publishers.

Buti, A. (2002). The removal of Aboriginal children: Canada and Australia compared. *University of Western Sydney Law Review*, 6: 25–37.

Carney, R. (1995). Aboriginal residential schools before confederation: The early experience. *Historical Studies*, 61: 13–40.

Cassidy, J. (2009). The Canadian response to Aboriginal residential schools: Lessons for Australia and the United States? *Elaw: Murdoch University Electronic Journal of Law*, 16(2): 38–71.

Claes, R. & Clifton, D. (1998). *Needs and Expectations for Redress of Victims of Abuse at Native Residential Schools*. Available online: https://dalspace.library.dal.ca/bitstream/handle/10222/10440/Sage%20Research%20Redress%20EN.pdf?sequence [Accessed April, 2019].

Clark, I. (2002). Indigenous children and Institutions: 'For the instruction and improvement of the natives'. In D. Mellor & A. Haebich (eds.), *Many Voices*. Canberra, Australia: National Library of Australia.

Coe, M. (1999). Windradyne: A Wiradjuri Koorie. In P. Newbury (ed.), *Aboriginal Heroes of the Resistance: From Pemulwuy to Mabo* (2nd edn.). Sydney, Australia: Action for World Development.

Collins, D. (1798). *An Account of the English Colony in New South Wales, with Remarks on the Dispositions, Customs, Manners etc, of the Native Inhabitants of that Country* (Vol. 1). Sydney: Terrey Hills. Reed, A.H. & Reed, A.W. in association with the Royal Australian Historical Society.

Cowan, J. (1992). *The Aborigine Tradition*. Brisbane, Australia: Element Books Ltd.

Cruickshank, J. (2008). To exercise a beneficial influence over a man: Marriage, gender and the native institutions in early colonial Australia. In A. Barry, J. Cruickshank, A. Brown-May & P. Grimshaw (eds.), *Evangelists of Empire? Missionaries in Colonial History* (pp. 115–124). Melbourne, Australia: eScholarship Research Centre in collaboration with the Schools of Historical Studies.

Das, P. (2013). 'The frontier spectrum': Colonial Australia and aboriginal resistance. *Galaxy: International Multidisciplinary Journal*, II(IV): 1–10.

Edwards, W.H. (2004). *An Introduction to Aboriginal Societies*. Melbourne, Australia: Thomson/Social Science Press.

Elder, B. (1998). *Blood on the Wattle: Massacres and Maltreatment of Australian Aborigines Since 1788* (Vol. 2). Sydney, Australia: National Book Distributors.

Find and Connect. (2019). *The Bungalow (1914–1942)*. Available online: https://www.findandconnect.gov.au/guide/nt/YE00019 [Accessed April, 2019].

Fletcher, J. (1989a). *Clean, Clad and Courteous: A History of Aboriginal Education in New South Wales*. Carlton, NSW: J Fletcher.

Fletcher, J. (1989b). *Documents in the History of Aboriginal Education*. Marrickville, NSW: Southwood Press Ltd.

Gladwin, M. (2012). Flogging parsons? Australian Anglican clergymen, the magistracy, and convicts, 1788-1850. *Journal of Religious History*, 36(3): 386–403.

Grant, E. (2014). The incarceration of Australian aboriginal women and children. In P. Ashton & J. Wilson (eds.), *Silent System: Forgotten Australians and the Institutionalisation of Women and Children*. North Melbourne, Australia: Australian Scholarly Publishing Pty Ltd.

Harris, J. (1994). *One Blood: 200 years of Aboriginal Encounter with Christianity: A Story of Hope* (2nd edn., Vol. 2). Sutherland, NSW: Albatross Books.

Hempenstall, H. (2018). *Kevin Rudd's Sorry Speech: Ten Years Later, Are Indigenous Australians Better Off?* October 3rd. Available online: https://www.who.com.au/kevin-rudd-sorry-speech [Accessed April, 2019].

Howard, J. (1997). *Transcript of the Opening Address to the Australian Reconciliation Convention Melbourne*. May 26th. Available online: https://pmtranscripts.pmc.gov.au/release/transcript-10361 [Accessed April, 2019].

Hunter, B. & Carmody, J. (2015). Estimating the aboriginal population in early colonial Australia: The role of chickenpox reconsidered. *Australian Economic History Review*, 55(2): 112–138.

Jacobs, M. (2006). Indian boarding schools in comparative perspective: The removal of Indigenous children in the United States and Australia, 1880-1940. *Faculty Publications, Department of History University of Nebraska-Lincoln*, 20: 202–231.

Jonas, W. (2000). *Submission to the Senate Legal and Constitutional References Committee's Inquiry into the Stolen Generation*. Available online: https://www.humanrights.gov.au/sites/default/files/content/pdf/social_justice/stolen_senate_submission.pdf [Accessed April, 2019].

Keating, P. (1992). *Transcript of Speech Delivered in Redfern Park*. December 10th. Available online: https://antar.org.au/sites/default/files/paul_keating_speech_transcript.pdf [Accessed April, 2019].

Keneally, T. (1987). Here nature is reversed. In E. Jagger (ed.), *Australia Beyond the Dreamtime* (p. 248). Richmond, VIC: William Heinemann Australia.

Kidd, R. (2002). Looking back: An historical overview of policy, legislation and administration relating to Indigenous child separation in Australia. In D. Mellor & A. Haebich (eds.), *Many Voices: Reflections on Experiences of Indigenous Child Separation* (pp. 247–264). Canberra, Australia: National Library of Australia.

King, J. (2009). *Great Moments in Australian History*. Sydney, Australia: Allen and Unwin.

Kociumbas, J. (1997). *Australian Childhood: A History*. St Leonards, NSW: Allen & Unwin.

Kohen, J. (1993). *The Darug and their Neighbours: The Traditional Aboriginal Owners of the Sydney Region*. Blacktown, NSW: Darug Link.

Kohen, J. (2006). *Daruganora: Darug Country: The Place and the People*. Blacktown, NSW: Darug Tribal Aboriginal Corporation.

Laidlaw, R. (1990). *Discovering Australian History to 1900: An Evidence-Based Approach*. Caulfield East, VIC: Edward Arnold (Australia) Pty Ltd.

Lemkin, R. (1944). *Axis Rule in Occupied Europe: Laws of Occupation, Analysis of Government, Proposals for Redress*. Washington: Carnegie Endowment for International Peace.

McHugh, S. (2002). The carers: 'To me they were children'. In D. Mellor & A. Haebich (eds.), *Many Voices: Reflections on Experiences of Indigenous Child Separation*. Canberra, Australia: National Library of Australia.

Mellor, D. & Haebich, A. (eds.). (2002). *Many Voices: Reflections on Experiences of Indigenous Child Separation*. Canberra, Australia: National Library of Australia.

Melville, W.I. (2006). *An Historical Analysis of the Structures Established for the Provision of Anglican Schools in the Diocese of Perth, Western Australia Between 1917 and 1992*. Perth, Australia: University of Western Australia.

Moses, A.D. (2004). Genocide and settler society in Australian history. In A.D. Moses (ed.), *Genocide and Settler Society: Frontier Violence and Stolen Indigenous Children in Australian History* (pp. 3–48). New York: Berghahn Books.

New South Wales Government Office of Environment and Heritage. (2019). *Bomaderry Aboriginal Children's Home*. Available online: https://www.environment.nsw.gov.au/heritageapp/ViewHeritageItemDetails.aspx?ID=5061330 [Accessed April, 2019].

Newbury, P. (ed.) (1999). *Aboriginal Heroes of the Resistance: From Pemulwuy to Mabo*. Sydney, Australia: Action for World Development.

O'Brien, A. (2008). Charity and philanthropy. *Sydney Journal*, 1(3): 18–28.

Parbury, N. (1988). *Survival: A History of Aboriginal Life in New South Wales*. Sydney, Australia: Bloxham and Chambers.

Parbury, N. (2008). *Survival: A History of Aboriginal Life in New South Wales* (Revised edn.) Surrey Hills, NSW: NSW Department of Aboriginal Affairs.

Perpitch, N. (2018). *A Journey into 'Hell on Earth'*. Available online: https://www.abc.net.au/news/2018-05-26/moore-river-aboriginal-settlement-journey-into-hell-on-earth/9790658 [Accessed April, 2019].

Prochner, L. (2004). Early childhood education programs for Indigenous children in Canada, Australia and New Zealand. *Australian Journal of Early Childhood*, 29(4): 7–16.

Ramsland, J. (1986). *Children of the Back Lanes: Destitute and Neglected Children in Colonial New South Wales*. Kensington, NSW: NSW University Press.

Read, P. (1981). *The Stolen Generations: The Removal of Aboriginal Children in New South Wales 1883 to 1969*. Sydney, Australia: NSW Department of Aboriginal Affairs.

Read, P. (2006). *The Stolen Generations: The Removal of Aboriginal Children in New South Wales 1883 to 1969* (Revised edn.) Sydney: NSW Department of Aboriginal Affairs.

Read, P. (2007). Shelly's mistake: The Parramatta Native Institution. In M. Crotty & D. Roberts (eds.), *The Great Mistakes of Australian History* (pp. 32–47). Sydney, Australia: UNSW Press.

Read, P. (2015). Dispossession is a legitimate experience. In A. McGrath & M. Jebb (eds.), *Long History, Deep Time: Deepening Histories of Place* (pp. 119–133). Canberra, Australia: ANU Press.

Reynolds, H. (2001). *An Indelible Stain? The Question of Genocide in Australia's History*. Ringwood, VIC: Penguin.

Reynolds, H. (2013). *Forgotten War*. Sydney, NSW: New South Wales Publishing.

Ritchie, J. (1986). *Lachlan Macquarie: A Biography*. Melbourne, Australia: University Press.

Rowley, C. (1970). *The Destruction of Aboriginal Society*. Canberra, Australia: Australian National University Press.

Sheehan, N., Martin, G., Krysinska, K. & Kilroy, K. (2009). *Sustaining Connection: A Framework for Aboriginal and Torres Strait Islander Community, Cultural, Spiritual, Social and Emotional Wellbeing*. Brisbane, Australia: Centre for Suicide Prevention Studies, University of Queensland.

Smith, K. (2001). *Bennelong: The Coming in of the Eora: Sydney Cove 1788-1792*. Sydney, Australia: Kangaroo Press.

SNAICC: National Voice for Our Children. (2017). *Understanding and Applying the Aboriginal and Torres Strait Islander Child Placement Principle*. Available online: https://www.snaicc.org.au/understanding-applying-aboriginal-torres-strait-islander-child-placement-principle/ [Accessed April, 2019].

Stanner, W.E.H. (1987). *The Dreaming*. Melbourne, Australia: The Macmillan Company of Australia Pty Ltd.

Sydney Gazette and New South Wales Advertiser. (1814). p. 2, December 31st. Available online: https://trove.nla.gov.au/newspaper/page/7240 [Accessed April, 2019].

Sydney Gazette and New South Wales Advertiser. (1819). p. 2, April 17th. Available online: https://trove.nla.gov.au/newspaper/page/494184 [Accessed April, 2019].

Tatz, C. (1999). Genocide in Australia. *Journal of Genocide Research*, 1(3): 315–352.

Tench, W. (1793). *A Complete Account of the Settlement at Port Jackson Including An Accurate Description of the Situation of the Colony; of the Natives; and Of Its Natural Productions*. Available online: http://setis.library.usyd.edu.au/ozlit/pdf/p00044.pdf [Accessed April, 2019].

van Krieken, R. (2004). Rethinking cultural genocide: Aboriginal child removal and settler-colonial state formation. *Oceania*, 75(2): 125–151.

Willmot, E. (1987). *Pemulwuy: The Rainbow Warrior*. Sydney, Australia: Allen and Unwin.

Wilson, R. (1997). *Bringing Them Home: National Inquiry into the Separation of Aboriginal and Torres Strait Islander Children from Their Families*. Canberra, Australia: Human Rights and Equal Opportunity Commission.

Chapter 5

Greenland

Stephen James Minton and Helene Thiesen

Greenland is, in two ways, a somewhat exceptional inclusion in this book. In the first place, it is to be acknowledged that, unlike the other countries that are featured, there was never a system of residential schools in which Indigenous children were forcibly enrolled in Greenland itself. Secondly, Greenland is the only country that is featured in this book in which the Indigenous population is today (and, as it has always been) in the majority. Yet as we shall see, Greenland has experienced a millennium of European colonisation; and, despite moves towards independence, including limited 'home rule' from 1979, and self-government from 2009, Greenland remains a territorial possession of Denmark. Some of the specifics in these respects are outlined in the first section of this chapter, 'Historical contexts'. It is also to be acknowledged that abusive attempts at forcible cultural assimilation through means of educational and social systems have been part of Greenland's story. To exemplify this, we will provide an account of the Danish state's taking, in 1951, of twenty-two Inuit children, from their homes and families in Greenland, to families and institutions Denmark, where they were to be 're-educated as 'model Danish citizens', in a section entitled 'The experiment'. Finally, and drawing on the recently concluded work of the Reconciliation Commission in Greenland, we will examine some of the 'Efforts towards processes of truth, restitution, reconciliation, and reclamation' in this chapter's final section.

Historical contexts

The 2019 population of Greenland (in *Kalaalisutt* [(Western) Greenlandic], *Kalaallit Nunaat* ['land of the Kalaallit'[1]]) was estimated at 56,673 (World Population Review, 2019). Greenlandic Inuit people (which include mixed-ethnicity people) make up between 85 and 90 per cent of the population, with a non-Inuit population (which is mainly Danish, so includes Danes and Danish Greenlanders,[2] and also other Europeans [the largest number of which are Icelanders], North Americans and other foreign nationals [chiefly Thai and Filipino]) making up the remainder (Statistics Greenland, 2018). The

Inuit (sing. *Inuk*) peoples are the Indigenous peoples who inhabit areas of the Alaskan, Canadian, and Greenlandic Arctic. Whilst archaeological evidence exists of a number of successive Paleo-Eskimo cultures living in Greenland from 2550 BCE (what Western anthropologists and historians have called the 'Saqqaq', 'Independence I', 'Dorset', and 'Independence II' cultures, who arrived from the landmass that is now Canada), the present-day Greenlandic Inuit population is believed to descend from the Thule culture, who arrived in Greenland from the east (Alaska) in around 1300 CE (Grønnow, 2017; Sale & Potapov, 2010). The Inuit native languages are part of the Eskimo-Aleut family (Kaplan, 2011), and since 2009, Western Greenlandic has been the sole official language of Greenland (Statsministeriet, 2009), although smaller populations traditionally speak the Northern (*Inughuit*; ca. 800–1,000 speakers) and Eastern (*Tunumiit oqaatit*; ca. 3,000 speakers) Greenlandic languages (Simons & Fennig, 2018).

The past millennium of Greenlandic history has been dominated by European colonisation. The first of these colonisers was the Norseman Erik Thorvaldsson (Old Norse: *Eiríkr Þorvaldsson*), better known by his nickname, Erik the Red (Old Norse: *Eiríkr hinn rauði*) (950–c. 1003), who first landed in Greenland (having travelled there from Iceland) in 982 CE. Four years later he returned, successfully landing fourteen ships (a further twenty-one ships were either turned back, or were wrecked), loaded with supplies and settlers. A year after that, more Icelanders arrived, and two settlements were founded (*Øysterbygd* ['East Settlement'] at Qaqortoq, and *Vesterbygd* ['West Settlement'] at Nuuk). After Christianity was established, the Norsemen built sixteen churches, two monasteries, and a cathedral (Sale & Potapov, 2010). The Norse settlement, which lasted until 1410, numbered 4,000 people at its peak; the Norsemen farmed and traded with the Greenlandic Inuit, although as Sale and Potapov (2010, p. 96) put it, 'Evidence from both the Norse sagas and Inuit tales suggest that dealings between the two peoples were not always friendly, each telling of conflicts, usually on a small scale, but involving deaths on both sides'.

The reasons as to why these early Norse settlements in Greenland died out are disputed; however, an expedition sent by the Danish king Christian I (which marked the beginning of Danish involvement in Greenland) could find no evidence of Norse survivors (Sale & Potapov, 2010). Modern-day Danish colonisation of Greenland (which Petersen (1995, p. 119) characterised as being '….synonymous with mission and trade station') began in 1721, with the arrival in Greenland of Hans Egede, a pastor from Bergen,[3] who had convinced the Danish king of the benefits to the crown of the acquisition of the island, and founded the settlement of Godthåb (which is now Nuuk). His fifteen years on the island, in which he attempted to convert the Inuit to Christianity, were marked by a smallpox epidemic caused by the visit of an infected child visitor from Denmark, which killed one-quarter of the Greenlandic population; widespread scurvy (due to the near impossibility of agriculture); and, instead of being Greenland being deliberately populated by 'good Danish Christians', Egede found that the settlement was used as '....a dumping ground for convicts, and the "women of easy virtue" who accompanied them' (Sale & Potapov, 2010, p. 97). However, Danish settlements were made, and a governor was installed, leading to the enrichment of Danish traders and the impoverishment of the Inuit population. The Danes completed their mapping of Greenland shortly before the First World War, and whilst there was periodic trading contact between some Greenlandic Inuit populations and the British (with their commercial and territorial interests in the Arctic, for example, neighbouring Baffin Island in Canada), and the Dutch (Petersen, 1995), it was not until the raising of the Norwegian national flag[4] by Norwegian fur-trappers in northeast Greenland (an area that they called '*Erik Raudes land*' [Erik the Red's Land]) that the Danish claim to the entirety of Greenland was seriously threatened. The International Court of the League of Nations ruled in favour of Denmark's sovereignty over all of Greenland in 1933 (Sale & Potapov, 2010).

As Denmark was occupied by Nazi Germany during the Second World War, the status of Greenland was, for a while, uncertain; however, the Danish ambassador to the United States, against the wishes of his government, signed an agreement that made Greenland a US protectorate, and the Americans built seventeen military sites on Greenland (Sale & Potapov, 2010). After the war, the United States signed a treaty with Denmark on the defence of Greenland, and began building an airport base at Thule in 1951. Significantly, in order to expand the defence area around the air base, the entire *Inughuit* population (the Thule people – twenty-six Inuit families, consisting of 116 people) were evicted from the villages of Pituffik and Uummannaq, and moved 81 miles (130 kilometres) north to the new town of Qanaaq. They were forced to leave behind their houses (which were later burnt down), a hospital, a school, a radio station, warehouses, a church (which was later moved to another village) and a graveyard (Environmental Law Alliance Worldwide, 2019), and to live in tents between May and November in 1953, whilst houses were being constructed for them in Qanaaq (Ehrlich, 2003).[5] In 2003, a legal case brought by 428 people from the Thule District in Greenland and '*Hingitaq 53*' (a group that represented the interests of relocated *Inughuit* people and their descendants) against the Danish Government was over-ruled by the Danish Supreme Court. An appeal was made to the European Court of Human Rights, who unanimously declared the application inadmissible (Environmental Law Alliance Worldwide, 2019).

The year 1953 was important for Greenlanders in another way, too; it was in that year that Denmark passed a new constitution, formally ending Greenland's status as a colony, and effectively making Greenland a constituent county within the Danish realm, being provided with nominal representation in the Danish *Folketing* (national parliament) (Ehrlich, 2003; Petersen, 1995; Sale & Potapov, 2010). Although this might have seemed significant in formal administrative terms, with respect to lived realities, Petersen (1995) noted:

> In fact, no real change occurred, as Denmark for a long time administered the common human rights or civil rights in Greenland and continued to govern Greenland with the same civil servants and the same administrative body as before. (p. 121)

The modernisation period in Greenland that followed this Danish constitutional change included a campaign to reduce tuberculosis (at that time, the leading cause of death), improvements to housing, the industrialisation of the economy and the reorganisation of the education system on a Danish model.[6] All of this relied heavily on the importing of Danish manpower and 'expertise'; it was paid for by the Danish state, and planned centrally in the Danish capital, Copenhagen (Petersen, 1995):

> Greenland was in fact more than ever governed politically, economically, intellectually and physically by another people....modernisation made Greenland economically more dependent on Denmark than ever. The Danish staff in administration, and not least in education, introduced Danish ideas concerning economic activities and organisation. The means of attracting Danish staff to Greenland were economic, housing, and social privileges. This created a really visible discrimination between colleagues according to their Danish or Greenlandic origin. (p. 122)

As Petersen noted (1995, p. 122), 'It was commonly said that any Dane working in Greenland "had come to help the Greenlanders". It was an old idea of the colonial civil servants that they had to do tasks which "the Greenlanders" could not manage for themselves'. Much political discourse about Greenland in Denmark following the 1953 changes to the constitution focussed upon Greenlanders now being considered 'Northern Danes', and an expression of faith that the modernisation measures would give Greenlanders their 'best chance', or even an 'equal chance', in the Danish realm.[7]

Home rule in Greenland was eventually established on 1 May 1979, after 70.1 per cent (of the 63.3 per cent of registered voters who turned out) had voted for greater autonomy from Denmark, in a referendum held on 17 January that year. The Greenlandic Home Rule Act gave Greenland the right to elect its own Parliament (the thirty-one-member *Inatsisartut*, or [in Danish] *Landsting*), which approves the executive government (*Naalakkersuisut*, or *Lansstyre*), which would have sovereignty and administrative responsibility in the areas of education, environment, fisheries, and health. However, under the Home Rule Act, the Greenlandic Parliament was not granted jurisdiction in the areas of civil rights law, defence and national security, finance and the monetary system, or justice (including policing, as well as the criminal and court systems) (Isbosethsen, 2007).[8] Although Greenland is a member state of the Council of Europe, it left the European Economic Community (EEC; the forerunner of the European Union) in 1985, primarily to maintain control of fishing in its territorial waters (although Denmark remained a member of the EEC and EU). Henceforth, EU law has applied to Greenland only in the area of trade (Isbosethsen, 2007).

On 25 November 2008, 75.5 per cent (of the 72.0 per cent of registered voters who turned out) voted for Greenlandic self-government, in a non-binding[9] referendum (*BBC News*, 2008). The result – the passing of the Self-Government Act (SGA) – took effect in June 2009, thus marking an end to exactly three decades of limited 'home rule' autonomy, and most significantly the taking over of the country's mineral and oil rights (which had previously been co-managed with Denmark). Denmark pays an annual subsidy to Greenland, which had been negotiated every two to three years, and which in 2008 stood at DKK 3.4 billion (then £395 million), or about 30 per cent of Greenland's GDP (Kuokkanen, 2017). The issue of the continued payment of the subsidy, which was fixed at the 2008–2009 level under the Self-Government Act, was probably one factor that underlay the negative comments made by some Danish politicians at the time. Per Ørum Jørgensen, a Conservative People's Party member of the Danish Parliament, opined that, 'Whether the Greenlanders can take over more political institutions themselves depends heavily on the natural resources. It could well be thirty to forty years', and worse yet, although somewhat predictably, the Danish People's Party[10] MP Søren Espersen stated that the Greenlanders voting for self-government had been '….brainwashed with unprecedented propaganda' (*BBC News*, 2008).

Kuokkanen (2017, pp. 180–181) argued that the freezing of the block grant has been '….a double-edged sword' because whilst it is no longer negotiated, and therefore '….cannot be used as political leverage by Denmark in other negotiations', on the other hand, it has '….created great pressure for the Greenland government to pursue an aggressive resource policy, in an attempt to find new sources of revenue as fast as possible'. Indeed, Kuokkanen (2017) stated that the economic aspect of implementing and fast-tracking self-rule was firmly grasped by the fifth (and first female) Greenlandic prime minister, Aleqa Hammond (who seems to have evidenced none of the self-deception that Espersen might have expected, had she been 'brainwashed by unprecedented propaganda', or been the agent of the brainwashing of others), who stated in an interview of 2013 (in Kuokkanen, 2017):

> Fully implementing the Self-Government Act would require us to become economically independent. In order to take control of all the new fields of jurisdiction requires us to become self-sufficient and self-governing in those areas. This puts a lot of pressure on us by ourselves. It is very important that the pressure comes from within and not from outside.

> The Self Rule Agreement is a fair agreement although achieving a full implementation is a very challenging task for us. If we are not able to do it, we also cannot achieve independence. The Agreement is an important undertaking for us. (p. 181)

Critically, Kuokkanen (2017) noted that in negotiating the self-government agreement, there had been '….no discussion of Inuit values or governance; there was no public or political discourse on the topic before self-rule, and [there has been] none since'. However, she argued that '….only some individuals today express criticism of the adoption of "Western" or "European" governance system', and that for many, Greenlandic self-governance *represents* governance based on Inuit values for two reasons: firstly, '….because of the central role of Inuit Greenlanders in drafting the self-government agreement', and secondly, '….because of the overwhelming Greenlandic support the agreement received in [the self-governance] referendum'. However, there was no explicit recognition of the Inuit *as a people* in the Self-Government Act,[11] and consequently, it did not (indeed, it could not) deal with the issue of the self-determination of the Inuit as an Indigenous people. Nevertheless, Kuokkanen (2017) concluded that Greenlandic self-governance has signified a greater autonomy and powers of decision-making for a country with an Indigenous majority, and that the Inuit are no longer subjugated by a colonising state; and further, that '….as an example of a successfully negotiated self-government agreement, Greenland's self-rule serves as an inspiration for other Indigenous peoples, especially other Inuit in the Arctic' (p. 193).

In terms of future aspirations, under the Self-Government Act, Greenland can declare full independence, providing that there is an approval to do so (via referendum) by the Greenlandic people (Kuokkanen, 2017). Whilst a poll conducted in 2016 showed that 64 per cent of respondents favoured full independence (Skydsbjerg & Turnowsky, 2016), 78 per cent of respondents in a poll conducted in 2017 were opposed to independence if it meant a fall in living standards (Bjerregaard, 2017). Some progress on meeting the challenges outlined by Hammond (interview, 2013; in Kuokkanen, 2017, p. 181 – see above) has been made, especially in the area of accelerated development in the extractive sector (which is considered to be the main condition of implementing self-governance (Kuokkanen, 2017). Nevertheless, the concerns about a fall in living standards are very real ones; on declaring independence, the subsidies paid to Greenland by Denmark will cease, a fact that current Danish Prime Minister Lars Løkke reiterated recently, along with requesting clarity from Greenland as to whether it wishes to remain a part of the Danish Kingdom, or to declare independence (Ritzaus Bureau, 2018).

The experiences, effects, and legacies of Danish colonisation have been, and still are, painfully evident in Greenland, not least in the area of health. Bjerregaard et al. (2004) pointed out that whilst it is unlikely that the Indigenous peoples of the Arctic had disease-free lives prior to European contact (e.g. early European observers had reported that the 'native' populations were 'healthy and vigorous'), the scattered populations of Indigenous peoples in the Arctic had no resistance to the infectious diseases (influenza, measles, smallpox, whooping cough) that the European explorers, missionaries, traders, whalers and, eventually, settlers, brought with them. The consequences of this were, predictably, devastating. Tuberculosis was one of the leading causes of death amongst the Inuit population during the nineteenth and twentieth centuries, and reached crisis proportions in the 1940s and 1950s, although after specific responses to combat the disease, apart from sporadic outbreaks, it has been under control in recent decades. However, Inuit people remain at an elevated risk for other infectious diseases, including pneumonia, meningitis, hepatitis, and sexually transmitted diseases (Bjerregaard et al., 2004).

Several chronic diseases – including specific forms of cancer, diabetes, heart disease, hypertension, obesity, and stroke – have been referred to as 'diseases of modernisation' or 'Western diseases', because, as Bjerregaard et al. 2004, p. 392 put it, '....they tend to increase in traditional societies (such as circumpolar Indigenous peoples) undergoing rapid social changes, with changes in diet, reduction in physical activity, and exposure to new environmental hazards'. All have been found to occur at greater levels of frequency amongst Inuit people than they do amongst their European counterparts. Traditionally, the lifestyle (hunting, vigorous physical activity), diet (high intake of fish and marine mammals), and genetic endowment of Inuit people had offered protection against many of these chronic diseases, but an increasingly Westernised diet, and the high prevalence of smoking and the use of alcohol, has reversed this. Chronic and acute abuse of alcohol has also, of course, been a factor in many incidents of abuse, accidents, interpersonal violence, and suicide amongst Inuit people (Bjerregaard et al., 2004). Furthermore, a representative cross-sectional study conducted amongst Greenland Inuit adults (n = 2,189) by Larsen, Curtis, and Bjerregaard (2013) showed that gambling, too, is a pervasive problem, and was associated with social transition and traumatic events in childhood (alcohol problems in childhood home, and sexual abuse in childhood (women only)), suggesting that people caught between tradition and modern ways of life are more vulnerable to such problems.

Hersher (2016) reported that, '....for more than thirty years, the suicide rate in Greenland has been *among* the highest in the world' (emphasis ours); however, data compiled by the World Health Organisation (2011) of reports between 1985 and 2011 showed that the suicide rate in Greenland was, in fact, *by far* the world's highest, at 83.0 suicides per 100,000 of the population,[12] which was more than twice the rate of the second placed country (Lithuania, with 36.7 suicides per 100,000 of the population).[13] Suicide was not unknown, but was not common, amongst the Inuit before the 1950s; traditionally, it had been practised mainly by the elderly and the infirm

(Bjerregaard et al., 2004). Furthermore, Hicks (2007) records that in 1935, Berthelsen had calculated an average annual suicide rate of 3.0 per 100,000 of the population in Greenland for the years between 1900 and 1930, and that as late as 1960, there were occasional years when no Greenlanders committed suicide. More recently, however, Lehti et al. (2009) recorded in their systematic review of studies of mental health, substance use, and suicidal behaviour amongst young Indigenous people in the Arctic not only that youth suicide rates were alarmingly high in many parts of the Arctic (particularly in Greenland and Alaska), but that rates were systematically and uniformly higher amongst Indigenous peoples than they were amongst non-Indigenous groups, across studies. Unlike what is the case in most Western countries, the suicide rate in Greenland decreases with age (World Health Organisation, 2011), and as suicide rates are higher amongst males than females, most of those who commit suicide in Greenland are boys between the ages of fifteen and nineteen years old (Bannister, 2010). They tend to do so by violent means (46 per cent by hanging, and 37 per cent by shooting (Björkstén, Kripke & Bjerregaard, 2009)). Björkstén et al. (2009) found that the clustering of suicides in the summer months was more pronounced in areas north of the Arctic Circle, and that suicide rates were higher in northern parts of west Greenland than in the southern parts of the country; thus, they proposed that seasonality (as well as alcohol abuse and impulsivity) was a risk factor. However, psychological (especially depression) and social factors (marital and domestic conflict, poverty) have also been implicated (Hersher, 2016). Hicks (2007) reports that Leineweber (2000) concluded, from his work with death certificates and police reports for deaths attributed to suicide between 1993 and 1995, that suicides of Greenlanders were most associated with '….frequent conflict within the family and with friends, a recent life-threatening experience, expressing suicidal intentions and the acute abuse of alcohol' (p. 34). Hicks (2007) further stated:

> The only logical explanation for the dramatic increase in suicide rates among Inuit living in different regions of the Arctic, with similar outcomes among the sexes and age groups, at different and distinct time periods, is that a similar 'basket' of social determinants has impacted heavily on Inuit societies at different times across the different regions and sub-regions. The manner in which Inuit in different regions of the Arctic in recent decades experienced history several decades ago may have had significant impacts upon the mental health of their children, the next generation of young Inuit,[14] who in some cases were the first Inuit to grow up in settled communities. (p. 34)

However, with a firmly held focus on the potential means of suicide prevention in the Arctic, as well as emphasising the importance of the role of historical experiences of colonisation, Hicks (2007, p. 35) also stressed the importance of '....some other reasons specific to Inuit societies as they exist today'. Factors that could, and should, be addressed as a matter of urgency include the full gamut of 'adverse childhood experiences' and '....weak health and education systems, poverty, high rates of all kinds of violence, high rates of substance abuse and generally poor living conditions' (Hicks, 2007, p. 36).

It is clear, therefore, that the appalling incidence rates of physical and mental health difficulties and suicide amongst the Inuit population in Greenland have warranted the not inconsiderable attention of researchers who have, in their attempts to explain (and sometimes point the way towards addressing) these problems, considered a number of factors, or sometimes proposed specific constellations of factors. What such sometimes disparate accounts have in common, perhaps, is a highlighting of external and internal conflicts that exist between traditional Inuit and colonial European traditions in Greenland – those that have existed historically, those that exert their contemporary effects through legacy, and those that persist through circumstances of social inequality in the present day. As we shall see in the following section, education – or rather, a 'social experiment' in attempted 're-education' – has also been a part of Greenland's colonial experience.

'The experiment'

In May 1951, the ship MS Disko set sail from Nuuk with twenty-two Inuit children on board, who were taken from their families in Greenland as part of a social experiment – the true nature of which remained concealed for decades – to have them '....re-educated as model Danish citizens' (Otzen, 2015), and after a year-and-a-half's schooling in Denmark, '....to return as Danish cultural bearers' (Karkov, 2019). The co-author of this chapter, Helene Thiesen, was one of these children.[15] In an interview with the BBC in 2015, Helene described her experiences. In 1951, she was living in Nuuk with her mother and two siblings,[16] and two well-dressed Danish men and their interpreter appeared at the door, asking whether Helene's mother would be willing to send her to Denmark for six months in order to learn Danish and to have the chance of a bright future. Ahead of this, school priests and headteachers had been telegrammed by the Danish authorities, who worked in association with Save the Children Denmark, and asked to identify bright children between the ages of six and ten years (such as Helene, who was then seven years old), who were to be fostered in Denmark, and re-educated there as 'little Danes'.

On arrival in Denmark (a place that Helene had never previously heard of), the children were quarantined at a so-called 'summer camp', known as *Fedgaarden* (which was run by Save the Children Denmark); such was the prestige of the project in Denmark that the Queen of Denmark visited, although photographs taken of the visit reveal that this was not a happy occasion for the Inuit children. Helene developed eczema at Fedgaarden; and for this reason, she was sent to live with a doctor, whose responses were to cover Helene's elbows and heels with a black ointment, and to forbid her from entering the living room, for fear of her damaging the furniture. Helene distrusted the adults who had sent her to Denmark, and answered the first foster family's questions only by nodding or shaking her head. Helene reported that the second foster family was much better than the doctor and his wife, the latter of whom suffered from mental health problems. A year-and-a-half later, of the twenty-two Inuit children who were sent to Denmark, six were adopted by their Danish foster families, and sixteen (including Helene) were sent back to Greenland. However, on her return, Helene had to contend with two tragic sets of circumstances: firstly, on meeting her mother again, Helene realised that they no longer spoke the same language (Helene had learnt Danish, and her mother spoke Greenlandic); and secondly, that she would not be returning to live at home. The Inuit children were, in fact, taken to live at an 'orphanage', which had been purpose-built by the Danish Red Cross whilst the Inuit children has been away in Denmark, in order to ensure that they who had 'enjoyed' the 'benefits' of living in Danish civilisation would not be returning to Greenland, only to live in what were presumed to be 'worse' conditions. In the children's home, according to a policy shared by institutions in other countries featured in this book, the Inuit children were forbidden to speak their native Indigenous languages, as were the mostly Greenlandic staff (Otzen, 2015).

By 2015, only eight of the children who had been transferred were still alive; some had died young; many had experienced difficulties in partner relationships; and some had experienced homelessness. They could not live as other people did, as they were never allowed to return home – to where they were born; to their parents, siblings, and other family members – and had therefore become strangers in their own country. As Helene explained: 'They lost their identity and they lost their ability to speak their mother tongue and with that, they lost their sense of purpose in life' (in Otzen, 2015, p. 9). Helene's relationship with her mother was never rebuilt.[17] And whilst the effects upon the children were immediately tangible, the truth about precisely what they had been involuntarily involved in did not emerge for nearly half a century. Whilst Helene received a letter in 1998 from the Danish Red Cross expressing its 'regret' for its role, and Save the Children Denmark (who in the meantime, had apparently 'lost' many documents, acknowledging that these documents could have been destroyed on purpose) eventually apologised in 2009, it was a Danish archivist, rather than a government or charity source, who first broke the news to Helene in 1996 (at which point, she was fifty-two years old) that she had been part of a social 'experiment'. Calls from the Greenlandic government for an independent investigation into this 'experiment', which were backed by *Socialdemokraterne* (the Danish Social Democratic party) when in opposition, but dropped when they entered government in 2011,[18] have remained unheeded by the Danish government

(Otzen, 2015). Subsequent Danish prime ministers have refused even to apologise on behalf of Denmark for these events. However, a Greenlandic member of the Danish Parliament, Aaja Chemnitz Larsen, made a resolution on 8 February 2019, to instruct the government to apologise '....to the persons who were removed from their families in Greenland in 1951 and sent to Denmark as part of a social experiment' (Hermann, 2019; Karkov, 2019).[19] On the basis of events to date, we can only conclude that, at the time of writing (April 2019), it would be prudent to await the results of this resolution with a measure of hope, rather than with unqualified expectation.

Efforts towards processes of truth, restitution, reconciliation, and reclamation

After the Self-Government Act (see above, section on 'Historical contexts') came into effect in 2009, considerable debate in Greenland ensued regarding both the colonial past, and the future relationship between Denmark and Greenland. One outcome of this was the decision in 2013, by the newly elected Greenlandic self-government, to establish a Reconciliation Commission, which would be assigned to investigate the effects and legacy of colonialism in Greenland (Rud, 2017). In the summer of 2014, it was announced that Greenland had indeed established the Reconciliation Commission (see Andersen, 2014; DIIS, 2015; Jacobsen, 2015; Rud, 2017), the aims of which included the initiation of a process of reconciliation with its Denmark, which were to be linked to the ongoing discussions on Greenland's future political status. Indeed, the previous August, Greenland's then-prime minister, Aleqa Hammond, had described the overall purpose of such a commission as being '....to break away from the colonisation of this country' (Andersen, 2014); and, on its establishment, Hammond stated that (in Jacobsen, 2015):

> Reconciliation is very important on a path where Greenland strives for independence....For a country that moves toward greater autonomy and independence, its people need to know about their own story.

Despite Hammond's expression of her view that 'This is not a question of making Denmark [look] bad, this is a question of bringing our lives and a discussion of our history to a higher level', this announcement met with opposition from some Danish politicians (from across the political spectrum), with Christian Friis Bach (a senior member of the Social-Liberal Party[20]) opining that, 'I see the Danish realm as a family. We've made mistakes together, we have created progress together, and therefore I see no need for a reconciliation commission', and Søren Espersen, the Danish People's Party's spokesman on Greenland, stated that the Commission was '....a deadly insult to Denmark' (Jacobsen, 2015). Nevertheless, in April 2016, it was reported in Norway[21] that the Reconciliation Commission in Greenland had already begun to map out the consequences of assimilation and colonisation, and that the Commission members would visit remote villages in order to collect testimonies and document events (Somby, 2016). However, despite the initial Greenlandic aims, and the optimism shown in certain (mostly Sámi) quarters in Norway, at the briefing meeting between Aleqa Hammond and then-Danish prime minister, Helle Thorning-Schmidt in Rig, Denmark on 29 August 2013, Thorning-Schmidt characterised efforts towards reconciliation as being a purely Greenlandic wish, rather than a Danish one. At the press conference that followed the briefing, she said (in Therkildsen et al., 2017; first author's translation)[22]:

> We do not need reconciliation, but I fully respect that it is a discussion that occupies the Greenlandic people. We will follow the discussion carefully from here. (p. 16)

To what extent the discussion was, in fact, 'closely followed' by the then- and subsequent Danish prime ministers is unclear; however, the report of the Reconciliation Commission in Greenland was clear in stating that, *'Danmark ikke med'* ['Denmark [is / was] not with [us]'], and that (Therkildsen et al., 2017):

> From being a reconciliation commission that would also bring about reconciliation between Denmark and Greenland, the Commission's task was narrowed to being a reconciliation process in Greenland alone. (p. 17)

From this gesture of non-participation in what was hoped and intended to be a truth and reconciliation process, it is hard to envision Denmark as having any intention other than to continue to govern Greenland as part of its northern realms – as 'Northern Danes', as part of the Danish 'family' – or, given its history, and particularly as experienced by its Indigenous population, as a quasi-independent incarnation of its long-standing colony. In its work, the thus-reduced Commission undertook to consider reconciliation as an overall process, which included the following aims (Therkildsen et al., 2017):

- To raise awareness of the people about Greenland's history and its impact on the present day;
- An understanding of the past to advance towards a common future;
- A long-term process of change of society;
- Generally, building relationships;
- A process of recognising and learning from the past; and that,
- Atonement is both a goal and a process. (p. 17)

Whilst the Reconciliation Commission undertook good and useful work along these lines, its members were surely correct in their assertion that the Commission '....should not be considered a commission of truth'

(Therkildsen et al., 2017, p. 17). Hammond's aforementioned ambitions for the Reconciliation Commission ('....to break away from the colonisation of this country' (Andersen, 2014), and for reconciliation itself being '....very important on a path where Greenland strives for independence' (Jacobsen, 2015)) were, remain, and in the foreseeable future look likely to remain, unfulfilled. In conclusion, as long as Greenland's former colonial master, Denmark, fails to engage – and given the restricted focus of this book, we have highlighted only its failure to meaningfully participate in a process of reconciliation, and its failure even to apologise for what was surely one of the most blatantly abusive episodes of deliberate social experimentation with children of the latter half of the twentieth century – Danish statements of Greenland forming a part of the 'Danish family' will, to Greenlandic and other ears, continue to ring hollow, and will likely be perceived as attempts to obfuscate the continued colonising mentality of Denmark towards Greenland and its Indigenous people.

Notes

1. Historically, *Kalaallit* referred specifically to Western Greenlanders, with Northern and Eastern Greenlanders calling themselves *Inughuit* and *Tunumiit* respectively.
2. The English-language term 'Danish Greenlanders' refers to Danish immigrants to Greenland and their descendants, whereas the related English-language term 'Greenlandic Danes' refers to residents of Denmark with Greenlandic Inuit background.
3. Bergen is in Norway, but between 1380 and 1814, Denmark and Norway formed a single kingdom. See Chapter 2, endnote 21.
4. Norway was ceded from the Danish crown to Sweden under the Treaty of Kiel (1814), and gained independence from Sweden in 1905. Again, see Chapter 2, endnote 21.
5. To have an idea of the climate that must have been experienced by the *Inughuit* people in their tents, November temperature readings at Thule Air Base (which it is to be recalled, is ca. 80 miles south of Qanaaq) between 1961 and 1990 show a mean maximum dry bulb temperature of minus 12.9 degrees Celsius; a mean minimum dry bulb temperature of minus 20.1 degrees Celsius; and, as the polar night has by then begun, zero hours of sunshine (National Oceanic and Atmospheric Administration, 2013).
6. Whilst Danish teachers were engaged to teach the mostly monolingual Greenlandic speakers, Greenlandic language was retained as a school subject (Peterson, 1995).
7. A familiar theme regarding the apparent intentions of colonising powers towards Indigenous peoples, as revealed in other chapters of this book.
8. That being said, within the framework of the 1979 Home Rule Act, the Greenlandic government could open representations with countries with special commercial interest for Greenland; and, under a 2005 Act, 'Concerning the conclusion of agreements under international law by the Government of Greenland', provided for full statutory powers for the Greenlandic government to conclude certain international agreements on behalf of the Kingdom of Denmark (Isbosethsen, 2007).
9. The referendum was non-binding on the Danish government, although the Self-Government Act was supported by the Danish Parliament, who promised to honour its results.

10. Jørgensen's party, *Det Konservative Folkeparti* (the Conservative People's Party) has a centre-right orientation, and at that time, was in power as part of the Conservative-Liberal government (2007–2011). Espersen's party, *Dansk Folkeparti,* has a right-wing orientation (populism, national conservatism); at that time, it was providing parliamentary support for the Conservative-Liberal government.
11. The Act refers only to 'the people of Greenland', a term which could, as one of Kuokkanen's (2017) respondents pointed out, equally apply to an Inuit person, or a Dane who had lived in Greenland for only the past six months.
12. The World Health Organisation calculates and reports most cross-national data as incidence rates per 100,000 of the population, and given that the 2019 population of Greenland was estimated at 56,673 (World Population Review, 2019), such an index is perhaps not as helpful as it might be. Another way to consider this is in terms of total figures – and Björkstén et al. (2009) report that 1,351 suicides took place in Greenland in the thirty-five years between 1968 and 2002. Still another way, and perhaps the most sobering of all, is that according to the review of government statistics conducted by the BBC World Service, in a country of just over 50,000 inhabitants, there was almost one suicide a week in Greenland, and one in five people in Greenland have tried to kill themselves (Bannister, 2010).
13. For interest's and comparison's sake, the suicide rate in Greenland's former colonial ruler, Denmark, was 8.9 per 100,000 of the population in 2016, ranking at number 89 in the world (World Health Organization, 2018), and approximately one-ninth of the rate in Greenland.
14. Such patterns have been referred to as 'the intergenerational transmission of historic trauma and grief' (Wesley-Esquimaux, 2007), and their legacy effects have been conceptualised as 'historical unresolved grief' by Brave Heart (2000), who has also developed systems of interventions for the grieving and healing of those losses with her own Lakota people (Brave Heart, 2000) and Alaskan native communities (Brave Heart & DeBruyn, 1998). Furthermore, in chapter seven of this book, Natahnee Nuay Winder outlines her own development of the *'Colliding Heartwork'* framework, in which a space is created for Indigenous descendants of boarding and residential school survivors to meet to talk, share how they feel about the ongoing effects of colonialism, and heal (see also Winder, 2020).
15. Helene is the author of a book entitled *For flid og god opførsel: vidnesbyrd fra et eksperiment* ['For Diligence and Good Behaviour: Testimony from an Experiment'] (2011), in which she documents her experiences as part of the 'experiment', and her investigations and reflections since, and to which the reader of this chapter (if she or he can read Danish) is referred. In the English language, in 2015 the BBC World Service programme *'Witness'* provided an account of this 'experiment', and of Helene's experiences in particular (see Otzen, 2015).
16. Sadly, Helene's father had died from tuberculosis a month previously.
17. Helene has reported that 'I felt very bitter about her decision to send me away. Really angry that she had let me go, and not just that – that she let me stay in the children's home, even though we lived in the same town' (in Otzen, 2015, p. 7); and, 'The relationship with my mother was never good again. I knew she was my mother and that we belonged to the same family, but we could never talk freely to each other, because I could only speak Danish, and she was not so good at it' (in Hermann, 2019; and in Karkov, 2019).
18. After the 2011 elections, the Social Democrats formed a minority government, a centre-left coalition with the Socialist People's Party (*Socialistisk Folkeparti*) and the Social Liberal Party (*Det Radikale Venstre*; see also endnote 20), and the Social Democrats' leader, Helle Thorning-Schmidt, became Denmark's first female prime minister.

19. As reported in Danish (Karkov, 2019) and Swedish (Hermann, 2019) daily newspapers, journalist Anne Kirstine Hermann, in a book to be published in the autumn of 2019, will position the modernisation of Greenland as a means by which the post-World War II UN mandate to nations with colonies to develop autonomy in the colonies was essentially subverted. In the book, Hermann will argue that Denmark felt its security policy and economic interests too great to permit Greenlandic independence, and instead instigated modernisation reforms, of which the experiment with the twenty-two Inuit children was one (Hermann, 2019; Karkov, 2019).
20. The Social Liberal Party (*Det Radikale Venstre* [literal translation, 'The Radical Left']) is a centrist social-liberal party, despite the implications of its name in Danish (which refers to its historical origins as a radical wing within its parent party, *Venstre* ['The Left']). After losing the 2015 general election, they had eight (out of 179) representatives in the Danish national parliament, and are currently (April, 2019) in opposition to the governing coalition.
21. Greenland's nascent truth and reconciliation processes were closely observed by some people in Norway, as calls had been made in that country to establish a similar process, with respect to the experiences of the Sámi and Kven peoples (see Chapter 6; also, Andersen, Idivuoma & Somby, 2016; Somby, 2016). Indeed, Henrik Olsen, a member of the Sámi Parliament in Norway, referred to the Reconciliation Commission in Greenland in addition to the Truth and Reconciliation Commission in Canada (see Chapter 2; also Truth and Reconciliation Commission of Canada, 2015) and in making such calls. Olsen also referred to meetings that had been held between members of the Reconciliation Commission in Greenland, and the Sámi Parliament in Norway (Somby, 2016). The Norwegian national parliament announced that a commission would be established to examine the past policy of the forcible assimilation of the Sámi and Kven peoples (see Minton & Lile, 2018, 2019; Stortinget, 2017). They announced the name (short version, 'The Truth and Reconciliation Commission') and mandate of the commission (threefold: (i) mapping the history, including personal accounts and stories; (ii) contemplating the consequences of the Norwegianisation policy; and (iii) giving advice for the future and mandate of that commission) a year later, in June 2018 (see Stortinget, 2018).
22. This report was published in Greenlandic (with the title '*Qanga pisut paasivagut. Ullumi pisut akisussaaffigaavut. Siunissaq pitsaanerusoq sulissutigaarput*') and Danish (with the title '*Vi forstår fortiden. Vi tager ansvar for nutiden. Vi arbejder sammen for en bedre fremtid*'), but (somewhat unusually) not in English, in which the Greenlandic and Danish titles translate as 'We understand the past. We take responsibility for the present. We are working together for a better future.' What appear here as quotes from the report are translations prepared from the Danish version by the first co-author.

References

Andersen, A.N. (2014). *The Greenlandic Reconciliation Process: Project Description*. Available online: http://www.martinbreum.dk/wp-content/uploads/2014/12/Carlsbergansøgning-2014-EV.pdf [Accessed April, 2019].

Andersen, S., Idivuoma, A.M. & Somby, L.I. (2016). Norskspråklige lærere var et overgrep fra norske myndigheter. [Norwegian-language teachers were an abuse by the Norwegian authorities]. *NRK Sápmi*. Available online: http://www.nrk.no/sapmi/professor_-_-norske-myndigheter-forbrot-seg-mot-barna-pa-internatskolene.-1.12906901 [Accessed April, 2019].

Bannister, M. (2010). Singing to end teen suicide in Greenland. *BBC World Service*, December 7th. Available online: http://www.bbc.co.uk/worldservice/programmes/2010/12/101207_outlook_suicide_greenland.shtml [Accessed April, 2019].

BBC News (2008). Greenland votes for more autonomy. Available on-line: http://news.bbc.co.uk/2/hi/europe/7749427.stm [Accessed April, 2019].

Bjerregaard, M. (2017). Redaktør: Grønlændere vil ikke ofre levestandard for selvstændighed. [Editor: Greenlanders will not sacrifice standard of living for independence]. *Danmarks Radio*, July 27th.

Bjerregaard, P., Young, T.K., Dewailly, E. & Ebbesson, S.O.E. (2004). Indigenous health in the Arctic: An overview of the circumpolar Inuit population. *Scandinavian Journal of Public Health*, 32: 390–395.

Björkstén, K.S., Kripke, D.F. & Bjerregaard, P. (2009). Accentuation of suicides but not homicides with rising latitudes of Greenland in the sunny months. *BMC Psychiatry*, 9: 20.

Brave Heart, M.Y.H. (2000). Wakiksuyapi: Carrying the historical trauma of the Lakota. *Tulane Studies in Social Welfare*, 21: 245–266.

Brave Heart, M.Y.H. & DeBruyn, L.M. (1998). The American Indian holocaust: Healing historical unresolved grief. American Indian and Alaska native mental health research. *Journal of the National Center*, 8(2): 56–78.

DIIS (Dansk Institut for internationale studier) [Danish Institute for International Studies]) (2015). New research project on Greenland's reconciliation process. Available online: http://www.diis.dk/en/node/4791 [Accessed April, 2019].

Ehrlich, G. (2003). *This Cold Heaven: Seven Seasons in Greenland*. London: Fourth Estate.

Environmental Law Alliance Worldwide (2019). *HINGITAQ 53 vs. Denmark, Application No. 18584/04*. Available online: https://www.elaw.org/content/denmark-hingitaq-53-vs-denmark-application-no-1858404-decision-european-court-human-rights-a [Accessed April, 2019].

Grønnow, B. (2017). *The Frozen Saqqaq Sites of Disko Bay, West Greenland: Qeqertasussuk and Qajaa (2400-900 BC)*. Copenhagen: Museum Tusculanum Press.

Hermann, A.K. (2019). Så gick det till när Danmark tog 22 barn från sina familjer på Grönland. [This happened when Denmark took 22 children from their families in Greenland]. *Dagens Nyheter*, March 10th.

Hersher, R. (2016). The Arctic suicides: It's not the dark that kills you. *National Public Radio*, April 21st.

Hicks, J. (2007). The social determinants of elevated rates of suicide among Inuit youth. *Indigenous Affairs*, 4(07): 30–37.

Isbosethsen, J. (2007). Politics in Greenland. Available online: https://web.archive.org/web/20090628203930/http://eu.nanoq.gl/Emner/About%20Greenland/Politics%20in%20Greenland.aspx [Accessed April, 2019].

Jacobsen, S. (2015). Greenland commission will probe Danish colonial abuses. *Reuters*, May 2nd. Available online: http://www.reuters.com/article/us-greenland-denmark-primeminister-idUSBREA410J920140502 [Accessed April, 2019].

Kaplan, L. (2011). *Comparative Yupik and Inuit*. Available online: https://www.uaf.edu/anlc/resources/yupik-inuit/ [Accessed April, 2019].

Karkov, R. (2019). Forfatter: Sådan blev 22 børn brikker i et storpolitisk magtspil om Grønland. [This was how 22 children became pieces in a major political game of power about Greenland]. *Berlingske*, March 10th.

Kuokkanen, R. (2017). 'To see what state we are in': First years of the Greenland self-government act and the pursuit of Inuit sovereignty. *Ethnopolitics*, 16(2): 179–195.

Larsen, C.V.L., Curtis, T. & Bjerregaard, P. (2013). Gambling behavior and problem gambling reflecting social transition and traumatic childhood events among Greenland Inuit: A cross-sectional study in a large indigenous population undergoing rapid change. *Journal of Gambling Studies*, 29(4): 733–748.

Lehti, V., Niemelä, S., Hoven, C., Mandell, D. & Sourander, A. (2009). Mental health, substance use and suicidal behaviour among young indigenous people in the Arctic: A systematic review. *Social Science & Medicine*, 69(8): 1194–1203.

Leineweber, Markus, 2000: Modernization and mental health: Suicide among the Inuit in Greenland. PhD Dissertation, University of Nijmegen.

Minton, S.J. & Lile, H.S. (2018). A conversation about the proposed truth commission in Norway for the Sámi and Kven peoples: What can be learnt from truth and reconciliation processes elsewhere? *14th International Congress of Qualitative Inquiry*. University of Illinois in Urbana-Champaign, USA, 16–19 May.

Minton, S.J. & Lile, H.S. (2019). Considering a truth commission in Norway with respect to the past forcible assimilation of the Sámi people. Due to appear in S. Wilson, A. Breen & L. DuPré (eds), *Research Is Reconciliation?* Toronto, ON: Canadian Scholars Press.

National Oceanic and Atmospheric Administration (2013). *Thule Climate Normals 1961–1990*. Available on-line: ftp://ftp.atdd.noaa.gov/pub/GCOS/WMO-Normals/TABLES/REG_VI/GL/04202.TXT [Accessed April, 2019].

Otzen, E. (2015). The children taken from home for a social experiment. *BBC News Magazine*, June 10th. Available online: https://www.bbc.co.uk/news/magazine-33060450 [Accessed April, 2019].

Petersen, R. (1995). Colonialism as seen from a former colonised area. *Arctic Anthropology*, 32(2): 118–126.

Ritzaus Bureau (2018). Løkke: Selvstændigt Grønland skal klare sig selv økonomisk. [Løkke: Independent Greenland must cope with itself financially]. *Sermitsiaq*, January 19th.

Rud, S. (2017). Toward a postcolonial Greenland: Culture, identity, and colonial legacy. In S. Rud (ed.), *Colonialism in Greenland: Tradition, Governance and Legacy*. London: Palgrave Macmillan.

Sale, R. & Potapov, E. (2010). *The Scramble for the Arctic: Ownership, Exploitation and Conflict in the Far North*. London: Francis Lincoln Ltd.

Simons, G.F. & Fennig, C.D. (eds.) (2018). *Ethnologue: Languages of the World* (21st edn.). Dallas, TX: SIL International.

Skydsbjerg, H. & Turnowsky, W. (2016). Massivt flertal for selvstændighed. [Massive majority for independence]. *Sermitsiaq*, December 1st.

Somby, L.I. (2016). Sametinget vil ha fokus på de tause historiene. [Sámi Parliament will focus on the silent stories]. *NRK Sápmi*. Available online: http://www.nrk.no/sapmi/en-kommisjon-som-skal-lufte-bort-skammen-etter-internatlivet-1.12911669 [Accessed April, 2019].

Statistics Greenland (2018). *Greenland in Figures*. Nuuk: Statistics Greenland.

Statsministeriet (2009). *Act on Greenland Self-Government*. (English Translation). Available online: http://www.stm.dk/_p_13090.html [Accessed April, 2019].

Stortinget (2017). Open Hearing in the Standing Committee on Scrutiny and Constitutional Affairs, 15 May 2017. Available online: https://www.stortinget.no/no/Hva-skjer-pa-Stortinget/Videoarkiv/Arkiv-TV-sendinger/?mbid=/2017/H264-full/Hoeringssal1/05/15/Hoeringssal1-20170515-091119.mp4&msid=0&dateid=10004071 [Accessed April, 2019].

Stortinget (2018). Innst. 408 S (2017–2018). Available online: https://www.stortinget.no/no/Saker-og-publikasjoner/Publikasjoner/Innstillinger/Stortinget/2017-2018/inns-201718-408s/#m3 [Accessed April, 2019].

Therkildsen, J., Olsen, D.K., Mathiassen, I., Petrussen, Î. & Williamson, K.J. (2017). *Qanga pisut paasivagut. Ullumi pisut akisussaaffigaavut. Siunissaq pitsaanerusoq sulissutigaarput: Saammaateqatigiinnissamut Isumalioqatigiissitamit isumaliutissiissut saqqummiunneqartoq. / Vi forstår fortiden. Vi tager ansvar for nutiden. Vi arbejder sammen for en bedre fremtid: Endelig betænkning af Grønlands Forsoningskommission.* [We Understand the Past. We Take Responsibility for the Present. We are Working Together for a Better Future: Final Report of the Greenland Reconciliation Commission]. Nuuk: Grønlands Forsoningskommission.

Thiesen, H. (2011). *For flid og god opførsel: vidnesbyrd fra et eksperiment.* [For Diligence and Good Behaviour: Testimony From an Experiment]. Nuuk: Milik Publishing, with Lene Therkildsen.

Wesley-Esquimaux, C.C. (2007). The intergenerational transmission of historic trauma and grief. *Indigenous Affairs*, 4(07): 6–11.

Winder, N. (2020). Post-secondary indigenous students' perspectives: Sharing our voices on how we fit into residential school history of Canada and the United States. PhD dissertation: University of Western Ontario.

World Health Organization. (2011). *Suicide Rates per 100,000 by Country, Year and Sex.* Geneva: World Health Organization.

World Health Organization. (2018). Suicide rate estimates, age-standardised estimates by country. Available online: http://apps.who.int/gho/data/node.main.MHSUICIDEASDR?lang=en [Accessed April, 2019].

World Population Review. (2019). Greenland population 2019. Available online: http://worldpopulationreview.com/countries/greenland-population/ [Accessed April, 2019].

Chapter 6

The colonisation of Sápmi

Jens-Ivar Nergård

Sápmi is the Sámi name for the territories that its people inhabit in four nations: Russia, Finland, Sweden, and Norway. Sámi settlements stretch from the Kola Peninsula of Russia in the north to Dalarna in Sweden and Hedmark in Norway in the south. The Sámi people have a common language, spoken in all Sámi territories. There are, however, significant differences between the various dialects. This means that certain dialects may not be understood in some parts of the Sámi region. The differences between Northern Sámi and Southern Sámi are comparable to the differences between Norwegian and German. The Sámi language is on the UNESCO list of endangered world languages.

The term 'colonisation' is usually employed to describe the annexation of a country's geographic regions. In Indigenous populations around the world, the term is also used to describe cultural colonisation. A reckoning with industrialised countries' abuses of Indigenous people, and violations of their ways of life, has given the term 'colonisation' a new meaning. Attempts by Indigenous people to liberate themselves from colonial powers, and the impact they have had on their population, are referred to as decolonisation (Smith, 2010). This chapter primarily addresses the situation in the North Sámi regions of Norway, although this shares many common features with the colonisation of the entire Sápmi area. Even with this limited focus, the subject can only partially be described within the constraints of this chapter.

The original settlements of the Sámi people were partitioned when the nation states they inhabited negotiated the current national borders between their territories. The border between Sweden and Norway, which were then in union with Denmark, was drawn in 1751. This border divided a large region which at the time was designated as 'shared territory' between Norway and Sweden, and used as grazing land for reindeer herds on both sides of the new national border. The same thing occurred when the border was drawn between Russia and Norway in 1826, when Norway was in union with Sweden. This border divided the East Sámi population living in communities known as '*siidas*' in Neiden, Pasvik, Petsjenga, and Suenjel. The East

Sámi, or Skolt Sámi, eventually settled in three countries: Finland, Norway, and Russia.

The consequences of the borders and the partitioning of the Sámi areas were striking, and the impact is still apparent today. The new national borders led to a splitting of the Sámi network and language, with the result that the Sámi communities became more vulnerable. The new borders had repercussions for the Sámi people's way of life, which was to a large extent based on the utilisation and harvesting of natural resources. While the new national borders regulated the territorial conditions between the nation states, they also paved the way for a more conspicuous and discernible colonisation of the Sámi areas. Sámi reindeer husbandry, which utilised areas on both sides of the new Swedish-Norwegian border and the Russian-Norwegian border, faced new challenges, as herders now belonged to different nation states and political regimes. Reindeer husbandry was given status as a 'cross-border' enterprise, with all of the problems that this entailed. The Sámi population became politically marginalised and the weaker party with respect to national interests in areas they had previously utilised and managed for years. National authorities now encroached on Sámi stewardship, and adapted it to meet competing interests. I call these encroachments the 'external colonisation' of Sápmi. The nation states also encroached on the inner life of the Sámi community. They drafted language and education policies for the purpose of assimilating Sámi cultural traditions. These policies had strong elements of abuse, particularly when viewed from a human rights perspective. Consequently, the policies had the effect of suppressing, undermining, and corrupting Sámi culture. In the most marginalised areas, the policies completely eliminated the Sámi language. The most radical idea of the policies was to eradicate Sámi language and traditions that many government authorities viewed as 'cultureless'. I call these encroachments aimed at Sámi culture the 'internal colonisation' of Sápmi.

In Norway, these policies had their own name: *Norwegianisation*. This has a specific historical and political background. When Norway became an independent nation in 1905, the country had a 500-year history of colonisation: a union with Denmark from 1380 to 1814 and a union with Sweden from 1814 to 1905. In the latter half of the nineteenth century, there were strong forces in Norway advocating for a dissolution of the union with Sweden. The struggle for national independence was an important context for the Norwegianisation of the Sámis, and for the Kvens, another minority group in Nordkallotten. Norwegianisation was at its most intense from 1850 to 1970 utilising harsh tactics. From 1905, Norwegian authorities began building boarding schools in order to make the language transition from Sámi and Kven to Norwegian more efficient. These boarding schools facilitated the cultural transformation of Sámi and Kven children. Over the course of more than one hundred years, Sámi and Kven communities were systematically diluted, dismantled, and in some places, utterly destroyed. At the beginning of the 1970s, when the Norwegian authorities altered their minority policies and attempted to clean up the cultural ruins caused by them, much of what needed repair had in many places already been destroyed or obliterated. In regions where authorities had not managed to complete its project (often referred to as 'the Sámi and Kven core areas') there was a drive and an initiative to reconstruct severely crippled Sámi and Kven communities. This, however, was no easy task. Colonisation had left deep and destructive footprints, which counteracted rehabilitation from within. The abuse had created forces from within the population that now actively resisted rehabilitation. This was a destructive counterforce that split the Sámi people. This duality, which will be discussed later in this chapter, was due to the colonisation policies themselves. It significantly complicated the challenges associated with the reconstruction of Sámi language and traditions in the modern Sámi community.

Key elements of Norwegianisation

Norwegian historian Henry Minde divides the Norwegianisation period into four phases, emphasising the aspects characterising these phases (Minde, 2005). He calls the first phase of the period (from 1850 to 1870) the *transition phase*. This was characterised by humanist beliefs that the Sámi people, like any other population, had the right to use their own language and maintain their own traditions. This position was emphasised by the church, and the school system being developed for the Sámi population. Theologian Nils Vibe Stockfleth, a key figure in the missionary work aimed at the Sámi people, assisted in producing texts in Sámi that could be used in educational instruction and in religious contexts. Respect for Sámi traditions characterised parts of this phase. However, this liberal approach also had its sceptics in the Norwegian Parliament (*Stortinget*), in certain Norwegian circles in Finnmark (which had been the primary area for Sámi coastal and inland settlements), and amongst Norwegian public officials.

In 1851, the Norwegian Parliament established '*Finnefondet*' ('the Lapp Fund'). This was a government budget intended to support Norwegianisation efforts in Sámi and Kven regions. The budget provided financial support to promote intensive efforts for educational instruction in Norwegian for Sámi and Kven students. Teachers in 'transitional districts' could seek financial support from this government budget for documented Norwegianisation activities (Grenersen, 2015). This initiative, which involved wage increases for teachers who promoted Norwegianisation in their instruction, was both viewed and used as a method of rewarding teachers' efforts in the Norwegianisation programme. Towards the end of the first phase, it became clear that Norwegianisation efforts in regular schools in Sámi and Kven regions were not entirely successful, and that the work to replace language (from Sámi to Norwegian, or from Kven to Norwegian) was moving too slowly. This was the primary reason for a new and harsher approach to Norwegianisation.

Minde (2005) refers to the period of Norwegianisation from 1870 to 1905 as the *consolidation phase*. According to Minde, this phase was characterised by the influence of security policies on Norwegianisation policies. The Norwegianisation strategy gradually became more evident, and policy measures were tightened. Between 1860 and 1898, government authorities issued four directives aimed at language instruction. These directives heightened the focus on school measures to replace Sámi and Kven with Norwegian. The directive from 1880 introduced a more severe Norwegianisation strategy (Niemi, 2017). The use of dual-language books, books with Sámi-Norwegian and Finnish-Norwegian texts, which had been common during the first phase, were eliminated from educational instruction. Students from transitional districts, with Sámi, Kven, and Norwegian inhabitants, were now required to learn to speak, read, and write in Norwegian. The majority of the children in these areas spoke Sámi or Finnish upon starting school. Teachers who were not able to show (document) good results of their Norwegianisation efforts were refused wage bonuses from the Lapp Fund. These tightened measures, particularly with regard to language policies, marked the beginning of a period where Sámi and Kven languages would gradually become more undermined.

A few researchers have pointed out that Sámi and Kven languages were never expressly prohibited as instructional languages during Norwegianisation. This is a strange argument if presented in support of these policies. In fact, the language directives clearly stated that minority languages were neither desirable nor supported. Sámi and Finnish were permitted as a method of assisting language instruction if students did not understand a single word of Norwegian upon starting school. Anything else would have been absurd. In many schools, however, teachers did not understand these languages. A Sámi teacher from Kautokeino who taught at a school there was dismissed because he used the Sámi language in his instruction, despite the fact that this was a community where Sámi was the native language of virtually the entire population. Two teachers who taught at Grensen boarding school in Karasjok in the 1970s, where all the children spoke Sámi, apologised for contributing to the students' 'long-term silence' from the age of seven. Today, they have acknowledged that they participated in a horrific project involving the psychological and cultural abuse of innocent children and their families. Given this perspective, it is pointless to bring up trivial arguments regarding whether Sámi and Finnish were 'prohibited' in a legal sense. In reality, these languages were in a far more difficult situation: they were expelled from the schools, partly because many teachers neither understood nor spoke them.

The sluggishness and poor progression of Norwegianisation efforts during the consolidation phase from 1870 to 1905 was the primary reason for the establishment of boarding schools as a final solution for the Norwegianisation process. Minde refers to this phase as the *culmination phase*. During this phase, Norwegianisation policies were tightened and placed under stricter government control. School policies in Sámi and Kven districts had not fulfilled government expectations, nor had they provided the desired results. The budget for the Lapp Fund was significantly expanded in early 1900 to cover the expenses of a large-scale development of boarding schools in Finnmark. This phase may therefore be referred to as the *boarding school phase* of the Norwegianisation of educational instruction.

The first boarding school began its operations in 1905, in Neiden in Finnmark county. This was not an arbitrary location. One of the intentions of Norwegianisation policies was to stem the assumed threat from the Kven population, which had strong bonds with Finland. Neiden was, therefore, the preferred location (Minde, 2005). Neiden also had a significant Skolt Sámi (East Sámi) population, with strong ties to Russian traditions. The border demarcation between Russian and Norway in 1826 had divided East Sámi settlements between the nation states. The same year the boarding school was completed and a new church was consecrated in Neiden. Norway opened two important institutions to mark Norwegian presence in an area where the majority of the population consisted of Kvens and Skolt Sámi. Present at the opening of the boarding school in Neiden was Finnmark's first Director of Schools, Bent Thomassen. Not only was he the first Director of Schools in Finnmark, but also the first in a Norwegian county. He was also appointed to an office with the task of monitoring and accelerating Norwegianisation efforts. Norwegian theologian Baard Tvete (1955) noted that the opening of a boarding school in Neiden must have felt strange to Thomassen:

> A Norwegian who came to Finnmark and noticed how un-Norwegian everything seemed in this part of the country could not help but feel insulted by it. His entire sense of nationality was outraged by it. No doubt this was how Thomassen, Director of Schools reacted. Coming to Neiden must have felt like coming to a foreign land. (p. 231)

After the first boarding school opened in Neiden, many others followed. Boarding schools were effective as a method of replacing language, and this was likely the measure with the greatest impact on the success of Norwegianisation in many areas. Boarding schools in Sámi areas were a tragedy for the Sámi community. The Norwegian authorities, however, held a different view. In 1920, a teacher, and later the head of an East Finnmark county school, wrote: 'The school policies carried out in Finnmark in the 20th century can be summarised with these words: Prudent and targeted efforts to overcome difficulties' (Reiersen, 1920).

Government authorities, and those who implemented the policies in practice, viewed them as a benefaction for what they considered a cultureless and 'primitive' people. With this perspective as a starting point, authorities proceeded to violate the rights of their own minority populations.

The major offensive of Norwegianisation did not limit itself to the eradication of Sámi and Kven as languages of instruction for the children. In fact, these languages were no longer desired in any form of speech and communication. It was a grotesque objective, which became even more attainable after the establishment of boarding schools. This goal must have been demoralising for teachers as well, as it was impossible to achieve without harming the children.

From 1901 to 1905, all school boards in Finnmark were required to submit reports to the Ministry of Church Affairs, which oversaw the national supervision of the school system. These reports give us an idea of the language situation in Finnmark, especially in central Sámi districts. In Karasjok, the population in 1904 was predominantly Sámi. Of the 148 schoolchildren, only one spoke Norwegian. It was therefore determined that instruction in Christianity should be conducted 'to a large extent' in Sámi, whilst all other instruction should be conducted in Norwegian. Kistrand municipality, which changed its name to Porsanger in 1964, reported in 1895 that of the 245 schoolchildren in the municipality, only 212 spoke Sámi. (In the source, it is questioned as to whether these figures are accurate.) The report from 1905 states that, '....the language's detrimental effect is gradually disappearing'. Textbooks no longer contained both Sámi and Norwegian text, as was previously the case (Tvete, 1955). The replacement of textbooks using both Sámi and Norwegian text was introduced in areas with a large Sámi population. This also applied to areas heavily populated with Sámi inhabitants and significant Kven settlements: Kvalsund, Måsøy, Hasvik, Loppa, Øksfjord, Talvik, Alta, and Lebesby. In Troms county, this applied to the areas of Lyngen and Kvænangen.

In Kautokeino, the reports describe two schools: the school for reindeer herding families (the 'Mountain Lapp School'), with 62 students, and the school for local residents, with 49 students. It was estimated in the report that there were many more school-age children in Kautokeino, but it had been impossible to trace them, as reindeer herding families migrated with their flocks to seasonal grazing areas, and were therefore constantly on the move (Tvete, 1955). Thomassen, the Director of Schools in Finnmark, made a derogatory comment on the reindeer husbandry community's migration patterns, writing that it didn't matter whether the mountain Sámi children learned Norwegian: 'They can herd reindeer without a smidgen of mental or spiritual substance' (Tvete, 1955). In Polmark, which at this time was inhabited solely by Sámi people, children were sent to school 'without the slightest knowledge of the Norwegian language'. Object lessons were conducted with the aid of pictures. It was stated in a school board report to the Ministry of Church Affairs that, 'It takes a fairly long time for the students acquire enough knowledge of the Norwegian language to follow educational instruction' (Tvete, 1955). This hopeless situation prompted some families to obtain textbooks from Finland, on the other side of Tana River, which made up the border with Finland. In 1902, Lauri Itkonen published a catechism in Sámi. Its use in instruction was prohibited, but some parents in Polmark acquired it and used it themselves. The book was written in Sámi, and although most people spoke Finnish, a book in Sámi was of great importance (Tvete, 1955).

The third phase of Norwegianisation, the *culmination phase*, from 1905 to 1950, was characterised by growing government control over Norwegianisation efforts in the schools. Previously implemented measures were enhanced and emphasised. Schools were now intended to 'spearhead' Norwegianisation efforts (Tvete, 1955; Minde, 2005). The budget for the Lapp Fund was significantly expanded in early 1900. This was to cover the expenses of the large-scale development of boarding schools in Finnmark in order to make the Norwegianisation efforts more efficient. During the culmination phase, the notion arose that there were differences between the Sámi and Kven peoples that would present a challenge for Norwegianisation policies. While Norwegian authorities viewed Kvens as a security risk in an area with multicultural settlements, they were still accepted as skilled farmers and fishermen. They posed a security risk, but no cultural threat. The Sámi people, however, were considered a cultural challenge, perhaps because their spiritual traditions were not fully understood. This was not viewed as cultural differences between Sámi and Norwegians. Rather, it became an excuse for derogatory and racist attitudes. In his letter to the Ministry of Church Affairs in 1923, Finnmark's second Director of Schools, Kristian Brygfeld refers to the Sámi in the following manner (Eriksen & Niemi, 1981):

> The few individuals left of the original Lappish tribe are now so degenerate that there is little hope of any change for the better. They are hopeless, and belong to Finnmark's most backward and wretched population, and provide the largest contingent from these areas to our lunatic asylums and schools for the mentally retarded.

The purpose of the government's attempts to achieve a 'language shift' for Sámi and Kvens involved more than just language. These policies chiselled away at the population's dignity and self-identity as a people with its own cultural traditions. In 1917, the Sámi language was the dominant spoken language in Kautokeino, Karasjok, Polmak, and Nesseby. In 1917, 66 per cent of schoolchildren starting school in Finnmark understood only Sámi (Tvete, 1955). There were 5,500 schoolchildren in Finnmark in 1917, and 2,000 of them had Sámi parents. There were several Sámi bastions in Troms and Nordland counties, where significant portions of the population spoke Sámi. This also applied to the Lule and South Sámi areas, which are discussed to a lesser extent in this chapter.

Norwegianisation efforts in the schools were supported by other political measures outside the schools. In the Land Sales Act of 1902, related to the sale of land areas in Finnmark that had become government property after the dissolution of the union with Denmark in 1814, Section 1c stated, 'The law solely applies to Norwegian citizens – who can speak, read and write the Norwegian language, and use this in their daily lives' (Tvete, 1955). Hence, Norwegianisation was not only aimed at language, but at the entire culture of which the language was a part. These policies had a strong impact on the Sámi and Kven population. After many years as a teacher, Anders Larsen, a Sámi, stated, 'There are few Lapp youth (Sámi) who have not in some manner had their souls damaged by the Norwegianisation policies' (Tvete, 1955).

The fourth and final phase of Norwegianisation is referred to by Minde (2015) as the *termination phase*. This took place from 1950 to 1970, and perhaps even up until the 1980s. The period is characterised by the struggles of the Sámi people, after more than hundred years of intense Norwegianisation efforts. Norwegianisation was incorporated into all areas of the Sámi community, resulting in numerous challenges at various levels of society. The termination of Norwegianisation consisted of curtailing efforts in the most vital areas, where policies were still fully in force. Initially, efforts were aimed at schools, the education system, and administration of territorial rights. Several official reports were initiated to determine the legal situation for Sámi people, their language, and their culture. The milestones of this work included the founding of the Sámi Parliament and the Sámi University as two key institutions. Work commenced on new Sámi curricula for compulsory schools, the administration of Sámi language, and the development of both new and traditional businesses. The challenges of new institutions and the problems involved in regaining what had been lost during the harshest Norwegianisation period required simultaneous efforts in several areas. The Sámi people lost their battle against the construction of a hydroelectric power plant in the Alta-Kautokeino River in 1979–1981. They did, however, win a moral victory against development interests and in both national and international public opinion. This battle was a determining factor in the growth of the modern Sápmi state.

Internal colonisation

The essential questions, and the ones that are the most difficult to answer, are: What impact did Norwegianisation and abusive policies have on the people? How does it affect them today?

Reports from school boards in Finnmark to authorities documented the struggles with Norwegianisation in public schools in Sámi and Kven villages. The idea of boarding schools gained momentum based on the recognition that Norwegianisation efforts in public schools were not achieving policy goals. Stronger measures were needed. This is the reason why boarding school was established, as early as 1905. At the consecration of Neiden chapel, the same year as the opening of the new boarding school, the Cabinet Minister for Church Affairs, Vilhelm Wexelsen, stated that the school in Finnmark would serve as a 'border guard': 'In Finnmark, we will build cultural border fortifications' (Tvete, 1955). The East Sámi population in Neiden, with its connections to Russian traditions through the orthodox St. Georges Chapel, built by Trifon in 1565, gave the area a unique cultural character with its Eastern aspects.

Boarding schools had dual objectives. One was to stem external political threats. Boarding schools in Neiden and other places were also meant to serve as 'cultural border fortifications', which would strengthen the population's Norwegian identity and loyalty. Many Sámi and Kven areas were considered a threat from within, from 'the great plateaus with a foreign population and foreign language'. It was feared that these people might give another national power the excuse to annex the region (Tvete, 1955). It was therefore 'necessary' to 'weed out' these foreigners by making the Sámi and Kven people essentially Norwegian. Boarding schools also gave the authorities an opportunity to tighten their grip. This may have resulted in better schools and better educational instructions, but also a tighter control and a harsher abuse of children and their families, which was hidden under the pretence of service for the 'good of the people'. A crucial aspect of the boarding schools' abuse was cloaked in the view that colonisation was solely a benefaction. It was meant to benefit a people who did not understand what was best for them. Boarding school policies were a collective measure aimed at individuals. For many who were subjected to this policy, it was the abuse that was most prominent. This abuse was most visible in the forced 'language shift' and the changing of the children's identity. Boarding schools were closed institutions and met many of the conditions for what the American sociologist Erving Goffman (1967) called the 'total institution'. The total institution is characterised by a large number of individuals being placed in an enclosed and formally administered existence, and cut off from wider society for considerable periods of time. A central feature of the total institution is that it violates what Goffman referred to as the 'territories of the self' (Goffman, 1967).

At their worst, boarding schools in the service of Norwegianisation came very close to becoming total institutions. There is reason to assume that they extensively violated the children's dignity and personal integrity. Boarding schools sought to break down Sámi and Kven children's self-identity and replace it with a Norwegian identity. Teachers and boarding school staff governed this process of upheaval, which, it must be said, was not equally brutal in all institutions. Nevertheless, the very idea of transforming the identity of Sámi and Kven children was in and of itself a violation. It is therefore not improbable that other types of violation and abuse also occurred. Language instruction and efforts to achieve a 'language shift' was the connecting thread for this work. It was the primary political directive put into practice by teachers in the daily running of the schools. Some boarding school students reported that staff attempted to stop them from speaking their own language after school hours at the boarding school. Such constraints were not possible to enforce in practice; however, the desire to carry them out was in itself a violation.

An inferno takes shape

In order to understand this aspect of the Norwegianisation and the boarding school operations, we must focus on concrete information. The Sámi community has a multitude of stories about the encounters Sámi children had with Norwegian authorities at school. There is a specific category of accounts I refer to as stories of pain (Nergård, 1992, 1994, 2004, 2006). These have been told and re-told as part of a collective memory of the harshest colonisation period. The stories live on in Sámi and Kven communities. Through more than thirty years of fieldwork, I have met some of the people who experienced Norwegianisation in both regular schools and at boarding schools. For some, encounters with the schools were extremely destructive. One of these involved a man then in his fifties, who I met for the first time at his home in Cuovddatmohkki in the late 1980s.

John Mienna was his name, and he lived in a simple, sparsely furnished house in a mountain village in Finnmarksvidda, about fifty kilometres south of Karasjok, on the way to Kautokeino. At that time, he lived with his father, who was over ninety years old. The two men resided in a small cluster of houses on two farms with a barn and shed, approximately one kilometre from the motorway. The wife of the older man, John's mother, was deceased. The smallholding had been their livelihood, along with hunting and fishing in the Lesjohka River that ran near the house. There are several fishing ponds in the area surrounding the farm, which are rich in trout and char. The household had worked a small patch of land, where they kept livestock and grew potatoes. John also worked as a hired hand or helper in a *siida* (a reindeer husbandry community), which had winter grazing grounds just an hour from the farm by snow scooter, towards the border with Finland. Several snow scooters and terrain vehicles were parked outside John's house, which had belonged to the herders in the *siida* where John had grown up.

The house had a lovely location, with all the facilities needed for cooking. They subsisted primarily on what they harvested from nature. John had a scooter that he used during summer when making purchases in Karasjok, about an hour's drive from the farm. In winter, he had to use his own means of transport, or take the bus that stopped once a day. The house had a wood stove, and they gathered wood themselves. The days were filled with household chores. John was a skilled knifesmith, and he spent much of his time during winter months crafting knives. He was a skilled craftsman. John purchased steel for the knife blades, but ground each knife himself into the desired shape. He made the knife handles from exquisite birch, obtained from the stubby birch trees he found on his walks through the woods and fields in the area where he lived. John was a friendly man, and the house had a peaceful atmosphere, even when filled with activity. John did not have an easy life. He belonged to a generation of children born during the Second World War, who did not receive a proper education.

John could neither read nor write Norwegian or Sámi. When a letter arrived, or a bill that needed to be paid, he relied on help from his sister's children, who lived about ten kilometres away, closer to Karasjok. His father could read, and he proudly displayed his own books from his schooldays which had Sámi text on one page and Norwegian on the other. During the war, he hid these books along with other important objects. He buried them in the woods, to prevent them from being destroyed by the ravages of German warfare in the area. This was a time when large areas of Finnmark were burnt to the ground.

During a visit to John's house, one particular episode made a strong impression on me. It was a winter's day, and the local book bus drove up to the house. John's father was deceased by this time, and John lived alone in the house. The book bus was a travelling library, and the driver knocked on the door and entered, even though he knew very well that the only occupant could neither read nor write. I was struck by the respect the driver showed to John, and that he never once mentioned the books he drove about to lend to other people. John served coffee, and conversation flowed easily between the host and his guest. They talked about everyday matters, and shared news and chit-chat about friends and acquaintances. When the driver got up to leave, John followed him to the door and reminded him he was welcome back any time. I was struck by the mutual respect between the two men during the visit.

This incident is linked to certain period in John's life. John received only thirty-three weeks of uninterrupted schooling. He was at school when the Second World War broke out and school services for children in the area where he lived were discontinued throughout the war period. This was the reason that John, like many other Sámi, did not receive an education during the war. The result was that he could not read and write (unlike his father), and also was unable to get a higher education after compulsory school, or to get a job that required education.

Nevertheless, the thirty-three weeks that John attended school left a lasting negative impression. John's family lived in Šuoššjávri at the time, before they moved to Cuovddatmohkki. About thirty kilometres away, across the mountain to Máse, there was a small boarding school. This is where John went to school for thirty-three weeks. When he started school, he spoke only Sámi, like many other Sámi children. Instruction was conducted entirely in Norwegian. John's teacher came from southern Norway, and neither understood nor spoke Sámi. John recalls that the teacher conducted his lessons with a significant degree of brutality against the children. This was something that

Figure 6.1 John in the kitchen of his house (photograph by Jens-Ivar Nergård).

he experienced first-hand. When there was something he did not understand, the teacher took his rod and struck John on his back. He recalls that his mother therefore sewed a pillow into the collar of his jacket to take most of the weight of these blows.

John lived at the boarding school in Máse. The school year was divided into 'autumn school', which ran from August/September until November, and 'spring school', which ran from January to May. The schoolchildren had a week's autumn holiday during the potato harvest, and an Easter holiday, which often lasted a couple of weeks. After the holidays, John and some of the other students returned to the boarding school in Máse from his home in Šuoššjávri. This was a distance of thirty kilometres across the mountains in difficult terrain. In the spring and fall, the children walked this distance on foot, and in winter they went on skis. John's thirty-three weeks of school lasted only a couple of years. He says that he never learned Norwegian, or anything else of value at school, but was left with upsetting memories of school. This amputated schooling, coupled with unpleasant school experiences, resulted in a life spent almost entirely at the farm in the little mountain village. Later, John completed sixteen months of military service at the Garrison of Porsanger, about a hundred kilometres from home. He said that his knowledge of Norwegian was solely derived from his military service experience.

From a very early age, John had worked as a *verdde* (a helper or hired hand) in the *siida* that had winter grazing grounds for its flock. This was in an area that could easily be reached from the farm where John lived. This short distance to the winter grazing grounds made it easy for him to make his way to the flock and see to the animals, either alone or together with the owners. In this way, he became part of the working community at the *siida*. He was also a very skilled craftsman, and made many knives during the year. The knives were crafted with a type of steel that he knew the herders preferred. These knives were popular, and customers often made personal visits to the farm to select the ones they needed for their purposes. John did not actively market his wares, but it was common knowledge that he made excellent knives of various sizes and designs to suit his customers and their needs. He had many regular customers who were reindeer-owners and herders, and some of them ordered knives with a specific design and shape, suited for a particular use. Knives used in daily reindeer husbandry must be made of steel that can be ground often, in order to be used as a work tool. John's knives were able to withstand rough use. This distinguished them from the type of knives often sold to tourists, which in many cases were merely decorative. John called them 'tourist knives'.

As John sees it, he has managed well enough in life. He is illiterate, but has an unshakeable faith in his ability to create his own way in life. The life he lost due to his lack of schooling is something he rarely talks about, but in all practical matters, he has been intent on preserving his own integrity. This was noticeable when he spoke about things that truly affected him. Now and then he would tear up, not only when relating his grief over his losses and defeats, but also when talking about his joy of kinship with and respect for

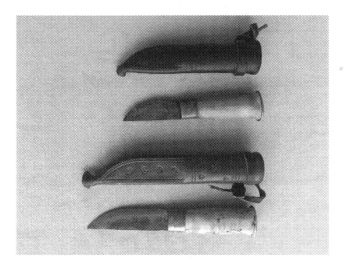

Figure 6.2 Collection of knives made by John (photograph by Jens-Ivar Nergård).

Sámi culture and traditions. He took pride in the way he had managed a life that in many ways had prevented him from flourishing. His accomplishments had made up for what he had lost. Through his strong connection with, and sense of belonging to, the Sámi community, life had strengthened him, and given him faith in himself.

John grew up on a farm with his parents, but never started a family of his own. When his father died, he was left alone on the farm, and almost alone in the little mountain village. There were no young people who wanted to settle there, and build homes and raise a family. This accentuated what he had lost in his life. As he grew older, he came to accept the life he was given, although the sense of loss still affected him. This was noticeable in his cautious demeanour when speaking with people who came to his house, and in the consideration that he showed to his guests. His hospitality and goodwill were apparent in these encounters, but he was also alert to anything that might threaten his self-respect.

John's losses have had an impact. The loss of an education robbed him of his opportunity to read and write, and perhaps also the confidence to start a family. His siblings' children have benefited from his warmth and kindness. He felt at home on his farm. A peaceful evening with his fishing pole in the river just a hundred metres from his home was sacred to John. He belonged to nature, and nature belonged to him. This close bond with nature was an important framework for his life. He did not seek out nature – he lived in it. He picked berries in the woods where he lived, fished in his 'own' river and hunted in his 'own' forest, where he also gathered wood for the winter. He did not care whether the government owned the land and resources he used to survive. No one else had laid claim to the area. It had been this way as long as he could remember. However, he did not need to travel far from the farm to realise that the Sámi community, with all its struggles for the right to the land they had used for generations, had changed. Perhaps this made him appreciate his home even more.

John's losses have left an impact. His brief experience of school was his first encounter with Norwegian authorities. The blows from his teacher's rod had scarred him for life. This was not only a blow from a rod across his back, but also a blow to child's soul. The rod told him he was a stranger in his own land, and that his language and the language of his family was not accepted. School was a foreign territory, and the power that the school wielded in denying him his own language was also an expulsion of his Sámi world. This brusque rejection of his Sámi identity in school denied him of his human right to learn to read and write. It emphasised his exclusion from the Norwegian community, and also from the Sámi community, in certain essential areas. It is difficult to ignore that this experience also shut him off from certain opportunities in his own life and his Sámi community. These losses could never entirely be compensated, and left John with a fundamental ambivalence in his relationship with Norwegian society, perhaps also with himself.

Figure 6.3 John fishing on a summer night (photograph by Jens-Ivar Nergård).

Bleak fate at a boarding school in the 1970s

Per Edvard Johnsen, or Molles Piera in Sámi, is currently the manager of Nedre Mollesjohka *fjellstue* (mountain lodge), located about seventy kilometres from Karasjok on the Finnmark plateau, and seventy kilometres from Alta. Here, he receives guests throughout the year and operates the lodge, complete with a café and overnight accommodations. His guests arrive at the lodge on skis or by snow scooter in winter, and on foot or by bicycle in summer.

Per was born and raised at the Mollesjohka mountain lodge. He had a secure childhood, as one of nine children. His family lived a free life in harmony with nature, fishing in the rivers and lakes in summer, hunting and trapping grouse, and ice fishing for char and trout in winter. The mountain lodge was one of many built for government officials that crossed the roadless mountains in their official capacity. In time, these mountain lodges were used by other people who crossed the plateaus and needed overnight accommodations before the roads were built. Per grew up accustomed to the open plateaus and a free life. When he turned seven years old, however, his life changed completely. It was time to start school. This was in 1969, and all of the children of the villages outside Karasjok were gathered together at one school. This is how Per came to Grensen boarding school in August, after two days of travel on his father's tractor, along with several older siblings. The long journey between Mollesjohka mountain lodge and Grensen boarding

Figure 6.4 Mollesjohka Fjellstue (photograph by Per Edvard Johnsen, reproduced with permission).

school near the Finnish border just past Karasjok, required an overnight stay for the children in Karasjok.

Per arrived at Grensen school with great expectations. His older siblings had already begun telling him exciting stories about school. He looked forward to slices of salami sausage on his bread: 'At home, we only had salmon and cloudberries on bread', he says with a smile. But life at Grensen school was not as he expected or hoped. He was not permitted to live with his

Figure 6.5 Mollesjohka Fjellstue today (photograph by Per Edvard Johnsen, reproduced with permission).

Figure 6.6 Fishing on Iesjávri in spring (photograph by Per Edvard Johnsen, reproduced with permission).

siblings, but was instead placed with four students his own age in the same room. Seven-year-olds accustomed to having their parents around from morning to night would naturally feel abandoned. 'Children were orphaned, and parents were made childless', says Per. He says that both his parents, especially his mother, were deeply affected by having to send their children away to boarding school. Per's mother died a few years ago, and he says that the last years of her life were haunted by memories of sending her children away.

Boarding school life was not the only challenge for the seven-year-old. Like most of the other children at Grensen school, Per only spoke Sámi when he started his first year. He recalls that he did not begin to understand or speak Norwegian until the end of his second year. The children spoke Sámi with one another at the boarding house at night, but the adults wanted them to speak Norwegian. Much of the contact with the adults involved speaking the Norwegian language. The road between Karasjok and Kautokeino was not completed until the mid-1970s. It was therefore not possible for the children from Mollesjohka to come home for weekends, in contrast with the other children, whose homes were connected by roads. This meant that Per and his siblings spent their weekends at the boarding school with a few other children. These were long periods of separation from their parents. The children from Mollesjohka arrived at the boarding school after the summer holidays in August and stayed until Christmas the same year. In spring, they stayed at the boarding house from New Year's Day to Easter, and then until summer holidays.

Per recalls the first months of the first school year, but the remainder of his time at school is enveloped in what he calls 'a deep darkness': 'I was locked within myself', he says. He believes that the teachers' strategy to facilitate language learning and educational instruction was to maintain a strict regime, with harsh discipline. This had numerous consequences, which left him scarred for life. Per recalls that one of his older brothers was directly subjected to violence by a teacher. He cannot recall what his brother was punished for, but remembers that the teacher took the boy out to the schoolyard. Several other boys had been gathered and forced to watch his brother being beaten. His brother had no opportunity to defend himself. Both he and his fellow students simply had to accept it. The teacher beat the boy until blood was running from his nose and mouth. Per believes that this violent episode was intended as a deterrent and reminder of the possible retaliations for anyone. In this way, the violence was a preventive measure. The children had no available course of action, and were helpless victims. Their parents were far away, not only physically and geographically, but also mentally. 'We were told to remain silent about the harsh discipline, which the boys especially experienced at the school and boarding house', says Per.

Per's experiences at school and the fact that he missed his parents caused him to gradually slip into the 'darkness'. Whilst he is not entirely sure what exactly this darkness entailed, he does offer a few glimpses into how his life has been impacted by his experiences. For a long time, he was unable to remember much of his time at school. Many of these memories were suppressed: 'There was only silence', he says. He noticed that his concentration was affected: 'I have never been able to read an entire book. I couldn't concentrate enough to read, and couldn't remember what I had read'. Much of what he experienced at school has been forgotten. Per believes this was because he missed his parents, and felt imprisoned at the boarding school, which was surrounded by tall pine trees. 'It was like being trapped in darkness', he says.

'Children were orphaned, and parents became childless', he repeats. This statement encompasses the bitter experiences from Per's time at the boarding school. School was not the exciting adventure that he had expected at the beginning. Instead, his traumatic experiences from school piled up, and caused him to behave strangely in situations with his own family, when he became a father. He was unable to understand or explain to his family why these situations, where he experienced a loss of control, occurred. When his own children started school, the memories of boarding school returned. He was distraught at not being able to help his children with their homework, nor being able to participate in other things related to school. This emphasised his sense of helplessness towards his children and towards himself. His own experience of loss was overwhelming. The boarding school experiences returned in what he describes as flashbacks. These 'ghosts' from the past, and Grensen boarding school, haunted him for many years. They obstructed him in his role as a supportive father and husband. 'My children did not have a boarding school experience. They attended "normal" schools', says Per. He had no idea why the 'darkness' came over him, and made him do things he didn't want to do.

One day, in despair over the situation, he brought along his eldest son and drove from the mountain lodge down to Karasjok, and from there to Grensen boarding school. Per had not been there since he was a student. He recalls that the weather was good, and it was a bright, moonlit evening. They did not get out of the car, but instead stayed parked outside the gate of the boarding school. Not much was said in the car, but both were crying. Per realised that his son understood the situation and what he wanted to tell him on that visit. Something happened between them that evening. Per had opened up about his own anguish, which he did not fully understand himself. His son, however, understood the purpose of the visit, and the story his father wished to tell him that evening at Grensen boarding school.

After six to seven years at Grensen boarding school, Per started middle school in Karasjok. This was a far better school experience. His father had bought a small house in Karasjok, where Per and his siblings all lived while attending school. After middle school, Per attended the *Sámisk Folkehøgskole* (Sámi Folk High School) in Karasjok. There he discovered what a school could be, and says the *Sámisk Folkehøgskole* was the reason he was still alive. Per has spent a long time processing his experiences from boarding school.

Figure 6.7 Per and his brother visiting Grensen boarding school as adults (photograph by Per Edvard Johnsen, reproduced with permission).

After his time at school, he realised how much his parents had suffered whilst their children were away at boarding school. He believes that his mother felt extreme guilt at sending the children away, although there was nothing else that she could have done. Their mother's guilt led the children to feel anxious, which often occurs when children feel that they may be the cause of their parents' problems. Experiences from school and the boarding house were interwoven in a confusing and impenetrable compound of problems, which people were neither prepared for, nor had the experience to deal with on their own.

Per was one of the boarding school victims who realised that he could not manage these experiences alone. For a long period, he attended therapy sessions. He believes that many boarding school victims should have done the same. He knows several other people who are struggling with trauma as adults from their time at boarding school, including his own brother. Per has four children, and felt that he could not be a good father or husband until he was able to process his own trauma. It had affected him in ways that he himself did not fully understand. During his early days of therapy, he felt a dam of emotions opening up. In these therapy sessions, he experienced a rush of memories, like a river thawing in spring. He was overwhelmed by these memories, and became physically restless. 'Things were boiling inside me, and I had all this energy', says Per. He bought a computer and, in a frenzy, began writing. Sometimes, the emotions produced in therapy got the better of him, and two or three computers ended up on the floor. He was surprised by everything that came out, but was also energised by it. He discovered that writing down his suppressed memories was a good way to organise them, and to keep them at a distance. After the therapy

Figure 6.8 An open and endless world (photographs by Per Edvard Johnsen, reproduced with permission).

The colonisation of Sápmi   133

Figure 6.9 An open and endless world (photographs by Per Edvard Johnsen, reproduced with permission).

programme ended, he continued his writing. He feels this has been good for him. Perhaps one day it will result in a book about his boarding school experiences. If he is not able to realise his dream of publishing his autobiography, these texts may still serve as an 'explanation' for his own children and family. They have also helped him to understand what he was unable to figure out or express a few years ago.

Per believes that therapy, which for a time made him quite ill, has paid off in the long run. He explains that it feels as though the pain he bore has been made visible to him. The process he went through has been beneficial. Per believes that the lives of many former boarding school students could be improved by going through the same process. He feels that he is now able to live with these experiences, because he has processed them. 'It felt good to get rid of the baggage', he says, as he knows what it is like to carry heavy baggage across the Finnmark plateau. For a long time, however, he still experienced unpleasant memories from his time at Grensen boarding school.

Today, Per feels his life is good. His eldest children are now young adults, have had educations, and live good lives. In Easter 2019, his youngest daughter was confirmed in the chapel at Šuoššjávri. This was a major event in a family that had been forced to deal with problems the Norwegian authorities had created for him, but which the same authorities had done little to repair. Per now operates Nedre Mollesjohka *fjellstue*. Here, he lives the life he feels he was born to live: in a timeless pact with nature, harvesting all that nature has to offer. He fishes as he did when he was a child, in rivers and ponds in summer, with ice fishing in the plentiful lakes in winter. He hunts and traps grouse in winter and obtains most of the food he serves to a large number of guests throughout the year at the mountain lodge: guests who seek close contact with untouched nature. Per guides them across the plateaus and teaches them about its natural resources, sharing his insights into a world that is quite foreign to most of the guests. He masters the plateau. In the last few years, he has also learned to master his own life.

Figure 6.10 Gifts from nature (photograph by Per Edvard Johnsen, reproduced with permission).

Figure 6.11 Gifts from nature (photograph by Per Edvard Johnsen, reproduced with permission).

Destructive consequences

The boarding schools and boarding houses in Sámi and Kven districts caused significant and lasting harm to individuals and communities. Norwegianisation was both a systematised political strategy against the Sámi and Kven people, and an assimilation process that attempted to replace their cultures with Norwegian culture. The language shift was a key part of this offensive, and became the very symbol of the strategy. The focus on a language shift was not arbitrary. Language was the backbone of the two cultures that the authorities wanted to destroy. A language is not only a linguistic system with a specific structure; it also involves a conceptual world where work and tasks, customs and traditions, beliefs and spirituality come alive. The world to which language belongs can be understood as the culture's 'depth grammar' (Wittgenstein, 1978). Not only does it comprise the language's foundation and references, but also contains the shared spaces where it is used, and obtains its meaning for communication and interaction. The concepts of language are the bedrock for how we think, understand and communicate. It is the very foundation for forming opinions in the community, and can therefore be considered the backbone of a community.

We now know that the violation of traditional Sámi beliefs regarding the management of vulnerable natural resources harms not only the Sámi people. The entire world needs to understand the balance between harvesting and protecting nature if it is to maintain its ability to feed people. The pioneers of Norwegianisation did not understand this balance, nor did they understand that their actions contributed to damage and destruction. This is not to imply that modern society should excuse and trivialise the damage done to individuals and communities. The worst cases of abuse were considered entirely understandable by the abusers, given their contemporary context. Punishing a child because he or she did not understand a foreign language was a blatant form of abuse. The abusers believed that they were following the practical implementation of Norwegianisation, which took place in the boarding schools until recent times.

Government authorities must bear a heavy responsibility for the lack of control and supervision, and for the lack of an apparatus that might have prevented these abuses. We now have adequate concepts to understand and judge much of what took place under Norwegianisation. There is little to indicate that this knowledge will not be applied when highlighting the abuses that have been, or can be, uncovered. The most fruitless manner of dealing with the abuses that occurred is to excuse or trivialise them. One of the most common ways of trivialising these issues is to argue, for the purpose of Norwegianisation, that many of the boarding school students did well, and enjoyed their time at school and boarding school. This zero-sum thinking, where victims of Norwegianisation were weighed against those who managed well, could almost be considered a new violation, one that attempts to mask the consequences of Norwegianisation (Nergård, 2019a).

The rejection of the Sámi and Kven languages was perhaps the most visible and definitive rejection of their culture. Children were unable to understand this collective rejection. Their option was to view this as a personal rejection, as illustrated in the biographic stories above. Children were only able to interpret the rejection of their language as rejection of themselves. With their parents partially out of the picture, the children became the true victims of Norwegianisation policies. Many of them developed a destructive self-identity, rejecting in themselves the very things the school rejected. The most extensive damage children incurred from Norwegianisation was at this personal level, which in practice functioned as a psychological razing of their cultural personalities. This is perhaps the most covert and least accessible aspect of colonisation. It is, however, possible to document this, as was done by the Canadian Truth and Reconciliation Commission's work (2015). The Commission was especially concerned with the fate of the children who were subjected to the worst abuses.

In Norway, the shame associated with this cultural devaluation has adversely affected individuals, families and local communities. The official rejection of Sámi and Kven languages and traditions, viewing them as worthless, led many of the victims to accept this perception of themselves. Colonial forces encroached upon both mental and spiritual aspects of their colonised victims. They came to identify themselves with their abusers, a phenomenon that we now refer to as 'Stockholm syndrome' (a condition where a victim of abuse seeks to develop a psychological alliance with the abuser as a survival strategy). Many victims of Norwegianisation passed on this alliance to their descendants, believing that the abuser was right. I have met these victims through my many years of fieldwork in the Sámi communities. Some of them have expressed that they agree with the opinion that Sámi language and traditions should not be protected and maintained. These views belong to the past, and have no place in our modern society. Many of those with such views appear to be in conflict with themselves. They deny their own history, yet are also drawn to it. This conflict leads many to not only deny their own Sámi background, but to reject it in others who do not do the same. It would seem, therefore, that many are struggling with inner conflicts. Some have an ambivalent relationship to both Sámi and Norwegian identities, and feel out of place in both worlds. The well-known Palo Alto Group, under leadership of Gregory Bateson, developed the double bind theory to describe this conflict situation (Bateson, 1972).

Under the reconstruction of the Sámi community after more than a hundred years of official rejection of its language and traditions, there are still traces of Norwegianisation that oppose reconstruction. The shame associated with Sámi culture is inextricably linked to the lack of recognition by Norwegian authorities. The absence of this recognition is noticeable in daily life – for example, when Sámi patients are admitted to hospital and institutions that neither understand their language, nor acknowledge their self-understanding associated with traditional beliefs of illness and health (Nergård, 2019b).

The Sámi community has a host of stories that place new experiences in a historical context. These stories have contributed to a collective memory and collective awareness of Norwegianisation. They have provided comfort and contributed towards reconciliation. They have also been of help in processing the incidents at schools and boarding houses that have made lasting impressions and scarred many for life. This material has had an important role in processing the degradation many have experienced, also on behalf of their Sámi culture. It was not until 2018 that the Norwegian authorities appointed a commission to review Norwegianisation policies, and to identify some of the consequences that it had for the Sámi and Kven populations. There are high expectations for the commission's analyses and proposals for reconciliation, and acknowledgement of the policies that were so destructive for so many people.

The milestones of reconstruction

Sámi reconstruction, following the colonialisation period from 1850 to 1970, is visible in many areas. Several official reports cleared the way for an extensive development of institutions, starting in the 1970s, when the Sámi community began preparing for a new era. The establishment of the Nordic Sámi Institute in Kautokeino in 1973 was crucial for continued reconstruction. The most important factor in this cultural rehabilitation has, without a doubt, been the development of new Sámi institutions over the past forty years. These have served as the cornerstone of the reconstruction. Nevertheless, some have been critical towards the development of institutions for the Sámi community. Prominent Sámi political activists believe that the new institutions open for new ways for Norwegian authorities to control their only Indigenous population. However, the development of modern Sámi institutions has contributed towards greater co-determination and has been vital for the reconstruction of the Sámi community, where the Sámi people themselves have been in charge.

In 1988, an amendment was made to the Norwegian Constitution, known as the Sámi paragraph, now stated in Section 108. This gave the Sámi people constitutional rights for the first time:

> It is the responsibility of government authorities to create conditions that enable the Sámi people to preserve and develop its language, culture and way of life.

In 1998, two important Sámi institutions were established in Norway: the Sámi Parliament of Norway, which was founded in Kárásjohka (Karasjok) and the Sámi University of Applied Sciences in Guovdageaidnu (Kautokeino). The first was crucial for the development of a political environment and a centre of administration for Sámi society. *Sámi Høgskole* (Sámi University of Applied Sciences) became a centre for higher education and research in areas that were important for the development of a modern society.

In 1990, Norway ratified the ILO Convention no. 169. The main principle of the Convention that applies to 'indigenous and tribal peoples' independent states' is that they have the right to preserve their own culture, and that government authorities have the duty to support this work. The provisions of the Section 108 in the Norwegian Constitution and Section 109 in the ILO Convention ushered in a new era for the Sámi people in Norway. The development of a Sámi society with a modern administration was both the key to a systematic reconstruction and a significant challenge. Many important areas required prioritisation. Resources, however, have been limited. Many have claimed, and with good reason, that the lack of funding for initiatives crucial for the development of a modern Sámi society indicates that Norwegianisation is still in progress. National developments and policies for the distribution of resources therefore continue to have a harmful impact on Sámi interests and the Sámi way of life.

Since the 1980s, the Sámi community has come quite far from Norwegianisation and degradation. An independent Sámi society with responsibility for its modern institutions of knowledge has prioritised the development of its own schools, education system and research. It was primarily through the schools and education system that the colonisation of Sápmi first began. It therefore seems only reasonable to embed the decolonisation process in institutions responsible for education and research. These efforts will be crucial for the future.

Figure 6.12 Freedom (photograph by Per Edvard Johnsen, reproduced with permission).

References

Bateson, G. (1972). *Steps to an Ecology of Mind. Collected Essays in Anthropology, Psychiatry, Evolution and Epistemology*. University of Chicago Press.
Eriksen, K.E. & Niemi, E. (1981). *Den finske fare. Sikkerhetsproblemer og minoritetspolitikk i nord 1860–1940*. [*The Finnish Danger: Security Problems and Minority Politics in the North 1860–1940*]. Oslo: The University Press.
Goffman, E. (1967). *Anstalt og menneske. [Institution and Human]*. Copenhagen: Paludan.
Grenersen, G. (2015). Finnefondet: et fornorskningsinstrument eller et ekstra lønnstillegg? En gjennomgang av fondets midler til lærerne 1901–1902. [Finnefondet: n exploration instrument or an extra salary supplement? A review of the Fund's resourcing of teachers 1901–1902]. *Norsk historisk tidsskrift*, 94: 609–633.
Minde, H. (2005). Fornorskninga av samene – hvordan, hvorfor og hvilke følger. [Assimilation of the Sámi – implementation and consequences]. *Gádu Cála, Tidsskrift for urfolksrettigheter*, 3.
Nergård, J.I. (2004). The sacred landscape. *Diedut*, 3: 85–92.
Nergård, J-I. (1992). *Den vuxna barndomen. Den psykotiska personen som vägvisare i vår kultur. [Adult Childhood. The Psychotic Person as a Guide in our Culture]*. Ludvika, Sweden: Dualis.
Nergård, J-I. (1994). *Det skjulte Nord-Norge. [The Hidden North Norway]*. Oslo: Pensumtjeneste.
Nergård, J-I. (2006). *Den levende erfaring. En studie i samisk kunnskapstradisjon. [The Living Experience: A Study in Sámi Knowledge Tradition]*. Oslo: Cappelen Damm Akademisk.
Nergård, J-I. (2019a). *Dialoger med naturen. Etnografiske skisser fra Sápmi. [Dialogues with Nature. Ethnographic Sketches from Sápmi]*. Oslo: The University Press.
Nergård, J-I. (2019b). Tradisjonens stemme. [The voice of tradition]. In J-I. Nergård & P. Vitebsky (eds.), *Kulturen som pasient: Uvanlige møter for vanlige folk. [Culture as a Patient: Extraordinary Meetings with Ordinary people]*. Oslo: The University Press.
Niemi, E. (2017). Fornorskningspolitikken overfor samene og kvenene. [The Norwegianisation policy towards the Sámi and the Kven]. In N. Brandal, C.A. Døving & I.T. Plesner (eds.), *Nasjonale minoriteter og urfolk i norsk politikk fra 1900 til 2016. [National Minorities and Indigenous Peoples in Norwegian Politics from 1900 to 2016]*. Oslo: Cappelen Damm Akademisk.

Reiersen, J. (1920). Skolearbeidet i Finnmark. [Schoolwork in Finnmark]. In C. Schøyen (ed.), *Nordlandet [Norselands]*. Oslo: Aschehougs Forlag.

Smith, L.T. (2010): *Decolonizing Methodologies: Research and Indigenous Peoples*. London: Zed Books.

Truth and Reconciliation Commission of Canada. (2015). Honouring the Truth, Reconciling for the Future: Summary of the Final Report of the Truth and Reconciliation Commission of Canada. Available online: http://www.trc.ca [Accessed April, 2019].

Tvete, B. (1955). *Skolebøker for samiske barn. Fra Thomas von Westen til i dag. [Schoolbooks for Sámi Children: From Thomas von Westen to Today*. PhD thesis, University Trondheim.

Wittgenstein, L. (1978). *Philosophical Investigations*. Oxford: Basil Blackwell.

Chapter 7

Colliding Heartwork
The space where our hearts meet and collide to process the boarding school experience

Natahnee Nuay Winder

Introduction

Pehnaho, Maik'w, Mique, Yá'át'èèh (Greeting in Shoshone, Paiute, Ute, and Navajo). My name is Natahnee, 'Naat'áanii', Nuay Winder. I am citizen of the Duckwater Shoshone Nation and am Paiute, Ute, Navajo, and African American. I grew up on the Southern Ute reservation in Colorado, and spent the summers at Pyramid Lake Paiute with my maternal grandparents in Nevada. I retain my connections to my family in Colorado and Nevada with yearly visits, and by participating in our seasonal ceremonies. I consider both Southern Ute and Pyramid Lake my home communities. 'Natahnee', ('Naat'áanii'), is my Diné (Navajo) name given to me by paternal great-grandma. It means an individual who is a leader or someone who has leadership qualities. My maternal great-grandmother gave in my middle name, 'Nuay', which means 'rain' in Paiute. According to research into my family history, 'Winder' is most likely a slave name given involuntarily to my ancestors by English settlers. I am a strong and passionate mixed-heritage Indigenous and Black warrior woman. I am also a daughter, granddaughter, sister, partner, and auntie. I am the oldest of six Indigenous siblings. I introduce myself before delving into the boarding school (residential school) system experience in the United States to ground and acknowledge my intertribal connections and tribal community. It is a both an Indigenous community practice and in some communities a cultural protocol. Most importantly, my introduction is '….an act of resistance' (Minthorn, 2019, p. 25), and a resilience within the academy to follow this cultural protocol and/or traditions. Many Indigenous scholars and students in the academy commit to this act of resistance and resiliency to acknowledge our ancestors and communities, and to bring them into academic spaces – whereas non-Indigenous academics acknowledge their educational training, title, and affiliation to establish prestige, and then may proceed to share their backgrounds.

For Indigenous scholars and students, there are similarities between the academy and the boarding schools, such as the practice of putting our identities and cultural protocols aside, in a diminished version, or last, in order to constrain and conform to the expectations in the institution. For instance, the type of 'education' Indigenous children in boarding schools in the United States received was a weapon designed to detach their culture and identity, and disrupt their social norms, because they were perceived as 'inferior' to settlers. In the academy, upcoming scholars are constantly pressured, or trained, to focus on their own research. The tenure-track process hierarchically ranks contributions as follows: (i) research, (ii) scholarship, and then (iii) service (at the bottom of the tier). My PhD programme's professional seminar emphasised this trajectory, and I have been told by some non-Indigenous academics that being an academic researcher carries more creditability for tenure than positioning myself as a community researcher. I have been fortunate, and supported by my supervisor to focus my efforts and position as an Indigenous community researcher who does research in the academy. I consider the tenure-track process a Venn diagram of scholarship, research, and services, where these pieces are equivalent. As an Indigenous community researcher in the academy, I see the importance of honouring, respecting, and working with Indigenous communities and students in order to maintain cultural protocols and privilege Indigenous voices. Both the boarding school system and the tenure-track system attempt to assimilate and transform Indigenous students and scholars into their institutional values and foundations.

Even though it may be problematic for Indigenous students and scholars, as they encounter difficulties in maintaining their identities and cultural protocols through the education system, they have retained and resisted contemporary forms of assimilation. Indigenous students and scholars have used secondary and post-secondary education to their advantage for personal and communal growth. My family instilled the notion in me that obtaining an education provided an opportunity to overcome challenges and to support the family and our community. When I decided to attend the University of New Mexico for my undergraduate degree, my Uncle Saa'swanis'his'waqs told me, 'We use our college education to give back to your community or another tribal community. It is the Native way to advocate, encourage, support, and create opportunities for Indigenous communities. Pursuing a college education is not an individual pursuit, and it is aids a larger community purpose'. I approach conducting research with Indigenous students and communities with my upbringing to use education to support and honour Indigenous voices and connections.

In this work, I share the life stories of Indigenous students,[1] who attended 'Southwestern University',[2] and how they expressed being impacted by the legacy of the boarding school system. The boarding school system and history has contemporary impacts on Indigenous peoples across the world. Schools funded by the United States government forged an atrocious process of assimilating and 'civilising' Indigenous children into Euro-American society by cutting their hair, limiting or eliminating the use of traditional languages, disconnecting families, and abandoning Indigenous ways of knowing, hence creating a loss of identity.[3] Indigenous peoples in the United States (and around the world) have survived not only the boarding school system, but also multiple forms of violence such as forced removal, wars, and genocide. Indigenous peoples have survived these forms of violence committed by the settler states. Thus, the boarding school legacy is not an event that only occurred in the past; for some Indigenous peoples, this institution is a living history, and a lived experience that they are still processing. The two terms 'residential school' and 'boarding school' will be used interchangeably to refer to the schooling system pursued by the United States and Canada to 'educate' Indigenous peoples.[4] There are lingering impacts of the boarding school system for Indigenous students who attended them, as well as for their descendants. When family members have the courage to share their boarding school experiences, it can become emotional and distressing for both the person sharing, and those listening to their truth in telling of an event. It is human nurture to provide comfort and alleviate the pain. This action is where our hearts reach out to support, which creates space for where our hearts collide. Boarding school and residential school histories are emotional and personal, and as scholars, especially Indigenous scholars and students, our families and communities' histories and personal testimonies are valid, and cannot be separated from our lived experiences. This chapter reflects the tradition of storytelling by showing how Indigenous students' hearts and mine collided to share their perspectives of the intergenerational aspects of the boarding school legacy through a process called '*Colliding Heartwork*'.[5]

A brief history of Indian boarding schools in the United States

Indigenous peoples had their own traditional methods and systems of education, which differ significantly from methods and systems used by Europeans. The American settler society endorsed and sought to *give* education to Indigenous peoples, because they were 'unaware of the extensive education systems already in place, or they deemed them *uncivilised*' (Hill & Redwing Saunders, 2008, p. 100). Indigenous children were forcibly taken and sent to boarding schools during the nineteenth century, and into the twentieth century, in an attempt by the American settler state to gradually eradicate Indigenous culture and identity. Indigenous children were mandated to attend Christian and US government-run boarding schools. The boarding school system goal was to create *suitable* Americans by assimilating and 'civilising' Indigenous children. The system of Euro-American education began in the 1600s, when Puritan missionary John Eliot established a reservation in Massachusetts to control Indigenous peoples by experimenting with the Christianisation of Indigenous peoples with 'praying towns' (Eliot & Morrison, 1974). Praying towns were designed to separate Indigenous peoples from their communities, so that they would receive Christianity as a form of 'civilising' method. Later colonists determined that adults had strong connections to their Indigenous ways of knowing, and it would be difficult to fully convert them to Christianity (Smith, 2006). As a result, Indigenous children were targeted for educating them through Christianity in designated schools.

The boarding school system during the 1600s and 1700s was based on missionary education primarily in the English colonies (before the establishment of the United States) where schooling for Indigenous youth focused on grammar, philosophy, divinity, and education offered by various religious societies and orders (Szasz, 1988). As the US nation state developed, Indigenous peoples were perceived as a 'problem' and an obstacle to settler expansion. Between 1783 and 1812, the US government entered into negotiations for more treaties that included policies for education and civilisation of Indigenous peoples. The US Senate established approximately 400 treaties with educational provisions (Reyhner & Eder, 2004). The 1819 Civilization Fund is considered to be one of the early approaches for the government's effort to educate Indigenous peoples by providing religious groups with financial support. The Civilization Fund established twenty-one schools within a span of five years, with 800 students until 1873 (Cate, 1995; Reyhner & Eder, 2004). The formalisation of the US boarding school system came into existence under President Ulysses Grant's Peace Policy of 1869–1870. The Peace Policy entrusted education and administration of reservations to various religious dominations by a means of watching over Indigenous peoples, and the creation of day and boarding schools (Getches, Wilkinson & Williams, 2005; Smith, 2006). During the late 1870s and early 1880s, the US government began investing in off-reservation boarding schools.

The escalation of off-reservation boarding schools ignited with the formation of the Carlisle Indian Industrial School and the General Allotment (Dawes)[6] Act in 1887. Richard Pratt founded the first off-reservation boarding school in 1879, with an initial enrolment of 138 Indigenous students. These students were Arapaho, Cheyenne, Comanche, and Kiowa prisoners from Fort Marion, Florida, who were introduced to reading and arithmetic, as well as part-time jobs (Child, 1998). Pratt was invested in an experimentation to 'civilise' prisoners from the Red River War of 1874 through the cutting of their hair, and introducing them to military drills and labour skills (Adams, 1995). His model of 'civilising' Indigenous adults was extended to include Indigenous children. Pratt argued that off-reservation boarding schools, where children would be taken far from their traditional homes at an early age and return as young adults, would be the best strategies for assimilating children and save them from 'savagery', so that they would become part of American society. Pratt's justification for off-reservation schooling was to '*Kill the Indian; Save the Man/Child*', and he believed that the '….transfer of the savage-born infant into the surroundings of civilisation [would allow a child to] grow to possess a civilised language and habit' (Pratt, 1973). Carlisle would later become a model for future off-reservation institutions throughout the United States and Canada. After the establishment of Carlisle, by 1909, there were over 25 off-reservation boarding schools, 157 on-reservation boarding schools, and 307 day schools operating (Adams, 1995). It is estimated that over 100,000 Indigenous children were forced to attend these institutions between 1879 and the 1960s. The US Congress also mandated laws to allow the Bureau of Indian Affairs to compel attendance on some reservations (Churchill, 2004; Coleman, 1993). Some Indian agents on reservations required Indigenous parents and communities to send children to boarding schools by withholding food rations and annuities, or sending parents to jail (Bowker, 2007). There are records of where the US Cavalry was used to enforce school compliance (TRC, 2015).

Indigenous children trained for domestic work (such as dairying, needlework, and cooking) for girls and manual labour (in the form of farming, agriculture, and mechanical trades) for boys, so that they would be absorbed in the American society for work at the bottom of the socioeconomic ladder. The boarding school system also utilised an 'Outing' programme developed by Pratt where children were leased to settlers for labour during the summers. The boarding school system permanently altered children by segregating them from their families, communities, and culture. Subsequently, these American principles of civilisation were intended to discredit and abolish well-established Indigenous lifestyles. This overall system brought upsetting emotional, mental, physical, and spiritual impingements and various forms of abuse to Indigenous children that attended these institutions. However, not all boarding school experiences were negative. Some Indigenous students recollected having positive experiences. My maternal grandmother[7] is one of the students who felt that boarding school benefited her. There are an overwhelming amount of lived experiences and testimonies that describe the negative outcomes of boarding schools. In addition, there were also Indigenous children who did not survive these institutions.

In 1928, the Meriam Report, also known as the *'Problem with Indian Education'*, was released, and documented the detrimental effects of the boarding schools on Indigenous children. The report's two major findings were that Indigenous peoples were excluded from management of their own affairs, and that the health and education services they were receiving were of a poor quality. The government's expenditures for the institutions were small; schools were underfunded, and exploited children as free labour (Child, 1998). In fact, the boarding schools had insufficient food budgets (i.e. 11 cents per child per day); they were overcrowded, health care was deficient, and children were extremely malnourished and overworked. As a result, Indigenous children were starving, and contacted contagious diseases such as tuberculosis, measles, pneumonia, and influenza, which routinely took many of their lives. At Carlisle, there are the graves of 184 students, who died at that boarding school (Zalcman, 2018).

Furthermore, there were many Indigenous children who experienced distress and/or forms of sexual, physical, emotional violence, and abuse at boarding schools. For instance, in 1987, the Federal Bureau of Investigation (FBI) found that John Boone, a teacher at a Hopi school, sexually abused over 142 boys, but the school did not launch any investigation into any allegations of abuse (Goodbye BIA, 1994). In addition, there was no policy on reporting sexual abuse established by the Bureau of Indian Affairs until 1987, a system of background checks for teachers was implemented only in 1989 (Child Sexual Abuse in Federal Schools, 1990; Smith, 2006). Indigenous children who attended boarding schools in the United States, and residential schools in Canada, experienced direct and indirect physical, psychological and sexual abuse. The Truth and Reconciliation Commission (TRC) of Canada was mandated to investigate and to record the residential school experiences of survivors (children who attended these institutions) in 2008 as part of the Indian Residential School Settlement. The initiative was to raise awareness of the mistreatment of Indigenous children and generate a public record of its legacy. The TRC's report in July 2015, *'Honoring the Truth: Reconciling for the Future'*, made visible expressions of cultural and language loss, death and disease, and emotional, physical, and sexual abuses of those who attended the residential schools (Winder, 2020). There are estimates of 38,000 residential school survivors who have claimed compensation for both sexual and serious physical abuse as children.

Currently in the United States there is a momentum for legal actions for the boarding school abuses. In addition, legal action in the United States for sexual and physical abuses represents a challenge, because of the combination of statutes of limitations, lack of documentation, and prevalence of conservatives in the Supreme Court (Winder, 2020). Furthermore, boarding school survivors in the United States are small in number compared to Canada,[8] and individuals are hesitant to speak openly share their experiences (Smith, 2006). However, the Native American Rights Fund (NARF) is working with the Native American Boarding School Healing Coalition and some Indigenous nations on ways of healing from the boarding school system, and policies in order to find some form of closure. In addition, boarding school survivors' descendants who are learning more details at university about the boarding school system have been forced, or are more willing, to self-reflect on how their families and themselves have been impacted by the legacy of the agenda of colonised education.

Overview of 'Southwestern University' students and the dissertation study

Sixteen Southwestern University Indigenous students consented to participate in a dissertation study entitled *'Post-Secondary Indigenous Students' Perspectives: Sharing Our Voices on How We Fit into Residential School History of*

Canada and the United States', to examine the effects of the boarding school system on their lives. The larger dissertation study is a comparative assessment of the impact the residential school history in Canada and the United States. The aim for the study is to contribute to our understanding of the impact of intergenerational trauma on the Indigenous students of today, by exploring the perspectives and lived experiences of the students at two sites: the United States and Canada. Furthermore, this dissertation study focused on Indigenous voices of boarding school descendants to investigate boarding school distress occurring in their generation. I conducted an examination of sixteen Indigenous students at Southwestern University's perspectives on the following:

- how historical unresolved grief had affected them;
- how they understood the aftermaths from boarding and residential school;
- their common knowledge about resilience and survival;
- their family and national experiences regarding the policies of assimilation and colonisation in Canada and the United States; and
- how reflecting on both their own, family, and community experiences impacted them.

Thus, there are sixteen different perspectives of the boarding school system's impacts on students' families and themselves, as depicted from their diverse Indigenous backgrounds; however, there are also similarities, which are shown in their pictures. Table 7.1 documents the various Indigenous nations, gender, and age brackets of students at Southwestern University who participated in the dissertation study.[9]

Furthermore, the entire dissertation study's findings included thirty participants'[10] perspectives from self-identifying Indigenous students. Data was

Table 7.1 Participants' characteristics

Indigenous nations	
Navajo	8
Pueblo	7
Other	1
Gender	
Female	11
Male	5
Age brackets	
18–27	7
28–37	7
38–47	1
48–57	1
Total number of participants	16

collected from group discussions, one-on-one interviews, and their photographs, by implementing three research methods (Indigenous research methods [IRM], participatory action research [PAR], and photovoice) and analysed using coded themes in Nvivo.[11] There were six research phases: (i) recruitment and information sessions; (ii) questionnaire,[12] photovoice training, and residential school history sessions; (iii) group discussions; (iv) individual interviews; (v) member-checking of interviews and input on photo-analysis; and (vi) a celebration feast. All sixteen Southwestern University voluntary participants completed the study information session, photovoice training, questionnaires, group discussion meetings, and one-on-one interviews. Eligibility for the study required participants to (i) self-identify as Indigenous to North America; (ii) be eighteen years of age or older; (iii) be an enrolled student at each study site; (iv) be willing and able to use a disposable camera and/or personal digital camera or smartphone camera; (v) be willing to be audio-recorded, attend individual interviews and group sessions; and (vi) be willing to share their personal experience of how residential school impacted them. All sixteen participants stated they had both family and community members who had experienced the boarding school system in the United States, and they were familiar with this history.

Methods and methodology

Reason for the dissertation study

The ideas for the dissertation study developed during my teaching assistantship with the First Nations Studies Program at the University of Western Ontario in 2011. In the residential school lectures and tutorials, residential schools dominated the conversations for the rest of academic year for many Indigenous students. Moreover, the impact of the residential school legacy extended beyond the classroom to spaces such as support centres, discussions with friends, media sources, and the sharing of families' encounters to express how Indigenous students feel they have been impacted on a personal level (Winder, 2020). After I completed my teaching assistantship in 2013, I started to develop a study for a comparative analysis of a collective and individual understanding of the intergenerational impacts of the boarding/residential school system on the lives of survivors' descendants. Indigenous students (descendants of survivors) are processing the remnants of these colonial institutions that attempted to strip, erase, and alter Indigenous identity, languages, and ways of knowing. At the same time, Indigenous students are either partially or fully aware of the negative, positive, and grey areas of the aftermaths of boarding and/or residential schools. Rather than dwelling on how Indigenous children and survivors were drastically changed, Indigenous students focused on how Indigenous peoples who attended these institutions survived, how they had empathised with their families and communities who went, on those children who did not return, and how Indigenous peoples are still present in Canada and the United States.

Indigenous research methods

IRM, PAR, and photovoice methodologies were employed to analysis Southwestern University Indigenous students' perspectives about boarding schools, and their lasting effects. IRM materialised in the early twenty-first century in the Western academy (Jordan, 2014). IRM is founded on the prominence of Indigenous knowledges, epistemologies, and methodologies to give voice to Indigenous experiences in the research process. Hence, IRM specify that there are mutual power relations and responsibilities between researchers and Indigenous participants, and that these are safeguarded in the research process – that is, that it is going be done ethically without inflicting harm. IRM is built on the foundation of six Rs: respect, relevant, reciprocity, responsible, relationships, and relational (Kirkness & Barnhardt, 1991; Kovach, 2009; White, 2013; Wilson, 2001, 2008). The six Rs that are explained by Kirkness and Barnhardt (1991) and White (2013) are as follows:

- Be *Respectful:* Of the distinction between each person and community's culture, values, worldview, and all things (animate and inanimate) as interdependent. To be respectful is to have an understanding of the diversity of the cultures and knowledge held by the people.
- Be *Relevant:* Consideration for the importance of a belief in unseen powers in the world, and the value of an Indigenous worldview; understand the people who are the subject of the investigation.
- Show *Reciprocity:* The relationship between people, animals, and all things is essential; there is a value created for the Indigenous peoples, and they can realise that value. It is a bilateral exchanging of learning processes and research activities.
- Be *Responsible:* To teach, learn, and behave in a moral and ethical manner for Indigenous peoples' ways, which means leaving the people stronger than when you entered into the process. The interests of research partners are protected, enhanced, and engaged in the process.
- *Relationship* and *Relational* refer to the sharing of knowledge (Kovach, 2009; Wilson, 2001, 2008).

These six Rs of Indigenous research guide the research process with working with Indigenous peoples. When working with Indigenous descendants of boarding school survivors '….the researcher assumes a responsibility that the story shared will be treated with the respect it deserves in acknowledging of the relationship from which it emerges' (Kovach 2009, p. 97). As an Indigenous community researcher in the academy, I ground myself in the principles of IRM and have an ethical responsibility to share and retell the participants' stories correctly, and, as such, researchers take on '....a role of a storyteller' (Wilson, 2008, p. 32). The boarding school system represents both a lived history and living testimonies among many Indigenous communities, nations, and individuals who can be engulfed by an amalgamation of emotions and feelings (Winder, 2020). Furthermore, IRM integrates subjective truths that allow Indigenous participants to produce a collective explanation of the boarding school impacts. Indigenous students' knowledge of these institutions include stories they heard from their families and community members, thereby making IRM significant in raising our consciousness of the boarding school life stories of the descendants.

Participatory action research and photovoice

PAR is a construct of reflection, data collection, education, experimental learning, and action-oriented towards research as a social transformation and practice (Baum, MacDougall & Smith, 2006; Kindon, Pain & Kesby, 2007; McTaggart, 1997). It represents a back-and-forth dialogue and reflective understanding between the researchers and participants throughout the entire research process, to emphasise participation and action. Indigenous students shared their expertise about familial boarding school experiences through a shared dialogue in group discussions, and one-on-one interviews with me. Photovoice is a research method that uses pictures to answer research questions using themes, and was developed by Wang and Burris (1997). Participants' pictures are used to document representations of their reality. The principles of photovoice are critical consciousness and empowerment, constructivism, and documentary photography (Guillemin & Drew, 2010; Hergenrather et al., 2009; Wang, 1999; Wang & Burris, 1997). The objectives for photovoice are to empower participants to (i) record and reflect their community's strengths and concerns; (ii) promote critical dialogue and knowledge about personal and community issues; and (iii) reach policymakers (Catalani & Minkler, 2010; Wang, 1999). Indigenous students took pictures representing how they have been impacted by the boarding school system. Each Indigenous student had a unique lived experience of how their family and their own lives have been multiply affected by the boarding school system.

Furthermore, how each individual engaged with historical unresolved grief shaped their lives differently. Historical unresolved grief originates from the loss of lives and land, forced abandonment of culture, and prohibited practices of ceremonies and traditional languages, as well as other vital aspects of Indigenous culture destroyed by the settler conquest of North America (Brave Heart & DeBruyn, 1998). Indigenous students relied on a self-reflective approach to investigate their life experiences about being a descendant of a boarding school survivor. The social consequences of the boarding school system identified by Indigenous students were issues such as alcoholism, identity, language, lack of cultural ties, and the ignition of their

'*Colliding Heartwork*'. '*Colliding Heartwork*' (see endnote 5) discusses the multiple layers of learning about the direct familial impacts of the boarding school such as the loss of Indigenous culture, knowledge, language, and identity for Indigenous descendants. '*Colliding Heartwork*' creates a space for Indigenous peoples to learn, to discuss, and to come together (with an intention of opening mind, heart, and emotions) to initiate and to continue processing the outcomes of the residential school system.

Findings

Interpretation of the boarding school impacts

Initial responses to boarding school from Indigenous students included the following: 'disruptive', 'hurtful', 'damaging', 'created loss' – which left them feeling 'anger', 'sadness', and 'empathy' (for children, family members, and parents who were forced to send their children to these institutions). For instance, in the one of the group discussions, Blackhorse[13] expressed that the boarding school system was '….hell, for our grandparents and our great-grandparents, and whoever went to [there]' (personal communication, 1 October 2014). Lisa added that some Indigenous parents willingly sent their children to boarding school due to '….all the poverty and the disease … on the reservations. [Families] or parents … said, "Here, take them. I can't provide for them." But then again, Europeans said if [Indigenous parents] don't turn in [their] kids, then no rations, food and stuff, to survive on. It was the domination of the Europeans' control' (personal communication, 30 September 2014). Indigenous students expressed that some parents did not have a choice, and due to the dire situation on some reservations, the boarding school represented a better opportunity to suffer in a new environment, at the expense of leaving behind Indigenous traditions and adopting a new education system and lifestyle. Hungry Turtle felt that the boarding school was a hidden agenda or '….humane way of getting rid of the Indian, because they couldn't kill us off. So, [Euro-Americans] would educate them' (personal communication, 30 September 2014).

Indigenous students in either the group or individual meetings voiced anger for the boarding school system and the mistreatment of their family members (see Winder, 2020, Chapter 5 for complete listing of photographs from the study). Students acknowledged that this institutional history was 'emotional', but the 'history needs to be told', and there are still 'physical remnants'. For example, Little Sun talked about train tracks near her home:

> I love them and I hate them. I love them because they helped my grandfather get home when he wanted to run away. But they also took him back where he was forced to go and I think about how many of our people get up on those tracks today and they're so fractured, you know; they're so conflicted because they don't know what to do. They are so lost.

Figure 7.1 Love/hate relationship.

Bluebird tied together the impacts of boarding school on children, and the lack of leadership opportunities, with the influence and incorporation of a church. She stated:

> [Indigenous] children were kept at boarding school… that tried to hinder the growth and development of young [Indigenous peoples]. Meaning boarding schools weren't created to make scholars. They weren't created to propel the next generation of [Indigenous peoples] up. They were created to make manual workers. […]Trying to hinder [Indigenous peoples] from growing and being leaders in our country.

Terrance communicated the outcomes of the boarding schooling system in Canada and the US targeted Indigenous children. Children were forcibly cut off from their languages, ideas, traditions, and cultures. He noted:

> This target represents how I get the feeling they knew exactly where to hit us by taking our language away. They did everything to take it away – beat us, or washed our mouths out with soap – or strictly forbid it to the point where our grandparents didn't want to teach us. All of our world-views are in our language; that's how we communicate our teachings, our behaviours in life. By cutting that off, I just felt like they knew just cutting the language part off. They knew that that was the key to assimilating us.

Colliding Heartwork 153

Figure 7.2 Keep gate closed.

Krystal and other Indigenous students imagined what the boarding school system might have felt like for Indigenous children. This form of empathy, which Indigenous students often expressed, was their connection to their ancestors, and their collective response to the boarding school. According

Figure 7.3 Right on target.

Figure 7.4 Lost in the classroom.

to Krystal, there are modern-day analogues of boarding school feelings in being in a different environment – sometimes as an Indigenous student, one's thoughts and opinions are thrown aside. She stated:

> I feel that sometimes going to a school with such a big student population I can feel lost in a big classroom. I can sometimes feel lonely, or that my thoughts or opinions are singled out/not acknowledged.

Insights into the intergenerational impacts of residential school

Indigenous students opened up about their families' lives and how family members who attended these institutions did not pass on Indigenous language to them. Furthermore, some students expressed the notion of 'loss' as a type of intergenerational impact from their parents' or grandparents' attendance at boarding school. The impact was also articulated as 'anger' for what happened to a relative, as well as feeling 'isolated'. April Thomas further noted the feeling of being isolated from cultural traditions, because they were not passed onto her since her grandmother attended boarding school.

Colliding Heartwork 155

Figure 7.5 Isolation.

> I was thinking about…how isolated I feel sometimes from my Pueblo. I thought my feeling this way could be from the boarding school experience. My grandmother went to boarding school. She felt like she needed to modernise herself and her family in order to succeed, which is what they really instilled in boarding schools: those traditions, living on the reservation, and staying within your own language isn't always going to let you be successful. You're going to have to assimilate and be modernised. My mother never learned the language as a result of that. She wasn't as close to the traditions as my grandmother. So I felt really isolated at times from my traditions because even though I go back often and I feel close to my family out there. I chose to take this [photograph] because the events following my ancestral people being forced into boarding schools have led up to this point in my life.

Jennifer articulated what she felt reflected a visual depiction of intergenerational trauma:

> This….drainage….related to intergenerational trauma. We have all this stuff happening, all this water building up then everything gets swept away. And, it goes down into this drain but there's still stuff left all this bad stuff that doesn't get washed away it just stays there….People say things like we have access to education, we have modernisation, we're not living in the dark ages, we have all these things but to me we have a lot of problems. We have a lot of depression. We have a lot of gang

activity. I relate gang activity to loss of identity that is a directly related to having our identity taken away from us and losing that concept of what means to be related to people. So, we have a lot of problems like that with drugs, alcohol people cannot deal with what happened to us even with all these advances and modernisation we're still poor on the reservation. I go out there and I see people living in shacks, looking poor and they don't have money for anything. What happened? They were supposed to make us better, bring us into civilisation, were still suffering all they did was assert their European authority over these people and put them within this structure that they will always be marginalised. And so, I'm angry when I start thinking about it like that and how social reproduction has reared its ugly head and we're still left with all this bad stuff. Yes, we have access to higher education. Yes, we have there are some positive changes but there's still a lot of disconnect and a lot of pain on the reservation. And to me, that is the echoing remnants of the boarding school experience.

Intergenerational trauma is expressed in Indigenous students' pictures as a type of loss, and linking to the negative experiences Indigenous communities are dealing with in the contemporary society. There still exists pain and sadness because the boarding schools took and slowly removed Indigenous identity and culture.

Figure 7.6 Not all is washed away – intergenerational trauma.

Expressions of cultural empowerment

There were various accounts of the boarding school experience in the United States. Some testimonies detailed the negative experience, others were neutral, and a few had positive experiences. These positive experiences reflected when Indigenous children learned certain skills, or were able to acquire a post-secondary education as a result of going to boarding school. However, the majority of the participants in the study interpreted a dominant narrative of the unfavourable outcomes of the boarding school system. Indigenous students' pictures also demonstrated how they were empowered, and exhibited resiliency, in the wake of boarding school history through paying tribute to their ancestors, re-learning their language, making cultural items, exerting their Indigenous identity, holding tight to their history, and wielding various aspects of their culture (Winder, 2020). For instance, Samantha spoke of the importance and continuation of prayer. She said:

> We're taught to offer prayers every morning and you're supposed to greet the day, greet the sun, and throw your corn meal and offer a prayer before the day....I think that's the first form of education for us as people to offer, to go out there to offer prayers.... Looking back of at the boarding schools....I think the reason we continue to still be here is because our ancestors offered prayers each day for us to be here.

Figure 7.7 Breath of prayer.

158 Natahnee Nuay Winder

Plain Jane articulated the importance of maintaining and fostering Indigenous identity. She acknowledged that the boarding school system was designed to strip away Indigenous identity, language, and culture. She is committed to teaching her children about what happened at these institutions, and that the bond between a mother and children would remain strong with her children. Plain Jane talked about her mother attending boarding school, and her feeling cold. She felt the boarding system school severed parental bonds with children. Her picture described:

> A representative of [her] faith in my Navajo culture and tradition and my protection because it's the talking guard rainbows. When [she wears the necklace] it's representative of being a child of the holy people and all things under the rainbow talking Gods are holy. It is a beautiful acceptance and peace that symbolises motherhood and life.

Figure 7.8 Symbol of my identity.

Concluding remarks

Indigenous students[14] involved in this project communicated distinctive facets of empowerment and survival tactics of Indigenous peoples who attended residential schools. They highlighted how these historical and contemporary reminders of this institutional system have created lasting impressions. By addressing how intergenerational trauma and historical unresolved grief functions in Indigenous students' lives we, as educators and staff who provide services at universities, can better enhance our knowledge and skills which will permit us to do a better job assisting Indigenous students with their success. We will recognise how learning or relearning about the boarding schooling system while Indigenous students are pursuing their studies can negatively trigger them (Winder, 2020). In closing the boarding schools, history is complicated. There are so many Indigenous experiences – many diverse and powerful life stories of survivors and family members. These stories shaped how we, as Indigenous peoples, see our families, our communities, and ourselves. There is not one story, but many numerous ones, and untold ones, which pull at the stings of our hearts, memories, and how our future will be formed when our hearts collide. Utilising the framework of '*Colliding Heartwork*' is a dedication to Indigenous community, and making oneself accountable to foster, to maintain, and to build relationships for benefit communities through selfless actions (Winder, 2020). '*Colliding Heartwork*' stems from the emotional residues felt by Indigenous peoples who experienced and empathised with their family members and ancestors who attended boarding schools, and is portrayed in Indigenous students' pictures. Furthermore, '*Colliding Heartwork*' is not only an exposition of empathy towards traumatic events or histories; it is a representation of the passion that Indigenous peoples are to uphold our communities – it bridges our hearts to reflect, and to come to a common understanding of where diverse Indigenous histories and lived experiences intersect. When I think of my own family and maternal grandmother's boarding school experience, I am a positive outcome of this history. If my maternal grandmother was not taken to boarding school, her job placement would not have been in Reno, Nevada and she would not have met my grandfather. My mom would not have been born, nor would my sister and I exist. My grandmother did not pass on the Shoshone language to us because she was taught that speaking our traditional language would not benefit us. As we can see, the boarding school system still prevents the use of Indigenous language and has created a lingering worldview that Indigenous languages are not as valuable as English. Yet, my grandmothers showed resiliency by giving me Indigenous names, and my family worked to foster a healthy Indigenous identity. The boarding school history represents an untapped geyser of emotions that can break through at any moment, and brings our hearts together.

Notes

1. I am currently finalising a dissertation study that compares post-secondary Indigenous students' perspectives of the intergenerational impacts of both the residential and boarding school system in Canada and United States (Winder, 2020).
2. 'Southwestern University' is a pseudonym for the dissertation study site for Indigenous students attending university in the United States, and is used to de-identify them.
3. The cutting of Indigenous hair symbolised a stripping away of their 'savagery', and for Indigenous children, held a negative connotation. (Editor's note: See also Chapter 2, endnote 16).
4. The term 'residential school' was used in Canada, whereas in the United States, the term (Indian) 'boarding school' was used.
5. '*Colliding Heartwork*' is a framework that I am developing, which explains how Indigenous descendants of boarding and residential school survivors empathise through storytelling, and how we are impacted differently and intersect. It is the space where our hearts meet to heal, talk, and share how we feel about the ongoing effects of colonialism. This framework builds on Dian Million's felt theory (see Million, 2009).
6. The Dawes Act stipulated that 160 acres be allocated to each family head, 80 acres to individuals over 18 years of age, and 40 acres to individuals less than 18 years of age. The act included a provision to double the size of the allotment if the land was suitable for grazing. After the land was divided among the tribe members, the excess was made available to white settlers.
7. My maternal grandmother attended boarding school during the 1940s.
8. Residential schools in Canada lasted until the late 1990s. In the United States, boarding schools were on the decline after World War II.
9. Personal information for Indigenous participants is confidential. Participants were given pseudonyms with generalised Indigenous affiliation and age brackets in order to protect their identity, instead of being specific.
10. The additional participants were also Indigenous students who attended a university in the United States or Canada.
11. NVivo is a widely used qualitative data analysis computer software package (produced by QSR International).
12. The questionnaire data provided demographic information, and a baseline of students' knowledge of either the boarding or the residential schools.
13. Blackhorse is pseudonym for an Indigenous student who voluntary consented to participate in the study. Indigenous students provided the pseudonyms.
14. Not all the data from the dissertation study is represented in this essay. For a more comprehensive analysis, refer to the forthcoming dissertation study.

References

Adams, D. (1995). *Education for Extinction: American Indians and the Boarding School Experience, 1875–1928*. Lawrence, KS: The University Press of Kansas.

Baum, F., MacDougall, C. & Smith, D. (2006). Participatory action research. *Journal of Epidemiology and Community Health*, 60(10): 854–857.

Bowker, K. (2007). *The Boarding School Legacy: Ten Contemporary Lakota Women Tell Their Stories*. PhD dissertation: Montana State University.

Brave Heart, M. & DeBruyn, L.M. (1998). The American Indian holocaust: Healing historical unresolved grief. *American Indian and Alaska Native Mental Health Research*, 8(2): 56–78.

Catalani, C. & Minkler, M. (2010). Photovoice: A review of the literature in health and public health. *Health Education and Behaviour*, 37(3): 424–451.

Cate, P. (1995). *Broken Vows, Broken Arrows: An Analysis of the US Government's Off-Reservation Boarding School Program, 1879–1900*. PhD dissertation: Boston College.

Child Sexual Abuse in Federal Schools (1990). *Ojibwe News*. January 17: 8.

Child, B. (1998). *Boarding School Seasons: American Indian Families, 1900–1940*. Lincoln, NE: University of Nebraska Press.

Churchill, W. (2004). *Kill the Indian, Save the Man*. San Francisco, CA: City Lights Books.

Coleman, M. (1993). *American Indian Children at School, 1850–1930*. Jackson, MS: The University Press of Mississippi.

Eliot, J. & Morrison, K.M. (1974). 'That art of coyning Christians': John Eliot and the praying Indians of Massachusetts. *Ethnohistory*, 21(1): 77–92.

Getches, D., Wilkinson, C. & Williams, R. Jr. (2005). *Cases and Materials on Federal Indian Law* (5th edn.). St. Paul, MN: West Publishing Co.

Goodbye BIA, Hello New Federalism (1994). *American Eagle*, 2: 19.

Guillemin, M. & Drew, S. (2010). Questions of process in participant-generated visual methodologies. *Visual Studies*, 25(2): 175–188.

Hergenrather, K., Rhodes, S., Cowan, C., Bardhoshi, G. & Pula, S. (2009). Photovoice as community-based participatory research: A qualitative review. *American Journal of Health Behavior*, 33(6): 686–698.

Hill, S. & Redwing Saunders, S. (2008). *The Urban Aboriginal Education Project Phase I: Research Study*. Oakville, ON: Commissioned by the Council of Ontario Directors of Education.

Jordan, S. (2014). Indigenous research methods. In D. Coughlan & M. Brydon-Miller (eds.), *The SAGE Encyclopedia of Action Research*. Thousand Oaks, CA: SAGE.

Kindon, S.L., Pain, R. & Kesby, M. (2007). *Participatory Action Research Approaches and Methods: Connecting People, Participation and Place*. New York: Routledge.

Kirkness, V.J. & Barnhardt, R. (1991). First Nations and higher education: The four Rs – respect, relevance, reciprocity, responsibility. *Journal of American Indian Education*, 30(1): 1–15.

Kovach, M. (2009). *Indigenous Methodologies – Characteristics, Conversations, and Contexts*. Toronto, ON: University of Toronto Press.

McTaggart, R. (1997). *Participatory Action Research: International Contexts and Consequences*. Albany: State University of New York Press.

Million, D. (2009). Felt theory: An Indigenous feminist approach to affect and history. *Wicazo Sa Review*, 24(2): 53–76.

Minthorn, D. (2019). Being brave in the Ivory Towers as 'Zape-tah-hol-ah' (Sticks with Bow). In M.C. Whitaker & E.A. Grollman (eds.), *Counternarratives from Women of Color Academics: Bravery, Vulnerability and Resistance* (pp. 25–32). Boca Raton, FL: Routledge.

Pratt, R. (1973). The advantages of mingling Indians with whites. In F. Prucha (ed.), *Americanizing the American Indians: Writings by the 'Friends of the Indian' 1880–1990* (pp. 260–271). Cambridge: Harvard University Press.

Reyhner, J. & Eder, J. (2004). *American Indian Education: A History*. Norman, OK: University of Oklahoma Press.

Smith, A. (2006). Boarding school abuses, human rights and reparations. *Journal of Religion & Abuse*, 8(2): 5–21.

Szasz, M. (1988). *Indian Education in the American colonies, 1607–1783*. Albuquerque, NM: University of New Mexico Press.

TRC (Truth and Reconciliation Commission of Canada). (2015). Canada's Residential Schools: The History, Part 1: Origins to 1939. In *The Final Report of the Truth and Reconciliation Commission of Canada*. Available online: http://www.myrobust.com/websites/trcinstitution/File/Reports/Volume_1_History_Part_1_English_Web.pdf [Accessed April, 2019].

Wang, C. (1999). Photovoice: A participatory action research strategy applied to women's health. *Journal of Women's Health*, 8(2): 185–192.

Wang, C. & Burris, M. (1997). Photovoice: Concept, methodology, and use for participatory needs assessment. *Health Education and Behaviour*, 24(3): 369–387.

White, J.P. (2013). Policy research: Good or bad? *International Indigenous Policy Journal*, 4(3).

Wilson, S. (2001). What is an Indigenous research methodology? *Canadian Journal of Native Education*, 25(2): 175–179.

Wilson, S. 2008. *Research as ceremony: Indigenous research methods*, Winnipeg, MB: Fernwood.

Winder, N. (2020). *Post-secondary Indigenous students' perspectives: Sharing our voices on how we fit into residential school history of Canada and the United States*. PhD dissertation: University of Western Ontario.

Zalcman, D. (2018). Carlisle and the Indian boarding school legacy in America. *Pulitzer Center*. Available online: http://pulitzercenter.org/reporting/carlisle-and-indian-boarding-school-legacy-america [Accessed January, 2019].

Chapter 8

Punishing poverty
The curious case of Ireland's institutionalised children

Jeremiah J. Lynch

> The Brothers shall regard themselves as the visible guardian angels of the children, among whose possession innocence holds the first place (Congregation of Christian Brothers, 1927).[1]

For a century up to the early 1970s, tens of thousands of young Irish children were taken from their families and communities and detained against their will in state-sanctioned residential industrial schools and reformatories. This system, which was to last over a century, involved the detention of generations of children in inhospitable penal institutions. They were operated entirely autocratically by, in the vast majority of cases, the Roman Catholic religious orders, and were socially (and often geographically) marginalised from the rest of Irish society (Maguire, 2009). They were characterised by the experience of child suffering (Arnold, 2009; O'Sullivan & O'Donnell, 2012) or, as Australian victim/survivor Penglase (2005, p. 48) recalled, a '….dehumanising institutional environment of fear, non-care, and bleakness'. This chapter is a journey through the strange and terrible history of how, in the hands of religious orders, industrial schools became an instrument of social control, and how these places, where children disappeared,[2] came to be a byword for cruelty and suffering. I draw on historical accounts of the industrial schools, as well as survivor memoirs, the findings of the Irish Commission to Inquire into Child Abuse (CICA, 2009) and the accounts of survivors I interviewed.

Historical contexts

Ireland is a small island nation located at the most western point of Europe. Before independence in 1922, Ireland was part of Great Britain, and for centuries, Roman Catholicism had been brutally repressed through what became known as the 'penal laws', under which (amongst much else) it was forbidden for Roman Catholics to set up schools and teach children (Raftery & Parkes, 2007). Oppressed Irish people subverted these laws by practising their faith in private, and by setting up secret schools, often in outdoor rural locations (to avoid detection); appropriately, these became known as 'hedge schools'. Raftery and Parkes (2007) noted that in 1824, there were 9,000 such schools scattered around the country. It was not until the late eighteenth century that these laws were relaxed, and that schooling and freedom of religious practice were possible once again. Primarily an agricultural economy up until the 1960s, Ireland's population was decimated by the Great Famine that occurred between 1845 and 1852, during which 1.1 million people died and a further two million emigrated (Kelly, 2012). According to data from successive censuses, post-Famine Ireland's population declined rapidly to an all-time low of under three million people in 1961, due primarily to prevailing poor economic conditions and the resulting emigration to places such as North America, the United Kingdom, and Australia. The exodus has been described as 'unprecedented in both scale and character' (Miller, 2013).[3]

Historically, the system of residential institutional care for children in Ireland owes much to the workhouse model established during the 1840s as a response to the poverty caused by the Great Famine.[4] Ireland's Industrial Schools Act (1868) was based entirely on the British Act of 1857, and it established residential institutions in Ireland to care for neglected, orphaned, and abandoned children from age six to sixteen years (Arnold & Laskey, 1985). The main objective of the system was to inculcate in children the habits of industry, regularity, self-denial, self-reliance, and self-control (Barnes, 1989; O'Sullivan & O'Donnell, 2007). The system comprised a network of denominational, religious order-managed institutions, supported by state aid (Barnes, 1989). Institutionalisation was deemed to be a legitimate and effective response to the large numbers of vagrant children orphaned during and after the Famine. Bucking the trend elsewhere in Ireland, Dublin, the capital city, grew in population post-Famine, becoming the destination of choice for thousands of people fleeing the rural districts. Children, too, were drawn to the cities where, in order to survive, they engaged in begging and theft (Barnes, 1989). Closely linked to vagrancy, therefore, was the issue of juvenile crime. In 1851, for example, the Inspector General of Irish prisons reported that 25 per cent of petty larceny cases brought to trial in Dublin during the previous year were committed by children and adolescents who had migrated to the city during the Famine (Miller, 2013).

In relation to similarly vulnerable Scottish children and adolescents in the first decade of the twentieth century, Mahood and Littlewood (1994) refer to the common pathologised image of the 'brutal father' and the 'feckless mother' that was also prevalent in Ireland. These impoverished people were regarded as 'work-shy beasts who neglect their miserable children if not actually schooling them in vice and crime' (p. 54). These authors concluded that these children were simultaneously pitied for their neglect, and feared for the crimes and vices they were destined to commit. The solution chosen was to detain such children in residential institutions and thus break the cycle of what Mahood and Littlewood call 'deprivation / depravation'. Emphasising the public perception of these children as 'other' and out of control, they were referred to as 'wild arabs' and 'savages' (Sargent, 2014). In a significant move in 1852, the report of the Inspector General of prisons introduced a new category of crime and a new category of criminal: 'juvenile crime' and 'juvenile offender', thus placing the spotlight on a new 'problem' that needed to be resolved (Sargent, 2014).

The perils of child crime escalating into a life of anti-social behaviour required a firm and comprehensive response. In 1870, the Lord Chancellor to the Statistical and Social Inquiry Society of Ireland justified the development of the extensive residential institutional complex as being necessary to prevent those children who were '....cast abroad as waifs and strays in the world ... from developing into the criminal preying upon society whilst he is at large and becoming a burden to it when it is forced to pay for his punishment' (in O'Sullivan, 1979, p. 211). Thus, the child in danger could soon become the dangerous child, posing a potential threat to society. There was no narrative of each child constituting a person with needs and rights; the challenge was to identify these children as early as possible and institute a programme of moral rehabilitation (Mahood, 1995). Criminal behaviour was seen predominantly as a masculine preserve, while in the case of girls, the emphasis was very much on (especially sexual) purity, and the perceived threat of 'moral failure', leading to sexual precociousness, prostitution and/or 'illegitimate' children (Cullen Owens, 2005; Jackson, 2000; Luddy, 2007; Mahood, 1995). Industrial schools for girls were, therefore, designed to halt what was seen as a general decline in the standard of public morals (Sargent, 2014). Industrial schools for boys were designed to re-direct them from a life of crime.[5] Adjudicating upon the morals for the Irish people (and their behavioural manifestations) was one of the self-appointed tasks of the powerful Roman Catholic Church.

The intervention of the state into family life as a modern social practice, particularly in the area of what we would today call child protection, was a phenomenon of the late nineteenth century. A century before that the issue of cruelty against children was noted, regarded as wrong, condemned by the judiciary and resulted in punishment, but only on a very small scale (Ferguson, 2004). The discovery of and concern about child sexual abuse in Victorian Great Britain (of which Ireland was a part) was gendered and linked to societal preoccupation with 'fallen' women[6] and young female prostitutes (Jackson, 2000). Thus, an alarmist public discourse on child crime prevailed in the Ireland of the mid-nineteenth century, as it did in the United Kingdom as a whole, that framed it, not just as a result of parental death, poverty or misfortune, but as a direct outcome of parental cruelty, neglect, or abandonment (Buckley, 2013; Jackson, 2000; Mahood, 1995). Other than by reason of death, the finger of blame was pointed firmly at parents, and separation from such unhelpful influences, segregation, reforming of the child's character and vocational training were the essential practice elements of the social risk model that prevailed (O'Sullivan, 1979).

The tendency to label parents of these children as inadequate, deserving of blame and even morally corrupt can be clearly seen in the files of the National Society for the Prevention of Cruelty to Children (NSPCC) and Irish Society for the Prevention of Cruelty to Children (ISPCC).[7] Buckley (2013) viewed the N/ISPCC files dating back to 1889, and noted the preponderance of negative ISPCC inspectors' descriptions of parents of children taken into care: 'careless', 'useless', 'lazy', 'immoral', 'excitable', 'foolish', 'indifferent', 'fond of drink', and 'quarrelsome'. Parents were, she states, viewed as 'degenerate, incapable and abnormal', while her examination of inspectors' case files revealed 'an aura of righteousness associated with their self-perception as saviours of the poor' (p. 56). Reducing social inequalities that may have been factors in the occurrence of abuse, and particularly, neglect, were not policy priorities of the London-based government, and later (post-1922) the fledgling Irish state. It was the moral panic and the avoidance of scandal that provided the impetus for the establishment of residential institutions in which a range of stigmatised individuals could disappear. Such a preoccupation with children who could upset the status quo may also have suited the interests of a Roman Catholic Church looking to re-establish itself (Ferguson, 2004).

During the Victorian era, and well into the twentieth century the desire to 'save' children in need coexisted with a morally ambiguous stance in relation to victims of neglect and abuse, and, in particular, sexual abuse (Ferguson, 2007; Jackson, 2000). Children were firstly viewed as having been contaminated by their morally corrupt parents. Child victims of sexual abuse were viewed as harmed, but also as 'impure', 'polluted', and being, or at least having the potential to become, 'dangerous' (Ferguson, 2004). Consequently, they were to be pitied as being akin to lepers; but they also required reforming, to mend their wicked ways.[8]

The operation of the residential schools system

In Ireland, the development of the industrial school system was inextricably linked to the vision of the predominant church.[9] Grzymala-Busse (2015) argues that the Roman Catholic Church in Ireland viewed itself as an active, equal, and sometimes superior partner in the process of moulding the nation. Its early nineteenth century efforts directed at educating the masses were aimed firmly at 'increasing its influence and control over the hearts and minds of its "flock", and the [religious] orders were its foot soldiers' (Chapman & O'Donoghue, 2007, p. 563). Post-Famine child-saving also included 'saving' them from the grip of other religious denominations. The unspoken motivation for institutionalising so many children was a concerted effort by the religious orders, acting as agents of the Roman Catholic Church, to counteract what they perceived as the 'proselytising fervour' of the Protestant institutions (Buckley, 2013). In this way, children were the unknowing pawns in a sectarian game for their souls (Luddy, 1995; Raftery & O'Sullivan, 1999).

The pact between the religious orders and the Irish state, whereby religious orders would build and operate the institutions, and the state would grant aid the religious orders and (nominally) hold them accountable, was a pragmatic one for the state, for it was cost-effective and convenient in terms of both financial and human resources to simply cede responsibility to the religious orders (Maguire, 2009).[10]

Within thirty years, the archipelago of industrial schools was extensive, with seventy-one scattered throughout the country and holding approximately 8,000 children at its peak operating capacity in 1898 (Kennedy Report, 1970). For its part, the Irish state ceded responsibility to the Church without any effective system of accountability or monitoring (Powell et al., 2012). With such lofty religious ambitions of saving children, it is perhaps of no surprise to find that their mass institutionalisation in the mid-nineteenth century coincided with a rapid expansion in the numbers of priests and of male and female members of Roman Catholic religious orders. The numbers of priests in proportion to the population rose from 1 in every 3,500 people in 1840 to 1 in every 600 people in 1960 (Cullen Owens, 2005). Female religious orders expanded particularly rapidly. In 1800, there were only 120 nuns in Ireland; by 1900, that number had increased to 8,000 (Cullen Owens, 2005). According to Luddy and Smith (2014, p. 18), the aim of the religious orders was to '....bind the Irish Catholic more to the practice of their religion', and to this end, many orders devoted themselves to the education of children.

By the end of the nineteenth century, religious teaching nuns and brothers staffed a growing number of Roman Catholic day schools and residential institutions, not just in Ireland, but throughout the English-speaking world (O'Donoghue, 2012).[11] By 1950 – the zenith of the system of child institutionalisation in Ireland – there were forty-four religious orders operating in the country that were involved in teaching (O'Donoghue, 2012). Adult souls, it seems, could be saved if the intervention occurred during the childhood years. Roman Catholic-managed residential institutions dominated the care system in Ireland for over a century, accounting for approximately 90 per cent of provision (Gilligan, 2014). In parallel to their control of residential institutional childcare, religious orders also dominated healthcare provision, and primary level education provision in Irish day schools (Inglis, 1998). However, although religious orders such as the Christian Brothers developed a fearsome reputation for rigid discipline in their day schools, their residential institutions containing children of little social value became the loci of endemic abuse and neglect that went beyond mere 'discipline'.[12]

Children could find themselves detained in an industrial school for a number of reasons. The N/ISPCC (see endnote 7) sought committal for cases involving 'lack of proper guardianship'. This category included neglect of the child, very often as a direct result of poverty. This was especially the case in Dublin, where run-down multi-occupancy houses (tenements or slums) were described as being the worst in Europe (Buckley, 2013; Kearns, 2006).[13]

Attendance officers sought committal for persistent non-attendance at school, and the *Gardaí* (*An Garda Síochána*, the national police force of the Republic of Ireland) sought committal for indictable offences. Hence, the *Gardaí*, the school attendance officer and the N/ISPCC representative (known colloquially as the 'cruelty man') were feared by many children, and were often used as a threat against them by parents, teachers, and other figures of authority (Buckley, 2013).[14] There are differing views on the extent of committal by the N/ISPCC of children to industrial schools. Whilst Ferguson (2007) estimated that only 2 per cent of children investigated by the N/ISPCC were committed to industrial schools, the Commission to Inquire into Child Abuse (CICA, 2009) calculated the extent of N/ISPCC committal involvement to be up to 37 per cent, indicating an alarming zealousness. The CICA (2009) concluded that the public perception of the agency as a conduit to the industrial school system was well-founded. For many Irish children, therefore, the threat of the 'cruelty man', the school attendance officer or the Garda and detention in an industrial school were not idle ones.

In the century from 1868 to 1969, over 105,000 children were detained in industrial schools, having been committed by the courts (Raftery & O'Sullivan, 1999). Section 58(1) of the Children Act 1908 (as amended by the Children Acts 1929 and 1941) allowed for the detention of a child or young person under three broad categories: 'lack of proper guardianship', 'non-attendance at school', and 'indictable offences' (Raftery & O'Sullivan, 1999). By 1966, a fourth category of 'uncontrollable' had been added (Tuairim, 1966). Children who had committed indictable offences were brought before the courts by the *Gardaí*, just like adults. Prior to the Children Act 2001, through which the age of criminal responsibility in Ireland was effectively raised to twelve years, it had been seven years. 'Offences' committed by children could be at the mild end of the scale, usually involving petty crime, or what has been referred to as 'minor acts of delinquency' (O'Sullivan & O'Donnell, 2012). Although a parent was required by law to be present at the hearing, the children were almost always legally unrepresented, and were usually not questioned or consulted in any way before the order for detention was made (CICA, 2009). Court proceedings involving children were perfunctory and the evidential basis for committal to an industrial school was rarely challenged (Arnold, 2009). Maguire (2009) notes that judges were only too willing to grant committal orders, with little investigation into family circumstances and background and few, if any, efforts to support needy families in ways that did not involve sending children to residential institutions.[15] A further 16,000 children (the vast majority of whom were boys) were committed to reformatories during the same period of time (Raftery & O'Sullivan, 1999). With the inclusion of children detained in other residential institutions such as county homes, it is estimated that the overall total of children so committed amounted to over 200,000 (Luddy & Smith, 2014), and therefore accounted for an estimated 1.2 per cent of the age cohort for that period of time (CICA, 2009). Indeed, in 1926, there were more children detained in Irish industrial schools than in all the residential institutions for children in England and Wales together (O'Sullivan & O'Donnell, 2012).[16]

Section 62 of the Children Act 1908 made it clear that no matter where a child lived, he could be detained in *any* industrial school that was willing to receive him or her. For many children, this meant not being detained in the nearest industrial school, which would have made it more convenient for parents, family, and friends to visit, but instead being detained far from home. Taking the Department of Education reports from the year 1946–1947 and one county (Cork), it is seen that only 31 per cent of boys and 53 per cent of girls were resident in industrial schools located in their home county (Morgan, 2009). When sentencing 'John' in Cork, the judge bypassed seven industrial schools in order to have him detained in Letterfrack, Co. Galway, an industrial school that was 320 kilometres from his home. For poor people, this would have involved a two-day journey with an overnight stay, something 'John's' parents, and most other parents of detainees, could not afford. Distance was important; given that one of the objectives of the industrial school system was that of character reformation, it was considered necessary to break the parent–child attachment bond to avoid their bad influence (Barnes, 1989). To the same ends, visits from parents were at the discretion of the Resident Manager of each institution, and were not encouraged. The CICA heard reports from fifty-five witnesses of parents being turned away or treated discourteously when they came to visit. The threat of being refused a parental visit, or not being allowed home to visit family in the summer, was used as a punishment and in order to induce children to keep silent about abuse (CICA, 2009).

Lest we forget that these children were criminalised by the judicial system, Section 64 of the Act specified that a child, once convicted and sentenced, should be conveyed to the relevant industrial school by a police officer. It is also clear that the judicial system effectively operated a maximum sentence policy. Children could be, and often were, detained from whatever age they were at entry up to their sixteenth birthdays, no matter why they had been committed. In this way, two men I interviewed, 'Matthew' was detained from thirteen years of age to his sixteenth birthday, and 'Mark' was detained from seven years of age until he reached sixteen. Survivors invariably report that they were released on the day before their sixteenth birthday, with 47 per cent of witnesses to the CICA (2009) reporting that they had little or no contact with any family members during their time in the institutions, and over half of boys (56 per cent) and over three quarters of girls (86 per cent) reporting that they had been detained for more than six years. By retaining children for the longest possible period, the service provider maximised labour and financial returns: State financial assistance known as the capitation grant was paid (per child, per week) jointly by the Department of Education and the relevant county council for the duration of their detention. Children worked without pay in enterprises operated by many industrial schools that provided services to local communities and sometimes turned a profit for the individual institution (Raftery & O'Sullivan 1999). Referring to what was effectively an effort to tout for business, the CICA report (2009) concluded that the managers of residential institutions demanded that more children be committed 'for reasons of economic viability' (CICA, 2009, Executive Summary, p. 19).

Rules were alarmingly lacking in detail when it came to the limits of the use of corporal punishment in residential institutions (Arnold & Laskey, 1985). The *Rules and Regulations for the Certified Industrial Schools* issued by the Department of Education instructed that punishments were to consist of the following: (i) 'forfeiture of rewards and privileges, or degradation from rank, previously attained by good conduct'; (ii) 'moderate childish punishment with the hand'; and (iii) 'chastisement with the cane, strap or birch' (Cussen, 1936, Appendix C, p. 63). Officially, punishment was to be carried out only by the Resident Manager of an industrial school or, in his or her presence, someone nominated by him or her. No punishment, other than those sanctioned above, was to be administered. The vagueness of the rules pertaining to corporal punishment meant that it was endemic and often excessive in ordinary Irish day schools, and generally supported by parents in a culture that viewed the physical chastisement of children as both normal and necessary (Maguire & O Cinnéide, 2005). Added to this, teachers could proceed with impunity. The Department of Education, even in the case of parental complaints of excessive force, tended to favour teachers and schools (Maguire & O Cinnéide, 2005).[17] All industrial schools were obliged to keep a punishment book in which the offences and the relevant punishments were to be recorded. These books were to be made available to Department of Education inspectors. Although there were fifty-two industrial schools operating in the twentieth century, only two of these books were ever made available to the CICA.

Ireland's Travelling community and the industrial schools

One group of people in Ireland that has traditionally been marginalised is the country's Travelling community. The proportion of Travellers in the general population has always been less than 1 per cent; it currently stands at 30,987, or 0.7 per cent of the general population (Central Statistics Office, 2017). Travellers have been referred to by a variety of derogatory names (including 'gypsies', 'itinerants', 'knackers',[18] and 'tinkers'), and have been the subject of anti-Traveller prejudice for centuries (Helleiner, 2003). Travellers are less likely to have completed secondary school education: Only 8 per cent have done so, in comparison to 73 per cent of the general population (Watson, Kenny & McGinnity, 2017). Amongst those Travellers in the 25–64 years age group, the unemployment rate was 82 per cent, compared to 17 per cent of the non-Traveller population (Watson et al., 2017). Poorer health outcomes have also been documented (All Ireland Traveller Health Study, 2010). Furthermore, Traveller men are between five and eleven times more likely than other men to be imprisoned, whilst Traveller women face a risk of being imprisoned of the order of eighteen to twenty-two times higher than that of the general population (Irish Penal Reform Trust, 2014). Between 2000 and 2006, the suicide rate among Irish Travellers was over three times that of the total population. It peaked in 2005, when it was over five times the national rate (Walker, 2008).

Like other children from other low socio-economic status groups, Traveller children were represented in the industrial school system (Bhreatnach, 2006; CICA, 2009). Helleiner (2003) draws our attention to the ethnic discrimination directed at a nomadic people. She notes that (i) some Traveller children were certainly detained in residential institutions during this period; (ii) threats of detention for not complying with the Childcare Act (1911), the School Attendance Act (1926) for and the Street Trading Act (1926) were used by the police as a means of forcing Travellers to move out of certain areas; and (iii) the law may also have been used in such a way to forcibly remove Traveller children from their parents, and detain them in residential institutions on the grounds of having no fixed abode. O'Sullivan (1976) interviewed forty boys who were detained in Letterfrack industrial school. Three boys (or 7.5 per cent of his sample) stated that they lived in caravans, so we can assume they were Travellers. In addition, and more importantly, his analysis of the admissions records pertaining to Letterfrack over a five-year period in the early 1970s revealed that Traveller children accounted for 3.1 per cent of the detainees.[19] Research carried out for the Kennedy report (1970, Appendix E, Table 31) on children detained in industrial schools showed that 62 out of 2,333 children in detention on 1 February 1968 across thirty institutions had fathers who were designated as 'itinerant'. This amounted to 2.7 per cent of the total number of children in detention on that date. By 1975, when the network of residential institutions was being dismantled and replaced by group homes and foster care, there was still evidence to suggest an over-representation of Traveller children in the system. A Department of Education audit of children in residential care, carried out in April 1975 (cited in O'Sullivan, 2009), showed that there were 104 Traveller children in care – or approximately 8 per cent – and O'Higgins (1993) found that for one Health Board area in 1989 Traveller children ($n = 63$) comprised 16 per cent of all children in care that year.

Whilst more research needs to be carried out in this area, Bhreatnach (2006) argued that if Traveller children were disproportionally subjected to institutionalisation measures, a charge of cultural assimilation could be made. This charge would not be an outrageous one, given that it was not until the early 1960s that the first government report recognising Travellers as a distinct group (the Commission on Itinerancy of 1963) was published, and that the explicitly stated main aim of that report was '….to inquire into the problems arising from the presence of itinerants, and to examine the problems inherent in their way of life' (p. 11). It was proposed that the integration of Travellers into Irish society be effected by a process of sedentarisation, using relevant social policy (McElwee, Jackson & Charles, 2003). Following this report, Travellers have been the 'objects' of official social policies that have failed to reduce anti-Traveller prejudice among the majority settled population, and have failed to enable Travellers to achieve inclusion in Irish society (Kenny & McNeela, 2010). Furthermore, it was not until 2000 that Ireland ratified the *UN International Convention on the Elimination of All Forms of Racial Discrimination* (Helleiner, 2003), and only as recently as 2017 when Travellers were officially acknowledged by the Irish state as constituting an ethnic minority (O'Halloran & O'Regan, 2017).

There is also some evidence to suggest that Traveller children suffered particular discrimination within the already discriminatory atmosphere of the industrial school. I interviewed a survivor who stated that one Christian Brother (who was later convicted for sexually abusing multiple children in his care) had a particular hatred for Traveller children, and treated them with particular cruelty. Seven witnesses to the CICA (2009) reported having been marginalised, verbally abused, and ridiculed about their Traveller backgrounds, most often in public: 'Brother X called me a "knacker",[20] and said my parents didn't want me. I felt worthless and degraded' (Vol. III, p. 107). Some industrial schools had what was known as a 'poor parlour', where particularly poor parents were directed if they visited. Traveller witnesses before the CICA reported it to be a common occurrence that their parents were directed to this room. It also seems that anti-Traveller sentiment was not confined to staff in residential institutions. Referring to their experiences in day schools, adult Travellers recalled being called names in school as children, and being harassed and beaten up by other pupils. Others described trying to avoid classmates at break time, for fear of bullying. Still others reported being treated by teachers as if they were dirty and, for instance, being forced to take showers, having their hair forcibly checked for lice, and having their clothes removed and replaced (Helleiner, 2003).

In Gmelch's (1991) biography of the Traveller Nan Donoghue, Nan recalled that when she separated from her husband Jim, he placed one of their children in institutional care – most likely an industrial school. She was impoverished upon separation, but was aware that if she went to the ISPCC, or 'cruelty' as she called it, her children would be taken from her. Not having enough money to support them on her own, she handed them into the care of her sisters and her mother. However, both children ultimately returned to their father, who voluntarily handed the infant Angela over to an industrial school in Cork. Nan subsequently had a number of children with another man, Mick, and when they separated after incidents of violence, her brother Pat arranged for them to be placed in care, saying (Gmelch, 1991):

> I want me sister's children taken into a home where they'll get their three [daily] meals and get well looked after….I want them educated so they won't have to ask anyone what road to follow. (p. 114)

The siblings were split up. Mary and Sally were sent to the industrial school in Clifden, Co. Galway, operated by the Sisters of Mercy. Joe, John, and Willie were sent initially to Drogheda, and then to the industrial school at Letterfrack, Co. Galway, operated by the Christian Brothers. It is quite likely that, although the two industrial schools were less than fifteen kilometres apart, the girls and boys did not meet again until they were released at sixteen years old. However, some cases have come to light of siblings not being reunited for sixty years post-release (Johnson, 2009).

I interviewed 'Luke', a Traveller and a former detainee of both the Letterfrack and Salthill industrial schools. In 1952, 'Luke' was detained in Letterfrack industrial school at seven years of age after an investigation by an inspector from the NSPCC. The order for his detention at an industrial school, which I have viewed, described his mother as being 'in very delicate health'. In his Letterfrack intake file, the reason for his detention at the industrial school was stated as 'having a guardian who does not exercise proper guardianship'. More than likely, the boy was sent to Letterfrack because (i) he was part of a large family (fourteen children); (2) the family was poor; and, (iii) it was believed at the time that without a healthy mother, the father could neither look after the needs of his children while working as a builder's labourer, nor could he arrange to have his family or friends support him in this endeavour. 'Luke' did not find out until he was released from Salthill industrial school at sixteen years of age that he had had two older brothers who had been resident in Letterfrack for some of the two-year period that he was detained there. The Christian Brothers, who would have been aware of the fact that there were three siblings from the same family from their intake files, never thought it worthwhile informing him.

I also interviewed 'John', a forty-eight-year-old Traveller. He was born in the large Labry Park Traveller encampment in Dublin, and was detained in St. Joseph's industrial school in Kilkenny for a period of fourteen years. He has thirteen siblings, and he recalled that at least two siblings (that he is aware of) were also detained in industrial schools. 'John' was physically, emotionally, and sexually abused (by both male and female staff) in the industrial school, and he was sexually abused by an adult farm labourer whilst being loaned out on unpaid work experience to a farmer. He recalls being violently assaulted in the industrial school for such 'small things' as having a runny nose, having unbrushed teeth, and his bedclothes not being straight and tidy. In fear, and in order to avoid the nuns, he hid under his bed, in the toilets, and even in a cupboard. Of the forty-four children who went through St. Joseph's together, only 'John' and one other man are still alive. He wouldn't say how many men and women killed themselves, or died as a result of drug overdoses, but indicated to me that the number is substantial.

The legacy of the residential schools system

Whilst many institutions were built in remote country areas, they were usually located near or in towns and villages. Although occurring almost in plain sight, what happened within the grounds or walls of each institution remained covered up by the religious orders and fawning local communities, tied to the religious orders by unquestioning reverence and the economic benefits that accrued from having a large institution in the area. Thus, the cover-up was facilitated by what was, in effect, a form of bystander apathy. In recent years this open-secret world has been exposed by journalists and scholars (Arnold, 2009; Raftery & O'Sullivan, 1999) as well as by survivors of these places (e.g. Clemenger, 2009; Coleman, 2010; Ellis, 2012; Fahy, 2005; Flynn 1983, 2003; Touher, 2001, 2008; Tyrrell, 2006). Apart from reformatories and industrial schools for children, other institutions in the carceral network for adults in Ireland have also recently become the focus of valuable research attention, for example, psychiatric hospitals[21] (Brennan, 2014), Magdalen laundries (Smith, 2007), county homes (Lucey, 2014), borstals (Reidy, 2009), and mother-and-baby homes (Earner-Byrne, 2013; Milotte, 2012). What we are still finding out is that for over a century, many vulnerable people, and especially children, lived a parallel and precarious existence in an Irish society that 'claimed to cherish and hold them sacred, but in fact marginalised and ignored them' (Maguire, 2009).

The creation and rapid proliferation of the institutions can be seen as either a desire to help those in need, or a means of controlling those whom the authorities viewed as a threat to the existing order (CICA report 2009). Pathologising the 'Other' was at the heart of the enterprise. So-called 'illegitimate' children were the focus of much prejudice. They were particularly tainted, as their very existence was seen to be in large part a result of the moral bankruptcy of their mothers, and they themselves were perceived as being more likely to become deviant/immoral (Luddy, 1995; Maguire, 2009). Indeed, some residential institutions refused admittance to the children of unmarried mothers lest it be construed as countenancing immorality (Luddy, 1995). Ferguson (2007) believed that these children in residential institutional detention were so stigmatised that they were seen as the 'moral dirt' of Irish society. He argued that preying on the fears of the general public was how the residential institution concept was 'sold', and how it thrived.

The CICA report (2009) found that 73 per cent of survivors reported receiving no second-level education and that 71 per cent reported being in non-skilled and semi-skilled work their entire working lives. Indeed, at the time of their attendance at the Commission, 33 per cent reported being unemployed with a further 19 per cent reporting that they were in receipt of disability benefit. Tobin (2015) also noted the consequences of the religious orders' limited commitment to the education of industrial school children in terms of the struggles of survivors to find reasonable and meaningful employment. Feeley's (2014) research with twenty-eight survivors found that just under half (*n* = 13) had attained little or no literacy following their experiences in industrial schools. O'Riordan and Arensman (2007) noted the number of survivors who had joined the defence forces post-industrial school, and speculated that other survivors who found themselves working in religious order-operated facilities, such as convents, monasteries, retreat houses, convalescent homes, and hospitals, may have, consciously or unconsciously, sought the familiarity of further institutionalisation.

Powell et al., (2012) noted that the most common factors that resulted in the detention of children in industrial schools, including '....combinations of poverty, illness, neglect, parental death, non-marital birth and unemployment'. Gwynn Jones added large families and mentally ill children to the list of factors (CICA Report 2009, Vol. IV, p. 208). He concluded that 'Children from the lower socio-economic groups were represented in disproportionately high numbers in schools'. However, the link to poverty had been noted many years before this. The Cussen Report (1936, p. 10) noted the connection in the public's mind between criminality and the industrial schools, and flagged that '....the main problem is one not of criminal tendencies, but of poverty'. The Cussen Report revealed that between 1930 and 1934, the vast majority (89 per cent) of children were admitted to industrial schools for 'poverty and neglect'. Over thirty years later, the Kennedy Report (1970, Appendix E, Table 31) showed figures for 1968. In terms of occupation of father, no man categorised as 'higher professional', 'lower professional', 'employer / manager', or 'commercial worker (e.g. agent)' had a son in an industrial school or reformatory.

The number of children committed to industrial and reformatory schools declined steadily after 1944, and by the time the Kennedy Report (1970) appeared, there were twenty-nine institutions holding approximately 2,000 children. The decline occurred for a number of reasons. Gwynn Morgan (CICA Report, Vol. 4, pp. 207–208) attributes it to the introduction of state provision of family supports, beginning with unemployment assistance and benefit (1933), widows' and orphans' pensions (1935), and continuing with children's allowance (1944). The advent of adoption (in 1952) was another factor in declining numbers entering the industrial school system.[22] Nearly fifty years after the system was dismantled, the nature and scale of what occurred in these places still challenges our understanding. With the enmeshed relationship that existed (and some would argue, still exists) between the (Roman Catholic) Church and State in Ireland, the publication of survivors' accounts of their experiences in these institutions (e.g. Clemenger, 2009;

Coleman, 2010; Cronin, 2010; Doyle, 1988 Ellis, 2012; Fahy, 2005; Finn, 2011; Flynn, 1983, 2003; Hayden, 1999; Hogan, 2008; Joyce, 2004; Touher, 2001, 2008; Tyrrell, 2006; Wall, 2013) and the official state investigation into what took place (CICA) have been a feature of only the last twenty years. However, what has emerged from these dark times is a catalogue of atrocities across institutions. In Ireland, in conjunction with the CICA, Carr and colleagues carried out the largest research project to date, with 247 adult survivors of the various residential institutions for children and adolescents (Carr, 2008; CICA Report, 2009, Vol. V, pp. 77–162). Almost all reported having experienced physical neglect (97.6 per cent), physical abuse (97.2 per cent), and emotional neglect (95.1 per cent) as children in these institutions; furthermore, almost half (47 per cent) reported having been sexually abused (CICA, 2009). Lynch and Minton (2016) attempted to expand the narrative about the institutional experience by revealing the existence of a culture within Christian Brothers-operated institutions of peer physical and sexual abuse. Among other explanations, we theorised that this feature was explicable in terms of the introduction by the Brothers of a category of older supervisor-detainee, known as a 'monitor'. Resembling the *kapo* system used in Nazi concentration camps (designed to do much of the 'dirty work' for the SS guards, and create terror among the inmate population)[23] many monitors became emboldened by their new-found power to be in charge of others and to punish them, and some abused their fellow detainees physically and sexually (CICA, 2009; Lynch & Minton, 2016; Tyrrell, 2006).

Such experiences had profound long-term impacts. All participants had experienced one or more significant life problems, with mental health problems (81.78 per cent had experienced anxiety, depression, or a personality disorder at some point in their lives), unemployment (51.8 per cent), substance use (38.1 per cent), and homelessness (21.1 per cent) being the most common. Carr (2008) found that participants with multiple co-morbid psychological disorders had experienced more institutional abuse (CICA, 2009). A cycle of poverty has been noted by clinicians and charitable support services working with survivors, but recently research carried out by Haase (2015), using address data provided to the *Residential Institutions Redress Board* (RIRB) on survivors living in the Republic of Ireland and a process of geocoding, confirmed the extent of this cycle. Half (50.4 per cent) of all survivors were found to be residing in the lowest two deciles, that is, the most disadvantaged areas of the country. In addition, results showed that the most disadvantaged decile (i.e. decile 1) contained the largest number of survivors (3,009 out of a total of 8,088). The author concluded that survivors' experience of residential institutional care '….may have compounded, and certainly did not alleviate, any baseline risks of poverty, deprivation and social exclusion that they may have inherited as a result of their social origins' (p. 7).

Codd (2016), in her statistical calculation of survivor life expectancy, noted that of the total number of survivors who had provided data, 34 per cent of males and 46 per cent of females had emigrated, most notably to the United Kingdom, Australia, Canada, and the United States. That such large numbers of survivors emigrated perhaps indicates that their intentions were to find decent employment and, perhaps, to try to escape certain memories. The fact that such atrocities were perpetrated by men and women of God in the context of a devoutly Roman Catholic country, where these representatives of God on earth were both revered and feared, has prompted me to posit that a uniquely damaging betrayal trauma impacted upon victims – *Clergy Betrayal Trauma* (see Lynch, 2018).

Processes of truth, restitution, reconciliation, and reclamation

The CICA (2009) took ten years to examine the evidence of how children were treated in institutional care. Its 2,600-page report chronicled the nature of abuses occurring over a period of a century. It concluded that physical and emotional abuse and neglect were features of the institutions. Sexual abuse, ranging from voyeurism to violent rape occurred in many of them, particularly residential institutions for boys, where it was described as endemic. In the minority of instances where sexual abuse came to the individual institution's notice, cases were handled with a view to minimising reputational damage to the individual clerical perpetrator and the religious order as a whole, with damage to the individual child and danger to other children disregarded. 'Discipline' was found to have been unreasonable and oppressive; regulations regarding the use of corporal punishment were simply disregarded. A climate of fear, using 'pervasive, excessive and arbitrary punishment', existed in the institutions: physical abuse was found to have been systemic, and not just the result of a few 'bad apples'. Standards of physical care were found to have been poor; children were frequently hungry and were provided with inadequate clothing. Accommodation facilities were found to have been cold and bleak; there was little or no privacy due to large dormitory sleeping arrangements and constant supervision. Education was not seen as a priority, and long hours of unpaid labour was a feature for both boys and girls (CICA, 2009).

Although industrial schools were referred to by the general public as 'orphanages', it is clear that children were not primarily detained as a result of being orphaned. For instance, in the 1935–1936 school year, the number of orphaned children admitted to industrial schools in Ireland was 54 out of a total of 905 (5.9 per cent) (Department of Education, 1936). A survey for the Kennedy Committee (Kennedy Report, 1970) found that industrial schools were aware that both of a child's parents were dead in only 1.5 per cent of cases and, alarmingly, were unable to say whether they were alive or dead in a further 10 per cent of cases. Although numbers were relatively small, it seems that orphans were over-represented in the industrial school system, as, for example, during the period of the Kennedy report in the late 1960s, orphans accounted for only 0.25 per cent of the general population (Morgan, 2009). One could argue, then, that referring to industrial schools as 'orphanages' gave the impression that they existed for a specific, necessary, and laudable purpose. Such impression management in the form of euphemisms was also used by religious orders operating residential institutions in other countries. For example, in Australia industrial schools were called 'homes', 'orphanages', and 'training schools' (Penglase, 2005). It was also found to be the case that children were not, in the main, detained because they were truanting from day schools. During the lifetime of the carceral system in Ireland, only approximately 10 per cent of children were detained for breach of the School Attendance Act.

It also appears that these institutions did not contain too many 'little criminals'. It is estimated that only 11 per cent of boys, and less than 1 per cent of girls, were detained as a result of being deemed to have committed a criminal offence (Raftery & O'Sullivan, 1999). The commonly held belief that significant number of poor Irish parents were voluntarily handing over their children to the care of the religious orders who operated the industrial schools, as a means of alleviating financial burden as well as providing the child with a better chance in life, is also called into question when we examine the statistics.[24] Between 1949 and 1969, for example, the largest number of boys admitted voluntarily in any one year was twenty-eight. The figure for girls that same year was eighty-six (Kennedy report, 1970). This is a mere 3.5 per cent of the total number of children institutionalised that year. An average of only 2.2 per cent of children were designated by the Department of Education as having been voluntarily admitted in the school years 1949–1950 and 1968–1969, according to my calculations. Therefore, because detention in industrial schools was overwhelmingly involuntary, it is appropriate to say that these children were, as Arnold & Laskey (1985, p. 35) described them, '*de facto* prisoners'. All of the survivors I have interviewed were clear that they had been detained in prisons for children. One described the industrial school where he had been detained as a concentration camp because of the isolation of the institution, the prolonged separation from family and friends, the brutality of the regime and the forced labour.

The persistent belief that industrial schools were populated by 'little criminals' is also disproved by the finding that approximately 80 per cent of all children and over 90 per cent of girls were placed in these institutions under the 'lack of proper guardianship' criterion (Raftery & O'Sullivan, 1999). In practice, this broad category could include 'illegitimate' children of unmarried mothers, children who had lost one or both parents, children whose parent or parents were disabled or incapacitated in some way (e.g. through illness), children whose parents could not provide for them due to extreme poverty, and children where a parent was in prison or had deserted the family. Children who were brought before a judge on the basis of the 'lack of proper guardianship' criterion (i.e. cruelty and/or neglect) were usually assessed by a representative of the N/ISPCC. However, in the vast majority of cases this was as a result of reports or allegations from third parties such as teachers, priests, the *Gardaí*, or neighbours, rather than their own investigations (Maguire, 2009). Maguire argued persuasively that the majority of children detained in industrial schools were, in fact, 'legitimate', and were committed because their parents could not look after them according to the standards of '....the middle-class court system and the middle-class ISPCC inspectors' (pp. 40–41). Furthermore, she expressed the belief that, typically, the neglect was directly attributable to the situation of poverty that the family lived in, rather than parental malice.[25] Supporting this view, Buckley's (2013) analysis of the 247 N/ISPCC files that had survived from the 1930s revealed that no case involved a family that was not poor, working-class, or both. Interestingly, she argued that an ideological shift away from identifying cases of cruelty to one of focusing on child neglect fundamentally changed the emphasis of the N/ISPCC child welfare mandate, and in doing so, effectively prejudiced the organisation against the poorer members of Irish society.

There is still a paucity of research on and with survivors of institutional abuse in Ireland. Many men and women have never spoken about their experiences. Some have spoken only to partners, immediate family members, and counsellors and their stories will go no further. As academics and researchers we are honoured that some brave men and women have published memoirs, have actively engaged in survivor support groups, have spoken to the media, and (in a small number of cases) have made themselves available to participate in studies. Research on survivors of clerical historical institutional abuse across many countries has consistently focused on the type, nature, severity, and long-term impact of abuse experiences (Blakemore et al., 2017). I believe that this is because the agenda for research and the parameters of that research have been set by state-activated enquiries that include a calculation of suffering and the linked element of financial redress. The limitations of such a process in terms of how the victim/survivor experiences the restorative justice system are being explored in other countries (see Daly, 2014) but remains to be comprehensively researched in Ireland.[26] Subsequent research on Irish survivors, mostly of a qualitative nature, has illuminated the lived experience of survivors post-release and has shown that alcohol and substance use, allied to social isolation, contributed to the risk of suicidal ideation and attempts. Survivors were found to be less likely to be employed, more likely to have a non-trusting/negative world view, more likely to have under-developed coping resources and a greater sense of hopelessness than those abused in non-residential settings (Gavin Wolters, 2006). Survivors felt criminalised, disempowered, and stigmatised (Pembroke, 2013). They equated affection with sexual abuse, felt unprepared for the world, and disconnected from the support of the Church. Perhaps disengagement from religion was an inevitable consequence for some as the experience of being taught the tenets of religion in residential institutions was inextricably linked to physical abuse

(Pembroke, 2017). The inter-generational nature of abuse was highlighted by O'Riordan and Arensman (2007) when they found that relationship difficulties and difficulties in parenting children were reported frequently by survivors.

My study of survivors who had been detained in the Letterfrack industrial school was the first study in Ireland in which survivors were asked about how they coped in an institution (Lynch, 2018). I found that, although they had lived their incarcerated lives in a state of fear, never knowing when and by whom they could be victimised, survivors revealed how creative they had been in trying to deal with their experiences. Coping strategies included seeking social support, separating oneself and acting alone, prosocial behaviour, finding blissful moments such as watching the weekly movie, enjoying the local scenery, or engaging in consensual sexual contact.[27] I also viewed both peer physical abuse and peer sexual abuse as part of the normal repertoire of coping strategies utilised in extreme environments, and that they were activated through such processes as the imitation of aggressive models (Bandura, Ross & Ross, 1961) and a compulsion to repeat previously experienced traumatic experiences (Freud, 1920; van der Kolk, 1989).

It should be noted that at the time of their contact with the RIRB in 2001, that 56.9 per cent were fifty years of age and older; and survivors now constitute an ageing population, for whom state reparations take on a particular urgency (Codd, 2016). In a more recent enquiry into historical institutional abuse in Northern Ireland, 65 per cent of those who gave evidence to the enquiry team were fifty-five years and older, with 10 per cent being over seventy-five years old (Hart, Lane & Doherty, 2017). Most of the survivors that I have interviewed live in conditions of poverty, and research by Haase (2015) confirmed my observations, and those of survivor advocates, that this is an economically vulnerable population. It is significant that in terms of practical services provided to survivors by the designated agency (Residential Institutions Statutory Fund), housing support accounted for by far the largest expenditure (Caranua, 2018). Transitional Justice (TJ) initiatives for victims/survivors of clerical institutional abuse contain elements of procedural justice – that is, participation and voice – but also the critical elements of validation, vindication, and offender accountability (Daly, 2014). Six guiding principles have been identified as critical in the delivery of a survivor-centred TJ process: (i) participation; (ii) accessibility; (iii) privacy; (iv) dignity and non-discrimination; (v) support; and, (vi) protection (Moffett et al., 2019). In Ireland, many survivors remain hurt and angry that their voices have not been heard in the decision-making process surrounding the various strands of the TJ programme initiated after the Irish state's apology to them in 1999 (Reclaiming Self, 2017). Indeed, some processes appear to have been so constructed and delivered as to be detrimental to victims of abuse (Reclaiming Self, 2017). For instance, it appears that legislation governing the operation of the CICA and the RIRB did not make it mandatory for these bodies to report any allegation of historical institutional abuse against named individuals notified to them to the Irish civil authorities.

From a human rights perspective, Holohan (2011, p. 7) described the abuse and neglect suffered by children in residential institutions as arguably constituting '....the greatest and most systemic human rights violations' in the history of the Irish state (p. 7). In particular, she noted the absence of effective organisational accountability mechanisms within the religious orders who operated the residential institutions, resulting in abuse continuing unchecked. The lack of individual offender accountability in the Irish context was highlighted on the world stage by the United Nations Committee Against Torture (UNCAT, 2017). In that committee's concluding observations on Ireland, it reported that its direction to the state to implement all the recommendations contained in the report of the CICA (2009) and to investigate allegations of torture and ill-treatment at residential institutions operated by religious orders of the Roman Catholic Church, prosecute and punish perpetrators of such abuse, and provide redress to the victims, had only been partially implemented.

By failing to fully implement the CICA recommendations (e.g. to create a memorial for survivors) and to sensitively apply, for example, the TJ mechanism of survivor participation in all decision-making processes pertaining to them, the Irish state has failed its children again (Reclaiming Self, 2017). The most recent manifestation of this betrayal is the announcement, without consultation, that survivors will not be able to access records of their testimony to the CICA or the RIRB. In a move that has shocked and angered survivors, it has been confirmed that the oral and written evidence presented to these bodies (upwards of two million documents) are to be sealed in state archives for seventy-five years (McGarry, 2019). The stated reason for such sealing the files was to provide survivors with anonymity and confidentiality for the testimony they had provided. Laudable though this sounds, it is imperative that survivors have the right to access their own testimonies – even with redactions to preserve others' confidentiality – and recent Irish data protection legislation may yet prove helpful in this regard. Up to this latest development, survivors have not been automatically provided with, or encouraged to request, transcripts of their testimony at hearings attended. I am aware of only two survivors who are in possession of transcripts of their testimony to the RIRB, so perhaps a case could be made that a precedent has been established.

Allied to this, the anonymising of alleged perpetrators in the CICA report,[28] and the suspicion that no allegations of sexual abuse against named perpetrators have been reported to the relevant civil authorities by the RIRB, has created a deep divide between the state and survivors. Given the concern that there was no reporting imperative on the RIRB in relation to allegations made against named abusers, and the sealing of files containing those allegations, survivors are justifiably concerned that many perpetrators of historical crimes against children may remain at large and a danger to children

(Reclaiming Self, 2017). This is particularly so as most survivors I have interviewed believed that (i) their allegations would be reported to the police by the RIRB; and (ii) they themselves were precluded from reporting experiences of historical institutional abuse to the police after appearing before the RIRB, and had signed what they believed to be an all-encompassing confidentiality contract.[29] Perhaps it will take an outside agency, such as the UNCAT to shame the Irish state into doing the right thing by victims/survivors.

Notes

1. From the *'Directory and Rules of the Congregation of the Christian Schools of Ireland'*.
2. I use the term 'disappeared' here in two distinct, but inter-connected ways. In the first case, I mean that children were detained against their will and incarcerated in secure residential institutions, with little or no contact with family and friends for months, and even years. Indeed, from interviews I conducted with victims/survivors I am aware that some children never returned home, either because the bond with family had been ruptured by the separation, or because they had died in detention. For example, the grounds of the industrial school at Letterfrack contain seventy-eight graves of boys who died and were buried far from where their families lived. In the second instance, 'disappeared' refers to children who were deprived of their identity as an individual boy or girl from a particular family and community, and forced to adopt an imposed shame-based identity of 'criminal' and/or 'sinner' and/or 'person involved in shameful behaviour'. For many survivors, therapy concerns itself with, amongst other themes, a reclaiming the original pre-shamed self through self-compassion. For an extensive psychological analysis of shame and guilt, see Tangney and Dearing (2002).
3. One of the main reasons for the extent of poverty pre- and post-Famine was that in rural Ireland, few jobs existed outside 'the over-manned agricultural sector' (Gray, 2007, p. 26). Agriculture was dominated by small landholdings. For example, by 1841, 45 per cent of the agricultural holdings in Ireland were less than five acres, and as subsistence farming grew, living standards fell (Kelly, 2012, p. 10). Poverty impacted on a significant proportion of the Irish population right up until the 1960s when the government of the day began to engage in economic planning in a coherent fashion (Maguire, 2009).
4. As part of what was known as 'poor relief', 130 large workhouses were built throughout the country to house impoverished and destitute families. These were bleak, austere places, and deliberately so. It was believed that if they were too comfortable, people might become dependent and want to stay. These places of mass confinement were based on the prejudicial belief that poor people were lazy, scheming, and intransigent. Each institution separated men, women, and children into basic dormitory-style accommodation, and families' lives within such places were tightly controlled to the extent that one historian noted that a 'radically new surveillance and disciplinary regime had been introduced to manage and control the Irish poor' (Smyth, 2013, p. 125). People were classified as 'inmates' or 'paupers' in all records; adults and children had to wear uniforms, and they were classified, confined, disciplined, and punished for their plight (Smyth, 2013).
5. In Germany at the same time, notions of 'born criminals' allied to medical and psychiatric interventions led to a prevailing view that some children would grow up to be unproductive, criminal and thus harmful to society. The word used for such people was 'asocial', which means anti-social. Such views and forecasts of doom were later to provide Nazi Germany with a 'rationale' for their form of pre-emptive action

'....regardless of the offences children did or did not commit' (Sheffer, 2018, p. 12). Sheffer demonstrated that the medical profession was co-opted into an eliminationist ideology and how they were culpable in the murder of thousands of children regarded as surplus to requirements. 'Difficult cases' were those children undeserving of life, while '*Behandlung*' [treatment] was a euphemism used by the euthanasia apparatus to describe the process of killing a child. Lifton's (2000) is the classic account of the role of that medical profession in Germany played in genocide, beginning with the sterilisation programme.

6. It is worth noting that girls and women could 'fall' but men and boys could not, despite knowledge of the existence of a market for male child/adolescent prostitutes (Jackson, 2000).
7. Based on the New York Society for the Prevention of Cruelty to Children, the Liverpool Society for the Prevention of Cruelty to Children was founded in 1883, and a national body, the National Society for the Prevention of Cruelty to Children (NSPCC) was founded in 1889, following the passing of the United Kingdom's Prevention of Cruelty to, and Protection of, Children Act of 1889. The NSPCC operated in Ireland from 1889, until the foundation of a successor organisation, the Irish Society for the Prevention of Cruelty to Children (ISPCC), in 1956. The NSPCC and ISPCC continue to function as national child protection charities of the United Kingdom and Ireland, respectively.
8. This ambivalent view of victims of abuse may have facilitated and even encouraged perpetrators to sexually abuse children, because we are now aware that viewing children as corrupt, and perceiving them as instigating adult-child sexual contact, would constitute offence-promoting cognitive distortions that 'justified' the assaultive behaviour, and allowed the offender to believe that the impact on the child was minimal or non-existent (Ward, 2000).
9. Ferguson (2007) reminds us that the system of mass institutionalisation of children was deeply patriarchal in nature, with a male-dominated police force, judiciary, Department of Education, N/ISPCC, and the Roman Catholic Church being the principal players in these children's experience of detention. In addition, Maguire (2009) is clear that the targeted population for intervention was a working class one, and that one goal of the intervention was to ensure that social mobility did not occur. These children would be taught to know their place in the social hierarchy, and to fulfil a useful function in employment terms.
10. In 1937, when the then *Taoiseach* (Irish prime minister), Éamonn de Valera, was re-shaping the constitution, he had two clerical advisors. No woman was involved in drafting the constitution. The feminist, Hannah Sheehy Skeffington, commented at the time that Ireland was 'rapidly becoming a Catholic statelet under Rome's grip' (In McCullagh, 2018, p. 124).
11. The spread of Irish religious orders across the globe was enormous. By the beginning of the twentieth century, one such order – the Christian Brothers – had, a presence in Aotearoa/New Zealand, Australia, Canada, Great Britain, Gibraltar, India, Italy, and the United States (O'Donoghue, 2012).
12. It has been suggested that exacerbating factors may have included the belief among religious nuns and brothers that working in the residential sector was a low status job and that less competent and 'troubled' clerics were assigned to that work (CICA, 2009; Dunne, 2002, 2010).
13. A typical Georgian tenement house in Dublin, for example, could be inhabited by between fifty and eighty people and in 1900 there were over 6,000 tenement houses in Dublin, housing one-third of the city's population (Kearns, 2006).
14. One man I interviewed recalled a troubled relationship with his mother, and that she had threatened him with being sent to the industrial school many times. On one occasion, however, she physically dragged him to the imposing gates and walls

of St Joseph's industrial school, Kilkenny, to increase his fear and induce compliance. As the psychoanalyst Alice Miller has shown, the prevailing child rearing philosophy of the time and one that, I would argue, was embraced by the religious orders in their residential institutions, was one of what she refers to as 'poisonous pedagogy': That of a total belief in the superiority of the adult, and a systematic effort to break the spirit of the child in order to gain immediate and total obedience (Miller, 1983).

15. Another man I interviewed forty years post-detention revealed that, in a clear breach of his human rights, he had not been represented legally in court, had not been allowed to make contact with his parents, and therefore his parents had not been present during the court hearing. In fact, his parents did not know the whereabouts of their son and were frantically searching for him, regarding him as a missing person and not knowing that he had been arrested for stealing sweets from a van, had been detained in a police station, had appeared in court, had been convicted, and had been driven to and detained in an industrial school approximately 300 kilometres from his home.

16. At this time, the general population in Ireland was 2.97 million, whereas the English and Welsh general population was over thirteen times this figure.

17. Corporal punishment across the Irish education system was prohibited in 1982 with the issue of circulars 9/82 to all primary schools and circular M5/82 to all secondary schools.

18. This is the most offensive of these examples. The word 'knacker' is a job title, used for those who trade in the removal and clear of dead and dying animals (particularly horses) from farms and roads, and render the carcasses into useful by-products (e.g. animal feed, bone meal fats, glue, and tallow). Historically, Travellers engaged in this trade, and the term is now used (by some) as a pejorative name for members of the Travelling community. The scale of the offence caused by its usage is comparable to that caused by a white American calling an African-American 'nigger'.

19. Perhaps reflecting the disrespectful and haphazard way Traveller children were treated by the Christian Brothers who ran the institution, O'Sullivan's (1976) examination of the admission records of Letterfrack industrial school drew him to the case of two Traveller brothers who had been detained after being convicted of larceny. It was stated that the first boy was detained in the industrial school in March 1968 because he was 'unable to be controlled' and that the other boy was detained in September 1969 for an 'indictable offence'. It seems that both boys had committed the 'offence' together; yet they were brought to court on separate occasions, and one boy served a longer sentence. The boys were nine years old at the time of the 'offence', and would not have been released until they had reached sixteen

20. See endnote 18.

21. The network of mental asylums in Ireland has been described as 'spectacular' in both scale and longevity, and by the 1950s Ireland had the dubious distinction of having the world's highest rate of asylum residency per 100,000 of population (Brennan, 2014).

22. Later, a raft of other initiatives were contemplated and ultimately activated in an attempt to deal with poverty and its social consequences: For example, disability benefits, contributory and non-contributory pensions, fostering, the development of social work as a profession (with an emphasis on child protection), maintenance orders, single parent allowance, the development of the probation service, free second level education, and legalised contraception. The CICA Report (2009, Vol. 1, p. 41) concludes that this decline was also due to '....improving economic conditions in the 1950s, and even more so in the 1960s'.

23. In the Nazi concentration camp system, *kapos* were prisoner functionaries who were appointed by the SS guards to supervise fellow prisoners. Part of their remit was to administer beatings, and in order to please their captors, they over-compensated and were extremely cruel in all their dealings with fellow prisoners. Privileges accruing included their lives being prolonged, better food and clothing, money, cigarettes, shoes, and a separate sleeping area. They were dreaded and reviled in equal measure by other inmates (Von Kellenbach, 2013; Wachsmann, 2015).
24. Taking Letterfrack as one industrial school, and 1952 as one particular year, I have discovered evidence indicating that when the then Resident Manager was admitting a boy on 9 May1952, he revealed on a form that there were no children in the school (out of a total of 164 boys) who had been voluntarily admitted by their parents.
25. Referring to Ireland in the period of the 1920s to the 1950s, Gwynn Morgan (CICA Report, 2009) noted the classic signs associated with poverty in the families of children detained in industrial schools: tuberculosis ('consumption'), rickets, anaemia, emigration, apathy, money-lending, and high unemployment, especially in the major urban areas. In addition, he notes that between 1930 and 1980, Irish fertility levels were the highest in Western Europe, but with coexisting high levels of infant mortality.
26. For an initial foray into how the system of restorative justice has failed survivors in Ireland, see the submission by the Irish advocacy group Reclaiming Self (2017) to the United Nations Committee Against Torture (UNCAT).
27. A parallel culture of older and stronger boys (not necessarily 'monitors') perpetrating predatory sexual assaults on younger, weaker boys, was also revealed (Lynch, 2018).
28. The anonymity of alleged perpetrators in the CICA (2009) report was guaranteed under the Commission to Inquire into Child Abuse (Amendment) Act (2005).
29. In a guide to the redress scheme (RIRB, 2005) the approximately 15,000 eligible applicants were informed that it was a criminal offence to disclose information provided to the Board, or to disclose the amount of financial compensation awarded, or to disclose information about their experiences at the Redress Board hearing. What became colloquially known as the 'gagging order' was perceived as being reminiscent of '….the bad old days where secrecy and concealment were the friends of child abusers' (Commins, 2010). Unfortunately, but perhaps not surprisingly, it was also interpreted by many survivors as preventing them from reporting their experiences of abuse to the civil authorities, if they had not done so prior to the RIRB process.

References

All Ireland Traveller Health Study. (2010). *Our Geels: Summary of Findings*. Dublin: School of Public Health, Physiotherapy and Population Science, University College Dublin.

Arnold, B. (2009). *The Irish Gulag: How the State Betrayed Its Innocent Children*. Dublin: Gill & Macmillan.

Arnold, M. & Laskey, H. (1985). *Children of the Poor Clares: The Story of an Irish Orphanage*. Belfast: Appletree Press.

Bandura, A., Ross, D. & Ross, S.A. (1961). Transmission of aggression through imitation of aggressive models. *Journal of Abnormal and Social Psychology*, 63(3): 575–582.

Barnes, J. (1989). *Irish Industrial Schools 1868–1908: Origins and Development*. Dublin: Irish Academic Press.

Bhreatnach, A. (2006). *Becoming Conspicuous: Irish Travellers, Society and the State, 1922–70*. Dublin: University College Dublin Press.

Blakemore, T., Herbert, J.L., Arney, F. & Parkinson, S. (2017). *Impacts of Institutional Child Sexual Abuse on Victims/Survivors: A Rapid Evidence Review of Research Findings.* Sydney: Royal Commission into Institutional Responses to Child Sexual Abuse.

Brennan, D. (2014). *Irish Insanity 1800–2000.* London: Routledge.

Buckley, S. (2013). *The Cruelty Man: Child Welfare, the NSPCC and the State in Ireland 1889–1956.* Manchester, England: Manchester University Press.

Carr, A. (2008). The psychological adjustment of adult survivors of institutional abuse in Ireland Report submitted to the Commission to Inquire into Child Abuse. Available on-line: http://www.childabusecommission.ie/rpt/05-03A.php [Accessed April, 2019].

Caranua. (2018). *Annual Report 2017.* Dublin: Caranua. Available online: https://www.caranua.ie/wp-content/uploads/2018/02/Caranua_Annual_Report_2017.pdf [Accessed April, 2019].

Central Statistics Office. (2017). *Census of Population 2016 – Profile 8: Travellers, Ethnicity and Religion.* Available online: http://www.cso.ie/en/releasesandpublications/ep/p-cp8iter/p8iter/p8e/ [Accessed April, 2019].

Chapman, A. & O'Donoghue, T. (2007). The recruitment of religious as teachers: A case study from 1960s Australia. *Cambridge Journal of Education,* 37(4): 561–577.

Clemenger, M. (2009). *Holy Terrors.* Dublin: O'Brien Press.

Codd, M.B. (2016). *Estimated Survival and Additional Years of Life Expected among Registrants to the Residential Institutions Redress Board (RIRB): A Report Commissioned by Caranua.* Available online: http://www.caranua.ie/attachments/CSTAR_Caranua_Report_Feb_2016_Fully_Integrated_Report-with-numbers.pdf [Accessed April, 2019].

Coleman, K. (2010). *Haunting Cries: Stories of Child Abuse from Industrial Schools.* Dublin: Gill & Macmillan.

Commins, S. (2010). Survivors of abuse must be allowed to speak freely. *Irish Times,* 18 March.

Commission on Itinerancy. (1963). *Report of the Commission on Itinerancy.* Dublin: Stationery Office.

Commission to Inquire into Child Abuse. (2009). *Report of the Commission to Inquire into Child Abuse* (Vols. 1–5). Dublin: Stationery Office.

Commission to Inquire into Child Abuse (Amendment) Act. (2005). Available online: https://www.irishstatutebook.ie/eli/2005/act/17/enacted/en/pdf [Accessed April, 2019].

Congregation of Christian Brothers. (1927). *Directory and Rules of the Congregation of the Christian Schools of Ireland.* Dublin: Congregation of Christian Brothers.

Cronin, T. (2010). *And I Thought I Could Fly.* Leicester: Matador.

Cullen Owens, R. (2005). *A Social History of Women in Ireland 1870–1970.* Dublin: Gill & Macmillan.

Cussen, G.P. (1936). *Commission of Inquiry into the Reformatory and Industrial School System, 1934–1936.* Dublin: Stationery Office.

Daly, K. (2014). *Redressing Institutional Abuse of Children.* Basingstoke: Palgrave Macmillan.

Department of Education. (1936). *Report of the Department of Education 1935–36.* Dublin: Stationery Office.

Doyle, P. (1988). *The God Squad.* London: Corgi.

Dunne, T. (2002). Seven years in the brothers. *The Dublin Review,* 6: 16–30.

Dunne, T. (2010). *Rebellions: Memoir, Memory and 1798.* Dublin: Lilliput Press.

Earner-Byrne, L. (2013). *Mother and Child: Maternity and Child Welfare in Dublin, 1922–60.* Manchester, England: Manchester University Press.

Ellis, D. (2012). *The Boy at the Gate.* London: Transworld.

Fahy, B. (2005). *Freedom of Angles.* Dublin: O'Brien Press.

Feeley, M. (2014). *Learning Care Lessons: Literacy, Love, Care and Solidarity*. London: Tufnell Press.
Ferguson, H. (2004). *Protecting Children in Time: Child Abuse, Child Protection and the Consequences of Modernity*. Basingstoke: Palgrave Macmillan.
Ferguson, H. (2007). Abused and looked after children as 'moral dirt': Child abuse and institutional care in historical perspective. *Journal of Social Policy*, 36(1): 123–139.
Finn, M. (2011). *In My Own Words: Still Running*. Milton Park, OX: Marston Gate.
Flynn, M. (1983). *Nothing to Say*. Dublin: Ward River Press.
Flynn, M. (2003). *James X*. Dublin: Lilliput Press.
Freud, S. (1920). *Beyond the Pleasure Principle and Other Works*. London: Vintage.
Gavin Wolters, M. (2006). Counseling adult survivors of childhood institutional abuse: A phenomenological exploration of therapists' perceptions and experiences in Ireland. *Person-Centered & Experiential Psychotherapies*, 7(3): 185–199.
Gilligan, R. (2014). The 'public child' and the reluctant state? In M. Luddy & J.M. Smyth (eds.), *Children, Childhood and Irish Society: 1500 to the Present* (pp. 145–163). Dublin: Four Courts Press.
Gmelch, S. (1991). *Nan: The Life of an Irish Travelling Woman*. Long Grove, IL: Waveland Press.
Gray, P. (2007). *The Irish Famine: New Horizons*. London: Thames and Hudson.
Grzymala-Busse, A. (2015). *Nations under God: How Churches Use Moral Authority to Influence Policy*. Princeton, NJ: Princeton University Press.
Haase, T. (2015). *Socio-Economic Mapping of Place of Living of Survivors of Institutional Residential Care in Ireland*. Available online: http://www.caranua.ie/wp-content/uploads/2018/02/CARANUA_SOCIO_ECONOMIC_MAPPING_RPT_150902.pdf [Accessed April, 2019].
Hart, A., Lane, D. & Doherty, G. (2017). *Report of the Historical institutional Abuse Inquiry*. Available online: https://www.hiainquiry.org/historical-institutional-abuse-inquiry-report-chapters [Accessed April, 2019].
Hayden, J. (1999). *The Winner in Me: The Don Baker Story*. Dublin: Marina Books.
Helleiner, J. (2003). *Irish Travellers: Racism and the Politics of Culture*. Toronto, ON: University of Toronto Press.
Higgins, K. (1993). Surviving separation: Traveller children in substitute care. In H. Ferguson, R. Gilligan & R. Torode (eds.), *Surviving Childhood Adversity: Issues for Policy and Practice* (pp. 146–156). Dublin: Social Studies Press.
Hogan, S. (2008). *In Harm's Way: A Childhood Lost – A Life Reclaimed*. London: Arrow Books.
Holohan, C. (2011). *In Plain Sight: Responding to the Ferns, Ryan, Murphy and Cloyne Reports*. Dublin: Amnesty International Ireland.
Inglis, T. (1998). *Moral Monopoly: The Rise and Fall of the Catholic Church in Modern Ireland*. Dublin, Ireland: University College Dublin Press.
Irish Penal Reform Trust. (2014). *Travellers in the Irish Prison System: A Qualitative Study*. Available online: http://www.iprt.ie/contents/2624 [Accessed April, 2019].
Jackson, L.A. (2000). *Child Sexual Abuse in Victorian England*. London: Routledge.
Johnson, H. (2009). Oh brother, where have you been? *Manchester Evening News*, 14 August.
Joyce, S.H. (2004). *Suffer the Captive Children*. Trafford: Victoria.
Kearns, K.C. (2006). *Dublin Tenement Life: An Oral History of the Dublin Slums*. Dublin: Gill Books.
Kelly, J. (2012). *The Graves Are Walking: The History of the Great Irish Famine*. London: Faber and Faber.
Kennedy, E. (1970). *Reformatory and Industrial Schools Systems Report*. Dublin: Stationery Office.

Kenny, M. & McNeela, E. (2010). *Assimilation Policies and Outcomes: Travellers' Experience.* Dublin: Pavee Point.

Lifton, R.J. (2000). *The Nazi Doctors: Medical Killing and the Psychology of Genocide.* New York: Basic Books.

Lucey, S. (2014). County homes took harsh toll on 'unmarried mothers'. *Irish Times*, 18 June.

Luddy, M. & Smith, J.M. (eds.) (2014). *Children, Childhood and Irish Society, 1500 to the Present.* Dublin: Four Courts Press.

Luddy, M. (1995). *Women and Philanthropy in Nineteenth Century Ireland.* Cambridge, England: Cambridge University Press.

Luddy, M. (2007). *Prostitution and Irish Society 1800–1940.* Cambridge, England: Cambridge University Press.

Lynch, J.J. (2018). *Hell in Connaught: Surviving St. Joseph's industrial school, Letterfrack, Co. Galway.* PhD thesis, Trinity College Dublin.

Lynch, J.J. & Minton, S.J. (2016). Peer abuse and its contexts in industrial schools in Ireland. *Journal of Aggression, Conflict and Peace Research*, 8(2): 76–85.

Maguire, M.J. (2009). *Precarious Childhood in Post-Independence Ireland.* Manchester, England: Manchester University Press.

Maguire, M.J. & O'Cinnéide, S. (2005). 'A good beating never hurt anyone': The punishment and abuse of children in twentieth century Ireland. *Journal of Social History*, 38(3): 635–652.

Mahood, L. (1995). *Policing Gender, Class and Family: Britain, 1850–1940.* London: Routledge.

Mahood L. & Littlewood, B. (1994). The 'vicious girl' and the 'street-corner boy': Sexuality and the gendered delinquent in the Scottish child-saving movement, 1850–1948. *Journal of the History of Sexuality*, 4(4): 539–567.

McCullagh, D. (2018). *De Valera (Vol. II). Rule: 1932–1975.* Dublin: Gill Books.

McElwee, N.C., Jackson, A. & Charles, G. (2003). Towards a sociological understanding of Irish travellers: Introducing a people. *Irish Journal of Applied Social Studies*, 4(1): 103–119.

McGarry, P. (2019). Over two million documents from redress bodies to be sealed in National Archives. *Irish Times*, February 28th.

Miller, A. (1983). *For Your Own Good: Hidden Cruelty in Child-Rearing and the Roots of Violence.* New York: Farrar, Strauss & Giroux.

Miller, I. (2013). Constructing 'moral hospitals': Improving bodies and minds in Irish reformatories and industrial schools, 1851–1890. In A. MacLellan & A. Mauger (eds.), *Growing Pains: Childhood Illness in Ireland 1750–1950* (pp. 105–122). Dublin: Irish Academic Press.

Miller, K.A. (2013). Emigration to North America in the era of the great famine, 1845–1855. In J. Crowley, W.J. Smyth & M. Murphy (eds.), *Atlas of the Great Irish Famine* (pp. 214–227). Cork, Ireland: Cork University Press.

Milotte, M. (2012). *Banished Babies: The Secret History of Ireland's Baby Export Business.* Dublin: New Island.

Moffett, L., Shilliday, P., Gilmore, S., Millman, S., Clarke, A., Coulter, A., Slane, D., Bousquet, K., Hearty, H., Kileen, R., Hearty, K., McAlinden, A. & Dowds, E. (2019). *Response to Historical Institutional Abuse Consultation by Queen's University Belfast Human Rights Centre and School of Law.* Belfast: Queen's University Belfast.

Morgan, D.G. (2009). Society and the schools. In *Report of the Commission to Inquire into Child Abuse* (Vol. IV, Ch. 3, pp. 201–244). Dublin: Stationery Office.

O'Ciardha, C. & Ward, T. (2013). Theories of cognitive distortions in sexual offending: What the current research tells us. *Trauma, Violence, Abuse*, 14(1): 5–21.

O'Halloran, M. & O'Regan, M. (2017). Travellers formally recognised as an ethnic minority. *Irish Times*, 1 March.

O'Higgins, K. (1993). Surviving separation: Traveller children in substitute care. In H. Ferguson, R. Gilligan & R. Torode (eds.), *Surviving Childhood Adversity: Issues for Policy and Practice* (pp. 146–156). Dublin: Social Studies Press.

O'Riordan, M. & Arensman, E. (2007). *Institutional Child Sexual Abuse and Suicidal Behaviour: Outcomes of a Literature Review, Consultation Meetings and a Qualitative Study.* Cork: National Suicide Research Foundation.

O'Sullivan, E. & O'Donnell, I. (eds.). (2012). *Coercive Confinement in Ireland: Patients, Prisoners and Penitents.* Manchester, England: Manchester University Press.

O'Sullivan, D. (1976). *An Irish Industrial School Viewed as a Socialising Agent with Particular Reference to Its Social Organisation.* PhD thesis, NUI Galway.

O'Sullivan, D. (1979). Social definition in childcare in the Irish republic: Models of the child and childcare interventions. *Economic and Social Review*, 10(3): 209–229.

O'Sullivan, E. (2009). *Residential Child Welfare in Ireland, 1965–2008: An Outline of Policy, Legislation and Practice.* Paper prepared for the Commission to Inquire into Child Abuse. Available online: http://www.childabusecommission.ie/rpt/pdfs/CICA-VOL4-10.pdf [Accessed April, 2019].

O'Sullivan, E. & O'Donnell, I. (2007). Coercive confinement in the republic of Ireland: The waning of a culture of control. *Punishment and Society*, 9(1): 27–48.

O'Donoghue, T. (2012). *Catholic Teaching Brothers: Their Lives in the English-Speaking World, 1891–1965.* Basingstoke: Palgrave Macmillan.

Pembroke, S. (2013). The role of industrial schools and control over child welfare in Ireland in the twentieth century. *Irish Journal of Sociology*, 21(1): 52–67.

Pembroke, S. (2017). Exploring the post-release experience of former Irish industrial school 'inmates'. *Irish Studies Review*, 25(4): 454–471.

Penglase, J. (2005). *Orphans of the Living: Growing up in Care in Twentieth-Century Australia.* North Fremantle, WA: Fremantle Press.

Powell, F., Geoghogan, M., Scanlon, M. & Swirak, K. (2012). The Irish charity myth, child abuse and human rights: Contextualising the Ryan report into care institutions. *British Journal of Social Work*, 43: 7–23.

Raftery, M. & O'Sullivan, E. (1999). *Suffer the Little Children: The Inside Story of Ireland's Industrial Schools.* Dublin: New Island.

Raftery, D. & Parkes, S.M. (2007). *Female Education in Ireland 1700–1900: Minerva or Madonna.* Dublin: Irish Academic Press.

Reclaiming Self. (2017). *Ryan Report Follow-Up: Submission to the United Nations Committee Against Torture.* Available online: http://tbinternet.ohchr.org/Treaties/CAT/Shared%20Documents/IRL/INT_CAT_CSS_IRL_27959_E.pdf [Accessed April, 2019].

Reidy, C. (2009). *Ireland's 'Moral Hospital': The Irish Borstal System 1906-1956.* Dublin: Irish Academic Press.

Residential Institutions Redress Board (2005). A guide to the redress scheme under the Residential institutional redress Act 2002. Dublin: RIRB. Available online: https://www.rirb.ie/application.asp [Accessed April, 2019].

Sargent, P. (2014). *Wild Arabs and Savages: A History of Juvenile Justice in Ireland.* Manchester, England: Manchester University Press.

Sheffer, E. (2018). *Asperger's Children: The Origins of Autism in Nazi Vienna.* New York: W.W. Norton & Company.

Smart, C. (1979). A history of ambivalence and conflict in the discursive construction of the 'child victim' of sexual abuse. *Social & Legal Studies*, 8(3): 391–409.

Smith, J.M. (2007). *Ireland's Magdalen Laundries and the Nation's Architecture of Containment*. Manchester, England: Manchester University Press.

Smyth, W.J. (2013). The creation of the workhouse system. In J. Crowley, W.J. Smyth & M. Murphy (eds.), *Atlas of the Great Irish Famine* (pp. 120–127). Cork, Ireland: Cork University Press.

Tangney, J.P. & Dearing, R.L. (2002). *Shame and Guilt*. New York: The Guilford Press.

Tobin, M. (2015). Literacy in the Irish reformatory school. *Irish Probation Journal*, 12: 179–204.

Touher, P. (2001). *Fear of the Collar: My Terrifying Childhood in Artane*. Dublin: O'Brien Press.

Touher, P. (2008), *Scars that Run Deep: Sometimes the Nightmares Don't End*. Dublin: O'Brien Press.

Tuairim. (1966). *Some of our Children: A Report on the Residential Care of the Deprived Child in Ireland*. Dublin: Irish Printers.

Tyrrell. (2006). *Founded on Fear: Letterfrack Industrial School, War and Exile*. Dublin: Irish Academic Press.

United Nations Committee Against Torture. (2017). *Concluding Observations on the Second Periodic Report of Ireland*. Available online: https://tbinternet.ohchr.org/Treaties/CAT/Shared%20Documents/IRL/INT_CAT_COC_IRL_28491_E.pdf [Accessed April, 2019].

Van der Kolk, B.A. (1989). The compulsion to repeat the trauma: Re-enactment, revictimization, and masochism. *Psychiatric Clinics of North America*, 12(2): 389–411.

Von Kellenbach, K. (2013). *The Mark of Cain: Guilt and Denial in the Post-War Lives of Nazi Perpetrators*. Oxford, England: Oxford University Press.

Wachsmann, N. (2015). *KL: A History of the Nazi Concentration Camps*. London: Little, Brown.

Walker, M.R. (2008). *Suicide among the Irish Traveller Community 2000–2006*. Wicklow: Wicklow County Council. Available online: https://www.hse.ie/eng/services/list/4/mental-health-services/nosp/research/suicidetravellercommunity.pdf [Accessed April, 2019].

Wall, T. (2013). *The Boy from Glin Industrial School*. Self-published.

Ward, T. (2000). Sexual offenders' cognitive distortions as implicit theories. *Aggression and Violent Behaviour*, 5(5): 491–507.

Watson, D., Kenny, O. & McGinnity, F. (2017). *A Social Portrait of Travellers in Ireland*. Dublin: Economic & Social Research Institute. Available online: http://www.esri.ie/pubs/RS56.pdf [Accessed April, 2019].

Chapter 9

Reflections

*Julie Vane, Stephen James Minton,
Tania Ka'ai, Rosemary Norman-Hill,
and Natahnee Nuay Winder*

A reflection by Julie Vane and Stephen James Minton

(Finding a) starting point

The contributing authors who have shared their histories and experiences in this book have told powerful stories of the abuses experienced by individuals, communities, and societies over generations. We have been struck by the dignity with which unspeakable abuses have been recounted, and also, by how the descriptions of attempts at 'reconciliation', and the carving out of spaces for existences to be expressed, have so often been crushed, ignored, or inadequately responded to by the relatively powerful Western/settler/dominant populations. This section represents our reflection on this sharing. It is, therefore, a response made by two relatively naïve Westerners, who are trying to learn by drawing on principles that our all-too-limited experience suggests to us might be common amongst Indigenous people – that is to say, the attempt to develop mutual understandings and solutions through respectful dialogue. We have reflected on alignment in common humanity, and the role of ally as an aspirational position, and wondered about how that might be practised. In our process, we noticed that the learning that has been opened up in the editing and compilation of this book as a whole has often arisen out of things that initially appeared as challenges. Some of the factors that appeared as such were

- lack of common language;
- our lack of knowledge and experience of the various Indigenous cultural reference points and world views; and
- our intention, or aspiration, to transcend different ontologies and epistemologies represented in differing mediums, including our attempts to negotiate differences between and within cultures and peoples, for example (i) those who have tended to emphasise the verbal, and those who have tended to emphasise the visual; and (ii) traditions of written histories (i.e. Western/settler peoples), and oral narratives (i.e. many Indigenous peoples).

We have also been struck by the relative time frames in which Western and Indigenous knowledge bases can be said to have been accumulated, and ways of being can be said to have been developed. To give an example of this difference, in his book *A History of Western Philosophy*, Bertrand Russell attempted to connect Western philosophical ideas to (as the book's full title suggests) 'political and social circumstances from the earliest times to the present day' (Russell, 1946). So just how early are these 'earliest' times? Well, Russell begins his consideration with the pre-Socratics, and first of all with Thales of Miletus, who was born in either 624 BCE or 623 BCE, and died somewhere between 548 BCE and 545 BCE – so in other words, a little over 2,500 years. In Chapter 4 of this book, Rosemary Norman-Hill, speaking of the European settlement of Australia, commented that 'In an Aboriginal understanding of time, 230 years is but a mere moment.' How true this is, especially when one considers that Indigenous peoples have a history in what is now Australia that reliably dates back 49,000 years (see Marcus, 2016). The origin of the native peoples in what are now the Americas has been dated to anywhere between 16,500 and 40,000 years ago (see Pauketat, 2012); as might be expected, this is a matter of continuing, and often politically motivated, debate. Yet the reality is that, whilst being by all reasonable estimations by far the junior, it is Western culture that has become, in a 'mere moment', politically and economically dominant in European and post-colonial settler states. Furthermore, when Westerners talk about the 'global culture', it is to specific manifestations of their own culture that they refer. But as the naïve Westerners we are, we have been inspired and exhilarated by the experience and the possibilities that opened up when we have dipped our toes into the oceans of Indigenous knowledge and experience that were previously unfamiliar to us, as well as by those more familiar streams that also drew us to what we hope are useful parallels.

In his famous book, *Lame Deer, Seeker of Visions*, John Lame Deer (1972) made regular reference to his attempts to negotiate his development as a *wičaša wakan*, a traditional medicine man for his (Lakota) people, with the seemingly all-consuming settler world in which he found himself living. With his characteristic humour – which is, as Western readers come to know through reading the book, a humour in which profound and often sacred truths are positioned – Lame Deer referred to the settler way of being and living as the 'green frog skin world':

> The green frog skin – that's what I call a dollar bill. In our attitude toward it lies the biggest difference between Indians and whites. My grandparents grew up in an Indian world without money. Just before the Custer battle[1] the white soldiers had received their pay. Their pockets were full of green paper and they had no place to spend it. What were their last thoughts as an Indian bullet or arrow hit them? I guess they were thinking of all that money going to waste, of not having had a

chance to enjoy it, of a bunch of dumb savages getting their paws on that hard-earned pay. That must have hurt them more than the arrow between their ribs. (p. 35)

Memorably, Lame Deer went on to illustrate the colossal arrogance in the assumption of their cultural superiority (over those they described as 'savages') held by settlers, in recounting one way in which he dealt with just some of its manifestations:

> The anthropologists are always saying that there's too much of the old buffalo hunter in us [Lakota people]. Share your food, share your goods, or the tribe will perish. That was good for yesterday. Today, it's saying, 'No, no, no' to a poor cousin. That's the practical thing to do. Trying to remake people in one's own image is a white man's disease. I can't cure that. I tell these anthros, 'You have green frog skins on your brains. If we Indians were such filthy savages, we should have eaten you up when you first came to this turtle continent.[2] Then I could have some peace and quiet now'. That shuts them up for a while.[3] (p. 41)

So in coming into largely Indigenous space, we have been, and still are, anxious in and about our attempts to finding our starting position. And in containing our anxieties about our abilities to do justice in this work, it has been personally comforting for us to keep in mind that the generosity of the principle that a 'step forwards' is helpful. We have tried to take care; we have tried (especially here) to speak honestly for ourselves, and from our hearts; and we have had no greater expectation of the contributing authors to do any more than that. The contributing authors were asked to summarise much historical information (see Chapter 1, the section 'The structure of this book'), and the ways in which they have done so are beautifully divergent. Expectations of representativeness are, therefore, held lightly in this response. The truths shared in each story are, of course, accepted, though we have done our best to ensure that none of the stories has been made subject to the weight of expectation of telling of the totality of experiences of populations over hundreds of years.

Therefore, with humility, curiosity, and respect, we have offered our reflection on the preceding chapters. We have concentrated on our identification of commonalities and differences of experiences shared about what our ancestors and powerful others said and did through residential schooling. As well, we reflect on some ongoing practices that maintain the power imbalances that made residential schooling possible in the first place. We have highlighted issues that struck us as needing to be better attended to by Westerners/dominant populations now, when we share thoughts about what we hope future Western contributions to processes of truth, restitution, and reconciliation might look like. We have suggested some actions to promote more meaningful responses to peoples who have been exploited and abused through residential schooling programmes' systems, in order that as a human community (rather than, say, as a neoliberal global economy) we never again permit the exercise of power in such abusive and destructive ways.

The most fundamental challenge of all in our attempts to negotiate the types of challenges we have outlined in this chapter has been our own limited, and limiting, position as Westerners. The positivist and scientific traditions to which we, as Westerners, are heirs to, encourage people to think (or are, perhaps, merely the latest outcomes of Westerners thinking) along the lines of the world/the universe/the cosmos containing 'universal truths', which apply to everything (including sentient beings) therein. According to these mindsets, therefore, it follows that if only we can correctly frame our enquiries, these 'universal truths' are 'ours' to uncover. But as Shawn Wilson has written (2008):

> The notion that empirical evidence is sounder than cultural knowledge permeates western thought but alienates many Indigenous scholars. Rather than their cultural knowledge being seen as extra intellectual, it is denigrated. It is the notion of the superiority of empirical knowledge that leads to the idea that the written text supersedes oral tradition. For Indigenous scholars, empirical knowledge is still crucial, yet it is not their only way of knowing the world around them. (p. 58)

As individuals, and especially with respect to some of the more fundamental questions raised in and by the contributing authors of this book, we two authors reject, and will continue to reject, the narrow pseudo-objectivist mindsets that privilege empirical knowledge, not least of all because of the power-abusive situations that have emerged from the social realisation of such mindsets, and the apparent blindness to, and obviation of, these same power-abusive situations that such mindsets have simultaneously permitted, and indeed continue to permit. Nevertheless, we are not Indigenous scholars, but Westerners; and in writing this section, we have been acutely aware of the words of Anaïs Nin[4] (1961), 'We do not see things as they are, we see them as we are'. Whatever our efforts as individuals may have been towards the widening of our experiences and understandings, the fact remains that this widening has been necessarily effortful; and it is precisely because we are who we are that we will have inevitably missed much of importance. And try as we might, we will equally inevitably miss much – although hopefully less – in the future. It seems (as it is) inadequate, and we offer our sincere regret for the outcomes of these realities. We are, therefore, delighted that three of the Indigenous contributing authors (Tania Ka'ai, Rosemary Norman-Hill, and Natahnee Nuay Winder [the authors of Chapters 3, 4, and 7, respectively]) will also offer their reflections, in the second and final section of this chapter. We think of this as a re-reflection – we have elicited feedback from these authors, including their indications as to how useful (or otherwise) they feel our reflection has been, and are grateful for them having agreed to do so. We also hope that this interaction, particularly as part of the overall collaboration between contributing authors in this multi-authored work, will serve as a stem of further, deeper, and wider conversations to come.

Residential schooling of 'Others': Who is the 'Other'?

One of the fundamental premises outlined in the Chapter 2 of this book (see sections 'Indigenous as "Other"' and 'Educational systems as agents of (cultural) genocide') is that the introduction and implementation of residential schooling systems is a reliable indicator of the practice of (cultural) genocide, and can be understood as an outcome of the extremities of 'Othering' perpetrated by settler/dominant populations. The accounts offered in Chapters 3–8 of this book have highlighted residential schooling as a feature of the experiences of people and cultures viewed as so different, and so much less, that their very survival was made contingent on their adherence to dominant values and the obliteration though education of any traditional/other identity and heritage. Critically, as Jeremiah J. Lynch's contribution ('Punishing Poverty – The Curious Case of Ireland's Institutionalised Children') so clearly demonstrates, one did not need to have been an Indigenous child to have been 'Othered' by powerful agents in a post-colonial society, and to have been (quite legally, under the laws of the day) separated from one's family and community, and to have experienced the indignities, neglect and abuses of residential schooling. During the same time period as Indigenous children were enduring similar horrors, in Ireland, one only needed to have been poor, and perceived or labelled as being a risk to established norms of law and order.

As we have seen, education through residential schooling served to limit the expectations and possibilities of its students/internees for their future positions within the Western/dominant cultures they were mandated to be part of. Time and again, we have seen that the people who were schooled in this way were not being educated to take a full part in society, but rather were being groomed for positions that would continue to hold them as lesser and in service to the dominant population.[5] Being identified by powerful others as 'non-productive'; of having ways of life and being that transcended the borders imposed by settlers who arrived generations, or millennia, after one's people had taken up their positions as the guardians of their lands; and of not identifying with staying in particular places because of a nomadic, or travelling heritage – these were all used as 'justifications', not only to act against individuals, but against whole cultures or societies. The unfortunate conclusion has to be drawn that any population or group which is identified as having interests that do not align with, or can be seen to challenge or act in opposition to, dominant cultural expectations is at risk of their annihilation through physical and/or cultural genocide. That being said, the fact that so many pervasive similarities exist in accounts of the practice of residential schooling in Indigenous people's experiences supports the conclusion that, in the face of Western 'progress' and 'civilisation', older cultures have been particularly and consistently vulnerable throughout the world.

Even within Western societies, we are still battling to redress some of the imbalances that modernist philosophy has introduced, strengthened, and continues to support. One of the key ways in which this world view is manifested is in the normative idea of the white, educated, heterosexual man as representing the rational position. Whilst Western women are assured that all is somehow well, demonstrable inequalities in pay, social roles and demands, and manifestations of abuse, continue to exist. A need highlighted in second-wave feminism was that of the recognition of different challenges existing for women in different circumstances, as well as the more general ideas of equality and recognising the commonalties of disadvantage, and the need for solidarity within and amongst societies. In parallel to this, it is of course possible to similarly position the struggle for Indigenous rights – as well as women's rights, LGBTQ+ rights, disability rights, civil (black) rights – within the more general context of human rights.[6] Because either we all have human rights, or none of us do. As human beings, with rights, and who would and should afford those self-same rights to others, we would do well to recall the well-known words of the German Lutheran pastor, Martin Niemöller, whose poem protested the inactions of his countrymen during the Nazi period (which exist in many forms, but are reproduced here from Gerlach, 2000):

> First they came for the socialists, and I did not speak out – because I was not a socialist.
> Then they came for the trade unionists, and I did not speak out – because I was not a trade unionist.
> Then they came for the Jews, and I did not speak out – because I was not a Jew.
> Then they came for me – and there was no one left to speak for me.
> (p. 47)

The particular problems of residential schools (as total institutions)

Time and again in Chapters 3–8, we have seen examples of what made the realisation of residential schools systems possible being the collaboration of Church and nation state. As was argued in Chapter 2 (the section 'Indigenous as "Other"'), when it came to the 'legitimisation' of colonisation and genocide perpetrated by Europeans against Indigenous peoples, Western 'scientific' and 'religious' value-systems were, for once, in agreement; and, as was stated in Chapter 1 (the section 'The scope of this book'), schools were generally run by Christian religious orders on behalf of, but with relative independence from, the governments of post-colonial nations. It is also noticeable that somewhat mixed discourses existed as certain trends in Western 'scientific' thinking competed for dominance in the fields of pedagogy and social philosophy. Whilst the Western 'scientific' views of culture being somehow in the 'blood' (what we might call 'biological determinism'), and of culture being formed through (especially early) experience (what we might call 'social constructionism') appear oppositional, and indeed, seem mutually exclusive, both of them informed the policy and practice of the residential schooling of Indigenous children. Whilst settler populations might have argued over these competing philosophies (the former predicting the extermination of, or physical separation from the savage, and the latter predicting educating the savage out of the child in order to 'save' her or him), or may possibly have reached some sort of unlikely intellectual accommodation that eludes us, the practices across country contexts appear to have been remarkably similar. As David W. Adams' reflects in the memorable title of his classic work, Indigenous children in residential schools experienced 'education for extinction'.

It has already been highlighted in this book, and in many other texts, that in the context of physical genocide and the forcible removal of lands, the practices surrounding residential schooling, being more covert, can appear – or, critically, can be made to appear – as somehow less damaging (see, e.g. Adams, 1995; Chrisjohn, Young & Maraun, 2006; Minton, 2016). However, it is significant that time and again across the various country contexts, residential schooling permitted – yes, an insidious, but also, a continual operation in fragmenting of families, 'legitimising' the direct abuse and neglect of children, and destroying language, histories, and cultures. In many contexts, we have seen that a distinct preference on the part of settler/dominant populations for residential schooling, rather than day schooling, emerged; it is hard to interpret this as anything other (and indeed, in some cases, the underlying policies were explicit to this effect) than deliberately increasing the geographical (and thereby, social and cultural) distance between the Indigenous child at school, and her or his parents and home community: in other words, separating the child from any and every aspect of life that was not informed by Western/dominant ideologies and practices.

Reflecting on her own experiences of beginning residential schooling, Lakota activist Mary Crow Dog stated that 'So the great brainwashing began, those who did not like to have their brains washed being pushed farther into the back country unto isolation and starvation' (Crow Dog & Erdoes, 1990, p. 14). In Chapters 3–7, we have seen that a common feature of the residential schooling of Indigenous children, and key component of this brainwashing, was the obliteration of native languages. The very essence of language, in the existence of Indigenous identities and cultures, was continually challenged, and we have seen that English (or in the case of Greenland, Danish, and in the case of Norway, Norwegian) was privileged above, and as more important/ better than the child's native Indigenous tongue. Of course, if one only wishes, as the settler populations invariably did, to judge and measure success purely in Western terms, then this was true; but this very assumption implied and implies that there is no or, at the most, only very limited value in knowledges, understandings, cultures, and identities represented through native languages. This privileging of English was, for example evident in Tania Ka'ai's account of the provisions made under the Revised Native Schools Code of 1897, which allowed for the Māori language to be spoken in junior classes for the express purpose of teaching English, and posited that the use of the Māori language should soon cease, and that English should become the sole language used in the classroom. To us, this seems to have been an overt expression of the debasement of a native language, in English forcibly replacing a native language as something juvenile, lesser, and something you can and should want to grow out of and beyond.

We have also seen that an effect of this privileging of the settler tongue was the disruption of communication within the family of origin. In Chapter 5 (the section 'The experiment'), we have documented the upset of that chapter's co-author, Helene Thiesen, on returning to Greenland after a year-and-a-half in Denmark (to where she had been removed at seven years old) to find that she and her mother no longer spoke the same language. Charla Bear (2008) reported on the experiences of the Bill Wright, a Pattwin man, who was sent to the Stewart Indian School in Nevada at the age of six years, and wrote that

> Students at federal boarding schools were forbidden to express their culture – everything from wearing long hair to speaking even a single Indian word. Wright said that he lost not only his language, but also his American Indian name. 'I remember coming home and my grandma asked me to talk Indian to her and I said, "Grandma, I don't understand you". She said, "Then who are you?"' Wright says he hold her his name was Billy. 'Your name's not Billy. Your name's TAH-rruhm', she told him. 'And I went, "That's not what they told me". (p. 3)

We have also seen that the settlers' devaluation of native languages were often internalised by the Indigenous children – and indeed, this shame was deliberately inculcated by the settler teachers. This corresponds in large part to what Jens-Ivar Nergård (the author of Chapter 6) has identified as 'internal colonisation'. As generations of Indigenous children were enrolled in residential schools, a reticence to share one's language and culture with future generations often (as it was no doubt intended to) emerged. Mary Crow Dog also related the following (Crow Dog & Erdoes, 1990):

> Many times I asked my grandmother, 'Why don't you teach me the language?' [Lakota]. Her answer was always, 'Cause I want you to get an

education, to lead a good life. Not to have a hard time ... you need a white man's education to live in this world. Speaking Indian would only hold you back, turn you the wrong way'. (p. 22)

One of the more distressing aspects in reading this book will undoubtedly be the documentation, which is consistent across all the country contexts that have been featured, of the pernicious and ubiquitous accounts of abuse and neglect perpetrated on children. To state that such sufferings were at complete odds with the protestations of the supposedly benign, beneficent, humanitarian, philanthropic, and religious motivations of the educators at these institutions is simply a statement of the obvious. Similarly sickening is that, even in the context of usually only subsequent (and even then, only partial) recognition of these abuses and deprivations, Westerners continued to maintain that what they were offering, or had offered, was somehow 'better' than what these native children's families and communities could and would have offered. Arguably, this is intellectually understandable as a psychologically defensive position, which was necessary on the part of settlers/dominant populations in order for them to continue to 'justify' their underlying belief that Indigenous, or otherwise 'Othered' peoples were, and remain, 'less than' dominant peoples. But this psychological positioning raises the possibility that the deep deception made by settler communities was not only perpetrated on Indigenous peoples (or, in the case of Ireland, made by religious elites, and perpetrated on the ungodly criminal poor), but also on themselves. Furthermore, it suggests that these deceptions would continue to be perpetrated down the generations, thus permitting direct Indigenous experience to be mystified, disavowed, and eventually confined to a perhaps unfortunate, but certainly long-forgotten (at least, by anyone who counts) aspect of history. As R.D. Laing (1967) said:

> It is not enough to destroy one's own and other people's experience. One must overlay this devastation by a false consciousness inured to its own falsity. Exploitation must not be seen as such. It must be seen as benevolence. Persecution preferably should not need to be invalidated as the figment of a paranoid imagination,[7] it should be experienced as kindness. The colonists not only mystify the natives, they have to mystify themselves. We in Europe and North America are the colonists, and in order to sustain our amazing images of ourselves as God's gift to the vast majority of the starving human species, we have to interiorise our violence upon ourselves and our children and to employ the rhetoric of morality to describe this process. In order to rationalise our industrial-military complex, we have to destroy our capacity to see clearly any more what is in front of, and to imagine what is beyond, our noses. Long before a thermonuclear war can come about, we have to lay waste to our own sanity. We begin with the children. It is imperative to catch them in time. Without the most

> thorough and rapid brain-washing their dirty minds would see through their dirty tricks. Children are not yet fools, but we shall turn them into imbeciles like ourselves, with high IQs if possible. (p. 49)

As a function of this self- and Other-deception, we have seen that residential schooling systems were indeed presented as benevolent and compassionate. As Mary Crow Dog wrote (Crow Dog & Erdoes, 1990):

> Oddly enough, we owed our unspeakable boarding schools to the do-gooders, the white Indian-lovers. The schools were intended as an alternative to the outright extermination seriously advocated by Generals Sherman and Sheridan, as well as by most settlers and prospectors over-running our land …. Just give us a chance to turn them into useful farmhands, labourers, and chambermaids who will break their backs for you at low wages. (p. 30)

Rosemary Norman-Hill has documented (see Chapter 3, the section 'The establishment of the residential schools system in Australia') that the fact that Indigenous Australian children could and did perform very well, and sometimes exceptionally well, within the education systems set up for them by settlers was merely greeted with surprise; unfortunately, this fact did not serve in any meaningful way to prompt the colonisers to question their definitions of Indigenous people as ignorant, savage, uncivilised; still less that Indigenous people they did things differently (and not worse), and appropriately within their own cultural contexts. Significantly, Charles Eastman (otherwise, Hakadah [at birth], and later named Ohíye S'a), a Santee Dakota physician (he graduated from medical school at Boston College, and was one of the first Indigenous people in North America to attain an MD) highlighted that the credit for achievements by Indigenous people were often claimed by settlers as their attainment, and the product of their 'good' systems and 'generosity' to the natives, in ways that obviated the effort, skill, character, perseverance, and forbearance of the Indigenous achiever (see Eastman, 1911/2018).

The experience of internment in a total institution is one of isolation – whilst it is true that one may be housed with others who share one's current experience, what is shared is a 'not-knowing', and an increasing institutional pressures towards 'non-being' – made manifest in the cutting off from one's pre-institutional identity and relationships, and the process of being disempowered. The possibilities for solidarity to develop and flourish are, thereby, limited,[8] and this is made deliberately so. Through all of these things, the practice of the residential schooling of Indigenous children – the total institutionalisation of the juvenile 'Other' – constituted an act of ontological and epistemological genocide. There was no curiosity about, or engagement with, what the 'Other'-ed knows or new, rendering moot any possible ontological discussion about what was useful, or even right or wrong, in a particular place. In the case of Indigenous societies, perhaps more undermining still was the epistemocide resulting from the deliberate attempts to disconnect children from anyone who knew, or had any means of knowing, truths and ways not privileged by Westerners. Implied in this is not only that nothing useful was known, but no useful ways of being or finding things out were, either. This is a curious, not to mention an appalling and unfoundedly arrogant, stance to take towards peoples who have found ways to survive and thrive in circumstances, and over periods of time which Westerners may struggle to fathom.

Where are we missing one another? Learning about ourselves, from one another, and developing shared understandings

We hold that it is essential to acknowledge the differences in the ways that different people live, and in the circumstances that they find themselves, before one can find ways of overcoming the tendency to be limited by our own views, perspectives, and experiences. Having acknowledged such differences in ways and circumstances, we can, perhaps, continue this process by looking, as honestly and accurately as our adult eyes permit, at ourselves in our formative years. Julie recollects that

> I grew up in a working/lower middle-class home, where no one had previously considered themselves to be an academic. I had the good fortune to have some aptitude for tests, and a mother interested to support me with practice papers. As a consequence, I passed an exam at the age of eleven or twelve which took me to a selective grammar school. I felt out of place and overwhelmed when finding myself in classrooms with many relatively privileged other young women; I felt not encouraged, but unworthy. I struggled at times to recognise the immense opportunities I was being offered, and failed to see purpose in studying some subjects; I could not imagine taking foreign holidays, or working abroad, so why would I need to learn other languages? With adult eyes, I can now see that these responses were unfortunate, childish, and naive; I have since learned that much of what I was taught then (however reluctantly I engaged with it) was rich and valuable in ways I could never have conceived or imagined. In preparing this chapter, I have noticed a parallel between my experiences, and those of Western cultural knowledge, expectations, and behaviour. As Westerners our cultures are, in relation to Indigenous cultures, young, keen to privilege their own interests, and to dismiss what does not immediately meet them. Throughout the accounts in this book are sub-textual stories of Westerners demonstrating a woeful lack of curiosity about, and valuing of, other ways of doing things demonstrated by older, and arguably wiser, cultures; or, in the

case of those spoken about by Jeremiah (Chapter 8), those finding ways to survive in without sufficient resources in communities, and being harshly judged for how they managed this. Perhaps this is because Western cultures are unable – as I was – to imagine the richness and possibilities in things they have no ready frameworks to understand. Whilst this was (I hope) forgivable in an adolescent girl, Western decision makers in governments and businesses need to hold themselves, and to be held by others, to a higher standard.

And Stephen recollects a specific memory, and his reactions to it then and now:

As a child in the late 1970s and the early 1980s, I attended my local (Anglican) primary school in the small English village where I grew up. Each morning would begin with a school assembly, which involved (usually, along with an unwelcome address from the generally despised headmaster, and sometimes, a much more welcome address from the generally loved and respected deputy headmaster) seemingly endless prayers and hymns. In making my own contributions to this book, and for a variety of reasons that are probably by now quite apparent, the words of one of those long-forgotten hymns came back to me, at least in part. The first line of the hymn, 'Over the sea there are little brown children', will provide direction enough for those who wish to consult its full text (see National Society, 2010); suffice it to say, the lyrics outline an apparent longing on the part of the frightened and ignorant 'little brown children' for those who will teach them the word of the Christian God, and the duty of Christians to meet that 'requirement'. The hymn was written by one Hetty Lee Holland in the 1930s; but clearly, it was still thought to be a fitting song for English primary school children to sing almost half a century later. The only concern that I can recall experiencing at the time, as the child that I then was, centred on how the single non-white child in the school might feel about his schoolmates and teachers singing about 'little brown children'. These days, of course, I have a host of other concerns, not least about what lay behind this attempt to instil – well, what? Christian missionary zeal? European supremacy? A post hoc justification for British Imperialism? Our responsibility to take on the 'white man's burden'? The list goes on and on – in yet another generation of children in English schools. And recalling Laing's (1967) words above – was this just one example of the 'rapid brainwashing' designed to turn children into imbeciles with high IQs? And if so, to what extent was this attempt successful? But like it or not (and I most certainly do not), this was part of my primary/elementary educational experience. In retrospect, I can see that the continued use of this hymn (and others like it) in the 1970s and 1980s indicates that the many of the messages and assumptions that made possible the abuses associated with the residential schooling of Indigenous children were still considered appropriate to be offered as received wisdom to Western children at formative stages of development.

As Westerners, we need to more protective of, and insistent upon, respecting shared humanity; we must be vigilant, speak up, and act, so as not to continue the repetition, denial, or excusing of the crimes of the past. One important way in which this could be done is through education; it is essential that honest accounts of colonial histories are taught in Western schools. (Despite the multiple abuses and atrocities of the British Imperial period, this did not happen when we were at school in the Britain of the 1970s and 1980s; and, to our certain knowledge, it still does not). Such education absolutely must involve being taught about the experiences of Indigenous peoples. Having acknowledged the importance of language in identity (for the individual, the community or a society), we hold that it is also critical that we attend to issues of translation. There has to be ongoing attention to how Westerners, and those empowered in (especially post-colonial) societies, can ensure that they can understand and respond to the other. The invite, for English speakers, is to rely on the dominance of that tongue, and this fosters a laziness and a limitation on what we can hear, and thereby come to know. So, when calling for efforts towards common understanding, we are in no way advocating that a *lingua franca* is the way forwards.

In her clinical role, Julie works with a group of people who can correctly be seen, both historically and in contemporary situations, to have been 'Othered' – those with learning disabilities. For a long while now, she valued the work of Phoebe Caldwell, who uses intensive interaction[9] as a foundation for relationship formation with people with profound and multiple learning disabilities (PMLD) and autism, who are unable to use standardised language, or other forms of communication such as signing. As people with learning disabilities and autism are also highly disadvantaged and marginalised in many if not all societies, there would appear to be useful lessons in the experiences of negotiating power and communication between them and others. Speaking about the dynamic between carers and people with learning disabilities and/or autism, Caldwell (1998) noted that

> One problem is that we frame our approaches to others based on our own realities and not with respect to how the other person senses and perceives their world …. Too often we try to teach the other person our language and concepts and then communicate with them in this language. We do this because we fear that [their] language may not contain the sophisticated concepts we need in the communication. (p. 40)

The importance of the people with the greater resources and positions of power taking the initiative, and responding proactively to the efforts of others to communicate, highlighted by this example, is essential, and we believe that this principle has a potential usefulness in work conducted between populations. Be it the use of media like gesture, touch, and sounds in communication with people with PMLD and autism, or engaging with other populations through the learning of their languages, and valuing their ways of knowing, life is richer when we get to know one another in ways, and on terms that make sense to, and are respectful of, the needs of both parties. If we fail to attend to the fact that things can be understood, known, and communicated in ways other than those we routinely use, we will continue to fall into the trap of using Western knowledge bases and languages to privilege dominant cultures.

Being able to learn from one another and work meaningfully together necessitates being able to hold realistic understandings of ourselves and others. Arguably, one result of Westerners' failure to do this, and their adherence to positivist, binary and oppositional stances with respect to knowledge, is a tendency to sometimes identify others as wholly 'good' or, more often, 'Others' as wholly 'bad'. Jeremiah J. Lynch's contribution (Chapter 8) highlighted the fact that in the poor finding ways to negotiate a world in which they do not have enough, there is a tendency for them to be blamed for the outcomes of their disadvantage. In many Westerners' attitudes towards Indigenous people, there have been similar polarising tendencies; interestingly, however, this would appear (in some Western circles, and with respect to some [usually dead] Indigenous populations, at least) to have undergone something like a reversal. For many years, the Indigenous person of what is now the United States was depicted, both in Hollywood and in what might generously called 'literature', as the 'dark menace' of the frontier myth. More recently, however, as Stephen said in his last book (see Minton, 2016, emphasis ours):

> ... the environmentalist, pacifist and even secular sage-like aspects of high profile Indigenous people are emblazoned on T-shirts, posters, coasters – practically anything one can print an image on – and a seemingly endless set of images and other depictions .... Sitting Bull, who was once seen by United States officials as too dangerous to leave at liberty across the border in Canada, or even in peaceful surrender on the Standing Rock reservation, is now perhaps the most prominent amongst Indigenous people 'celebrated' in this way. For example, of the thirty-five quotes attributed to Sitting Bull at the popular website 'Brainy Quote' on 6th January, 2016, thirty-four were of the ecological or pacifist (e.g. 'Let us put our minds together and see what life we can make for our children') types, with the sole exception being, 'I wish it to be remembered that I was the last man of my tribe to surrender my rifle' .... His statement [at the time of the Battle of the Little Bighorn] – 'We want no white men here. The Black Hills belong to me. If the whites try to take them, I will fight' – was recorded, but

is absent .... Nineteenth century Indigenous people were neither the mindless, bloodthirsty savages of innumerable Westerns of the early twentieth century, nor the embodiment of some sort of latter-day hippy/New Age ideal of the past three decades ... *like every human being before and since, individual nineteenth century Indigenous people were complex, fully-formed personalities, embodied souls existing and acting within their social and historical contexts.* (pp. 117–118)

Truth, reconciliation, restitution, and reclamation

Throughout the preceding chapters, stories have been told of how much has been lost, and of the limitations that have been placed on peoples' hopes and expectations for recognition, or reparation. The magnitude of loss has been so huge as to sometimes seem unspeakable – at least, within the context of an academic work. It is possible to imagine that for some people, and as hard as others have worked to preserve their cultures, the sheer effort involved in dealing with the harsh realities of the present could mean that histories do not have much resonance now – even if those histories are, in no small part, determinative of those present realities. To engage with the past might seem an equivalent gesture to trying to save as much as you can whilst your house is burning down. Some of the many hopes expressed in this book's 'Preface' centred around the book being read by Indigenous peoples; that they would experience it as having been written for, with and by them; and that they might take an interest in, and perhaps even drawn strength from, reading about certain commonalities in experience. However, with a view towards processes of truth, restitution, reconciliation, and reclamation, unless this book is similarly read and understood by, and provokes responses from, members of Western populations, it is eminently possible that the book's impact might be limited to preaching to the converted. Whilst it is both impossible and undesirable to generalise about Indigenous peoples, we feel it likely that they are, by and large, less likely to need convincing of the desirability of Indigenous truth, restitution, reconciliation, and reclamation than are Westerners. Indeed, in Chapter 5, we saw an illustration of this very disparity, in a statement made by the then-Danish Prime Minister, Helle Thorning-Schmidt, in 2013, in response to the proposed Reconciliation Commission in Denmark's former colony:

> We do not need reconciliation, but I fully respect that it is a discussion that occupies the Greenlandic people. We will follow the discussion carefully from here.

As we saw in Chapter 5 (the section 'Efforts towards processes of truth, restitution, reconciliation, and reclamation'), the distance from which Thorning-Schmidt and her successors 'followed' the discussion is hard to determine, but it was almost certainly not proximal; what was a definite finding was the recording in the final report of the Reconciliation Commission in Greenland that *Danmark ikke med* ('Denmark [is/was] not with [us]'). And yet despite such disappointments, and whilst different possibilities might exist regarding reclamation, in the effecting of meaningful processes of truth, restitution, and reconciliation (as we have seen, the work that was possible for the Reconciliation Commission in Greenland to engage with, and the ambitions for that process, was very much reduced), Indigenous peoples have no choice but to continue to try to work with settlers. To cite similar examples from this book, we have also seen the work, and reactions to that work, of the Truth and Reconciliation Commission of Canada (see Chapters 1 and 2); *Te Tiriti o Waitangi* (the Treaty of Waitangi) in Aotearoa/New Zealand, which was seen by the Māori people as a solemn agreement on which a national planning system inclusive of both Māori and Pākehā values could be based, although the mistranslation and misinterpretation of *Te Tiriti* has permitted the dominance of the latter values (see Chapter 3); apologies on behalf of the State in Australia (see Chapter 4); and the announcement of a truth commission in Norway to examine the past forcible assimilation of the Sámi and Kven peoples (see Chapter 6). What all of these are characterised by, in our view, are the voicing of apparently good intentions on the part of settler/dominant populations, but those good intentions, and the apologies and processes (in instances when these were forthcoming) were informed mainly, or in many cases solely, by Western understandings. What has become evident in each of these examples is a sense of the inadequacy of the process, and feelings, fears or outright critiques of tokenism and obfuscation. Suggestive here is that the needs of Westernised societies have continued to be privileged in these processes to such a degree that it appears that an essential motivation has been the appeasing of Western guilt. The interests of the powerful, in seeking, expecting or even demanding 'forgiveness', or at the very least, in absolving their consciences, remain prevalent, and this, of course, is an unacceptable basis upon which to proceed in future. In the 'Preface' to this book, Stephen advanced that feelings of shock, horror, or shame on the part of Europeans, and those of European descent, on reading this book were to be in some senses welcomed, as those feelings can be signifiers that the functions of unveiling, owning, and demythologising the truths about the residential schooling of Indigenous peoples by settler populations may be served. But settlers finding ways to absolve those feelings is not enough. It is essential that the co-construction and shared evaluation of outcomes (i.e. inclusive of Indigenous and settler populations, and their respective cultural understandings) is a defining feature of future efforts towards truth, restitution, and reconciliation. If what is done is not understood to be meaningful by all participants, any resulting work cannot be expected to elicit any worthwhile outcomes; and unless future efforts are founded on such premises, then they will risk continuing the patterns of inadequacy, tokenism, failure, and obfuscation.

A cautionary lesson can be taken here from common judgements of the Nazi Holocaust. Although children in many countries are taught about this history, there was, and there still remains, evidence of modifications made in the narrative that appear to serve Westerners' comfort with their own identities. Despite the persuasive laboratory demonstrations by Stanley Milgram (1965, 1974), which highlighted Westerners' all-too frequent acquiescence to 'power', even to the point of 'harming' or 'killing' another,[10] there remains a huge temptation, which is often given in to, to assume that the Nazi Holocaust was a particular problem, for a particular people, in a particular place and time, and that it could not happen, or have happened, anywhere else, at any other time. We must not allow ourselves to continue to let ourselves off the hook in such ways; particularly not as history, and particularly Indigenous history, disputes the foundations of those assumptions.

As with the mechanised slaughter of Europe's Jewish population, it should be a matter of no argument whatsoever that the physical and cultural genocides directed towards Indigenous people by settler populations must never be repeated. But the insidious and hidden nature of the operation of the residential schooling systems over such long periods of time is a reason for caution. Unless, or more optimistically, until such time that the power imbalances that underpinned residential schooling systems are addressed, our vigilance will need to be broader. In many of the increasingly populist, neoliberal societies of the West, and in other areas of the world that have adopted philosophies and political systems derived from Western thinking (e.g. Chinese communism), we have noticed dangerous and increasing tendencies towards 'Othering'. We must find ways to oppose, and to guard against, people and organisations peddling ideas about the relative values of different peoples at every level of the social ecology. We note here the exceptional efforts of Jacinda Ardern, the Prime Minister of Aotearoa/New Zealand at the time of writing (April, 2019) and others to preserve a sense of shared humanity in that country following the terrorist attacks against Muslims in Christchurch, memorably encapsulated in her statement: 'They are us'. In contrasting this response with those to similar atrocities perpetrated in the UK and USA, there would appear to be a much greater strength in, and more possibilities for, better common futures in Aotearoa/New Zealand. One cannot, and of course should not, underestimate the potentials for opposition to such responses, nor how much resolve and effort is needed to tread such paths.

At the beginning of this section, we commented that it has been comforting for us, in containing our anxiety, to keep in mind the generosity of the principle that a 'step forwards' is helpful.[11] Right or wrong, we feel that it is consistent with a principle of Indigenous research methods articulated by Natahnee Nuay Winder in her chapter in this book (Chapter 7) – that is to say, the principle of being responsible: 'To teach, learn, and behave in a moral and ethical manner for Indigenous peoples' ways, which means *leaving the people stronger than when you entered into the process'*. What we are confronted with now, at the end of this book, is how big (or small) that step has been. The stories of what happened to the children forced into situations of residential schooling, or similar, in six countries (Aotearoa/New Zealand, Australia, Greenland, Ireland, Norway, and the United States) across three continents (Australasia, Europe, and North America) have been told by contributing authors who have proven themselves to be eminently qualified to tell them. These narratives have included reflections on how and why this happened, and what these histories have meant for those directly affected by them. As the editor of this book, Stephen had the task of engaging/inviting potentially contributing authors for this book, and in this, exerted a level of choice over which country contexts were featured. So he would like to speak directly to the reader now:

> I am limited, as many British people are, in my command of languages, and as a native English speaker, it was predictable that I would be better able to access countries in which the settler populations spoke, and most accounts were written in, English. As I have a specific interest in the situation of the Sámi people in Norway, and have accrued something approaching a basic competence in Norwegian, and the fact that written Danish has few appreciable differences from written Norwegian,[12] this meant that Greenland and Norway were more immediately possible for me to include than they might have been for some others. However, I have wondered – hopefully, in a constructive way - about what might have been the immediate possibilities for a native Spanish speaker, who had had similar concerns to me? In all likelihood, she or he would have been more able, and perhaps more likely, to access the histories of countries in Central and South America, regions which have, of course, similar histories of European colonisation. In turn, a French speaker would have been more able, and again, perhaps more likely, to access the histories of countries that were formerly French colonies. A Dutch speaker might have been likely to consider the colonial histories of Indonesia, Surinam, various parts of the Caribbean, and (should she or he be able to manage Afrikaans) southern Africa, and a Portuguese speaker might have been more likely to consider the colonial histories of Brazil and Angola. I would like to meet these hypothetical Spanish, French, Dutch and Portuguese-speaking counterparts.

The reason why such wonderings are held to be constructive is because, as reasonably lengthy as this book is, we believe that its subject matter deserves and requires a more expansive treatment. As indicated above, many European nations colonised the lands of, and thereby displaced, Indigenous peoples. It is impossible to believe that the residential schooling of Indigenous children did not form part of these colonisation efforts, and whilst our knowledge is somewhat patchy, we do know for a fact that this was the case in certain country contexts. So, we believe that what we've made is a start. To Western/settler readers, we would like to repeat the words of a widely circulated Amnesty International campaign advertisement of the early 1990s: 'Take a good look. Don't ever say, "I didn't know it was happening"'. We hope you've had a good read ….

So yes, we have tried to make a start, and we hope that it's been a respectful start. As we have stated above, the second section of this chapter has been written by three of the Indigenous contributing authors. Their responses have been included in the second section with no editorial involvement, save for making adjustments in formatting where necessary. In these authors' highlighting of where they feel that we have heard and understood correctly, and where we have made mistakes and oversights, or fallen into the age-old traps of privileging Western perspectives, we hope that our collaboration on this chapter, as part of the collaboration between the contributing authors to this book as a whole, can serve as part of further, deeper, and very necessary conversations, in which we might consider further meaningful possibilities for truth, restitution, reconciliation, and reclamation. And we extend an invitation to others – Indigenous and Western/settler peoples alike – to join us.

Reflections by Tania Ka'ai, Rosemary Norman-Hill, and Natahnee Nuay Winder

Tania Ka'ai

The authors of the first section of this chapter have taken great care to capture the voices of the contributors' truths and stories about the impact of residential schooling on the Indigenous communities in their respective countries and communities. They go to great lengths to express the way that *Western privilege* manifests itself in the accounts provided by the authors weaving the effects of this privilege through their reflections, like an ocean tide ebbing and flowing backwards and forwards. They touch on the different manifestations of Western privilege, including

- the privileging of Western knowledges, world views, and languages to maintain the dominance and power of the dominant cultures;
- the privileging of Western values over Indigenous values;
- the privileging of Western power to 'legitimise' the abuse and neglect of children;
- the privileging of Western resources to implement archaic and draconian methods of control over the Indigenous, such as 'brainwashing' and

'assimilation' to affect children's identities, and in many instances, their ability to function as Indigenous peoples; and lastly,
- the privileging of Western education to legitimise educating Indigenous children in a way where they were simply being groomed for domesticity and in-service positions for the dominant population.

Of particular significance for me is the utmost care taken by the authors in writing the first section of this chapter in recognising that as Western scholars, they do not see things as they are for the Indigenous people through an Indigenous lens, because they are not Indigenous. Instead, they can only see these things as they are in the Western world, through a Western cultural lens (c.f. Nin, 1961). This positioning of themselves is evident throughout the section in the way they reflect on the writings of the contributors and their desire to be *just* and *fair* in their interpretations, because '[they] we have dipped [their] our toes into the oceans of Indigenous knowledge and experience that were previously unfamiliar to [them] us, as well as those more familiar streams that also drew us [them] to what we [they] hope are useful parallels'.

The authors' acknowledgement of the dignity of the contributing authors in writing their stories is quite affective, because it is often difficult to write as an Indigenous scholar in a dignified and respectful manner about the horrors of cultural genocide and the effects of inter-generational cultural trauma experienced by our Indigenous communities instigated by settler populations. Western education was one vehicle for this to occur, as we know. Recognition is also afforded by the authors of the attempts by Indigenous people to address the inadequacies and injustices of Western education with the dominant culture through reconciliation processes, and that these attempts have largely been ignored, or reframed to ensure the dominant culture maintains power. The authors understand the impact of colonial imperialistic practices and mindsets that have caused immense pain to successive generations of Indigenous families resulting in these communities being pushed to the fringes of our societies to function through the colonial and outdated practice of 'Othering'.

It is refreshing to have worked alongside these two Western scholars on this book. In the first section of this chapter, they demonstrate that they are open to critically reflecting on their own cultural boundaries, and are willing to interrogate the tensions between Western values and behaviours of the settler populations as the colonisers of Indigenous populations, and the impact of residential schooling on these populations. What is also equally important is the authors' acute understanding that there is a need for 'courageous conversations' to occur not just in our societies but amongst academics within the academy. Transferring these conversations into print is a powerful medium from which to effect change. Perhaps it is the responsibility of Western scholars to lead these conversations, to be agents of change, to create new and safe spaces within the academy where equity, diversity, and human rights are recognised, where the dominant population within the academy are tolerant, kind, and generous, and where Indigenous languages and cultures have a chance to thrive, and become hubs for the revitalisation of Indigenous languages and cultures. Herein lies the challenge.

This multi-authored book is a collaboration of scholars from across a range of disciplines. Hopefully, it will inspire other scholars, both non-Indigenous and Indigenous, to have these 'courageous conversations', and be part of the solution to effect transformational change amongst our communities across the world that have been affected by colonisation, and where successive generations of families live in hope that they can recover from past abuse and neglect, and create new and safe spaces for the education of their children in the future:

> Kia matomato te tupu o te reo o te pā harakeke
> [May the language and culture of our families flourish and thrive]

Rosemary Norman-Hill

First, I would like to thank Stephen for allowing me the honour of being a contributing author for this thought-provoking book. I also consider it a privilege to be able to offer my considerations on the work undertaken by Stephen and Julie as part of the 're-reflection' of this chapter. Bringing together a collective group of Indigenous authors from across the world to share the storying of native residential school systems privileges our voices. Seeking feedback creates a sense of inclusiveness, of greater understanding, and a shared knowing. As explained in Chapter 1, this book is distinct in that it provides an 'extended multi-country focus' whilst considering the 'transnational phenomenon of genocide through schooling'. In this way, the book becomes a ceremony of sharing and learning, of truth and reclamations. It venerates our truths as Indigenous peoples, whilst acknowledging both the differences and commonalities surrounding this part of our history.

As co-authors of this chapter, Stephen and Julie write candidly about the challenges they faced as non-Indigenous peoples entering into Indigenous space. Whilst admitting to being 'relatively naïve Westerners' with 'all-too-limited' experience, they approach this issue in a raw and candid way, not from a deficit perspective but as a learning tool. By courageously dipping their toes into 'the oceans of Indigenous knowledge and experience', they have found a starting position from which to engage in conversation, a way of developing mutual understandings and solutions. This has the effect of opening the door for the reader to challenge their own ways of knowing and being; a way of bringing together these truths about our Indigenous histories. Throughout this chapter, Stephen and Julie offer their reflections with 'humility, curiosity, and respect', initiating a conversation that comes straight from the heart, and goes straight to the heart. Through the rejection of the 'narrow pseudo-objectivist mindsets that privilege empirical knowledge', Stephen and Julie have caught the essence of the storying in an insightful way. Although they have limited experience with Indigenous knowledges, as co-authors, they have managed to encapsulate those messages. Their summarisation skilfully links together the imbalances and brings to light the insidious intent that lay behind the establishment of native residential school systems.

Highlighting the issues in this way allows the reader to look deeper into these stories to the reality that is the true history of Indigenous peoples' oppression at the hands of Western civilisation. However, challenging modernist philosophical thinking and Western ways of being means challenging peoples' thought processes on a deeper ontological level. The acknowledgement of these truths creates a deeper awareness of the abuse and trauma inflicted on the children placed in residential schools. It was a calculated attempt by Europeans to break down familial bonds and relationships to Country,[13] kin, and culture. Perpetrated wherever this method of schooling was established, these were not kind acts of benevolence by Church or State. The stories are real, they happened and had tragic consequences for Indigenous peoples across the globe. The trauma of separation, the loss of language, the denial of culture, and the denigration of heritage continues to impact on families and communities today, as all the stories in this book demonstrate so clearly.

By reflecting on their own challenges as non-Indigenous people immersed within Western constructs of knowing and being, Stephen and Julie have opened the door for a deeper and very necessary conversation. They ask the reader to be more 'protective of, and insistent upon, respecting shared humanity', heeding the lessons of the past so as not to repeat them in the future. Taking care through their reflectivity, they identify education as the catalyst for the (cultural) genocide that came as a result of the imposition of native residential school systems. They also see education as a way of providing honest accounts of colonial history within our respective countries. They recognise that the common intent across the globe for Europeans to use education as a tool to civilise the 'savage' child and inculcate them into the Western ways of life is not in dispute. Although each country's story and experience is different, their 'alignment in common humanity' allows the reader to move forward from the horrors of the past to a place of truth.

Bringing together Indigenous authors from three different continents to share our stories in our own way is a huge undertaking. The learnings for the reader are immense. They have the potential to pave the way for a new awakening, a rekindling of the spirit, and an opening up of the mind, away from Western thought processes. This book is a 'testing of the waters', and a step in the right direction in my view. I suggest it goes a long way to opening up the conversation and in creating a greater awareness of the impact native residential schools had on Indigenous peoples, not only in the six countries included in this publication, but in every country around the world where Indigenous child removal and cultural eradication through education took place, and in many ways continues to this day.

As a contributing author, I would like to acknowledge that Stephen and Julie, as two non-Indigenous champions, have walked with us on this journey. Dealing sensitively with each author's storying process, Stephen and Julie have courageously stepped away from Western perspectives, finding their own truths. Their reflections in this chapter demonstrate this shift in understanding, identifying that these practices were indeed (cultural) genocide. They now ask the reader to find their own truths within those stories and move to a place that allows for restitution, reconciliation, and reclamation. While the stories are tragic, our storying will not remain in 'the tragic'. For to do so disrespects and displaces the thousands of years of 'knowing, being, and doing' that our ancestors passed down through the ages to ensure a healthy future for our peoples.

Natahnee Nuay Winder

This book is a collection of Indigenous sister scholars and allies whose voices bring us, and others, into the circle of understanding, empathy, and healing. As a descendant of various family members who attended residential schools, I struggled in contemplating how to properly articulate concluding thoughts about the ongoing impacts these institutions have had on Indigenous peoples. Four aspects that pull the strings of my heart, spirit, and mind when reflecting on residential schools are: this was a lived history, it is our shared living history, these are stories of survival, and these are stories of resiliency.

It is part of our recent past that Indigenous knowledge systems, languages, cultures, and traditions were forcibly erased and attempted to be eliminated from the Western landscape of 'progress' and 'development' for Westerners. We must remember and honour all the students who survived residential schools to continue to advocate for the enhancement of educational systems and policies that privilege Indigenous knowledges.

The legacy left by residential schools is part of an ongoing conversation where Indigenous lives were inter-generationally affected. This topic reminds us of the ongoing structural colonialism Indigenous peoples encounter today (i.e. racism, prejudice, and the alarming rates of Indigenous peoples going missing and murdered). Tanaya Winder's poem *Extraction* (2018) represents a glimpse into the 'felt experiences' (Million, 2009), or the emotional experiences of residential schooling as

> Before I was born they tried to silence us,
> pierced our tongues with needles then taught
> our then-girls-grandmothers how to sew

like machines. Even then, they saw our bodies
as land, full of resources
waiting to be extracted and exploited.
[...]
For as long as I can remember, we've been stolen:
from reservation to Industrial boarding schools
and today our girls, women, and two-spirit still go missing
and murdered. I could find no word for this.
But yáakwi is to sink or disappear. Where is it we fall?
When did we first start vanishing?

Some descendants of residential school survivors are no longer fluent in, or do not speak, their traditional languages, resulting in language loss as evidence of how colonisers and settlers 'tried to silence' Indigenous peoples 'before they were born' (Winder, 2018). The lived experiences and testimonies of residential school survivors hold a deep affect that not only extends to their descendants, but also to their community members and allies. Indigenous peoples were silenced across generations from speaking their traditional languages because English was deemed more valuable to progress and a necessity to fit into the Western society.

These histories of education and educational policies were based on a structure that Othered Indigenous peoples, which deemed them culturally inferior to their non-Indigenous counterparts. Residential schools were based on a model for the extraction and assimilation of Indigenous peoples from their communities, families, and traditional territories. As stated by Anishinaabe writer, scholar, and activist Leanne Betasamosake Simpson (in Klein, 2013):

> ....[t]he act of extraction removes all of the relationships that give whatever is being extracted meaning. Extracting is taking. Actually, extracting is stealing – it is taking without consent, without thought, care or even knowledge of the impacts that extraction has on the other living things in that environment. That's always been a part of colonialism and conquest.

Residential schooling interrupted Indigenous peoples' lives across the globe through this process with complete disregard of the long-term effects such as the forced removal of Indigenous children from their homes. Indigenous children were stolen to become colonised bodies. Their lives were drastically changed and, in some cases, altered from a path that once embraced their Indigenous ways of knowing, replaced by Western knowledge and English-based societal norms. Indigenous students were trained to commit to working class positions; however, there are cases where attendees become medical doctors, musicians, teachers, and writers.

We must be consciously aware that there is still a large amount of work to be done in order for us to heal from the aftermath of these institutions. Healing is a continual process for both Indigenous and non-Indigenous peoples who want to learn. This book is also for Indigenous peoples and scholars who are doing hard work and heartwork[14] to ensure educational policies no longer target Indigenous peoples through assimilation and/or extraction. On a global scale, many Indigenous communities have a shared experience of the different types of colonial education and policies that were harmful and disruptive to their communities. Yet, there are commonalities and injustices that unite both Indigenous peoples and allies to fight and form a collective voice to challenge ongoing colonialism, assimilation, and extraction agendas.

By weaving together our hearts to have a better understanding of what happened at these institutions and the ongoing structural colonialism, this book helps its readers learn equitable ways to move forward as agents who empower positive change. Beyond that, it also provides a space where our hearts, minds, and spirits can be vulnerable enough to engage in Colliding Heartwork.[15] These collisions are the work of continuous healing, ongoing awareness, and understanding of the residential school legacies across the countries highlighted in this book. From an Indigenous perspective, these collisions can also resemble one's willingness to learn more about residential schools, and to reflect on how they fit into the history as an Indigenous person, an ally, or settler. This process of understanding collisions (residential schools) can be unsettling because it may lead to small fractures, huge awakenings, or go unnoticed for a long time before feelings of acceptance, empathy, and/or healing can occur. With responsibility to the survivors, we need to ensure educational policies going forward include Indigenous voices and perspectives. It is my hope that this book provides a pathway for our hearts to collide and the artwork to emerge collectively.

First, I would like to thank Stephen for bringing all the authors together into a shared space, to take up the heartfelt work to discuss the legacy and history of residential schools, and to honour the Indigenous children who attended these institutions. Second, it is a privilege to contribute to this chapter along with Stephen James Minton, Julie Vane, and my Indigenous sisters in academia, Tania Ka'ai and Rosemary Norman-Hill. I acknowledge that my contribution occurred on the unceded traditional territories of the Musqueam (xʷməθkʷəy̓əm), Squamish (Sḵwx̱wú7mesh Úxwumixw), and Tsleil-Waututh (səlilwətaʔɬ) Nations. I acknowledge Melissa Jackson, Alejandro Lopez, Denver Lynxleg, Daniel Ramirez, and Tanaya Winder for their feedback with my first academic publication as a collaborator on this work. Last, I thank Roe Bubar for connecting me with Stephen, and making a path for me as an emerging Indigenous scholar. Bubar is a leader and example for other scholars to both support and encourage the new generations of Indigenous scholars, bringing them into the academic circle. These acknowledgements represent my heartwork to serve and privilege Indigenous voices and perspectives as well to demonstrate gratitude and cultural protocol. I also highlight my connections to my colleagues and relations.

Notes

1. Here, Lame Deer referred, of course, to the Battle of the Little Bighorn in 1876, when 1,500 to 2,500 plains Indians (Lakota, Northern Cheyenne, and Arapaho) warriors defeated the 700 strong US Seventh Cavalry Regiment under Lieutenant Colonel George Armstrong Custer.
2. Turtle Island is a name for the landmass that is now North America, used by some of the native peoples of those lands (it appears, e.g. in the oral traditions of Anishinaabe and the Iroquois peoples), and some Indigenous rights activists.
3. Amongst Western readers, and certainly amongst politically left-orientated ones, *Seeker of Visions* has become as important as a dire warning about the ethical, human, and environmental consequences of unrestrained global capitalism (or the 'green frogskin world') as it is a beautifully written autobiography in which fascinating insights into the author's traditional Lakota culture are so generously provided.
4. Although sourced to Nin here, she did not claim credit for this adage. Her character in *Seduction of the Minotaur*, Lilian, is recalling a teaching from the Talmud.
5. A key outcome of the inclusion of the Irish experience of residential schooling was the highlighting of the practice of trying to rid society of 'Others' in this way has not only been inflicted upon Indigenous people by colonising populations as a follow-up to war and physical genocide.
6. Such identifications of commonality as being key in opposing 'Othering' by dominant groups is hardly a new idea in the struggle for Indigenous rights. In the late 1960s, this was evident in the contact between some members of the Black Panther Party for Self-Defense (BPP) and the American Indian movement (see Wyler, 1992). It is significant that whilst the majority of the COINTELPRO (portmanteau derived from COunter INTELligence PROgram) actions conducted by the FBI (Federal Bureau of Investigation) from 1966 onwards were directed against the BPP, who COINTELPRO labelled a 'Black nationalist hate group', several initiatives were directed at AIM (see United States Congress, 1976). It is to be recalled that COINTELPRO methods included infiltration, psychological warfare, harassment via the legal system, the deliberate undermining of public opinion, and the use of illegal force (including assaults, beatings, and assassination) (Glick, 1989; United States Congress, 1976).
7. The psychiatrisation of Indigenous peoples (see Chrisjohn, 2018) constitutes a prime example of the invalidation of 'persecution as the figment of a collective paranoid imagination'. Whereas our best chance of destroying our species these days is probably man-made environmental catastrophe, rather than thermonuclear war, we feel that much of Laing's statement (made over half a century ago) serves as an accurate assessment of how things continue to stand today.
8. There have been some exceptions to this, though. Davis (2001, p. 22) noted in an autobiography written by a Shoshone teacher, Esther Burnett Horne; she revealed that her students included '… Dennis Banks, George Mitchell and Leonard Peltier [who] became leaders of the American Indian Movement, through which they worked for Indian people's political self-determination [and] advocated a return to traditional spirituality, and cultivated cultural pride.' However, the possibilities of and for pan-Indigenous solidarity are still – and seemingly, deliberately so – silenced in mainstream news coverage. The 2016–2017 protesting of the construction of the Dakota Access Pipeline by the Standing Rock Sioux Tribe (whose

lands the pipeline runs across, and whose water supply remains under threat by leaks from that pipeline) and their supporters was a matter of immense significance across the Indigenous world (see Akande, 2018; Snyder, 2018), and yet was scarcely mentioned in the mainstream news. To my knowledge, the gestures of solidarity shown towards the Standing Rock Sioux protestors by the visiting Māori people – both the fact of their visit, and in ceremony – were visible to those who were not physically present only via social networking channels.

9. Intensive Interaction is a process based on primary caregiver/child interactions, and the normal development of communication and sociability (Nind & Hewett, 1994, p. 8). It encourages the use of imitation as a gateway to relationship formation, by establishing a vocabulary that has meaning for the person with a learning disability, allowing her or him to access a social world, and opening up possibilities for social change (Caldwell, 2006).

10. The details of Milgram's initial experimental set-up (1965) are well known amongst social scientists, but to non-psychological audiences, bear repeating. His demonstration involved duping genuine participants into believing that they were acting in a 'teacher' role in delivering, via an electroshock generating machine, shocks of increasing severity to what they were told was a fellow participant in a 'learner' role in the room next door (the 'learners' were actually actors) according to the 'learners'' 'errors' in a 'word-association learning task'. The genuine participants' apparently 'random' assignation to the 'teacher' role was fixed; the 'shock generating equipment' was bogus; and the people who were actually under investigation were the genuine participants. They were instructed to give the 'learner' a 'shock' each time he made a mistake, which were to increase in severity by fifteen volts each time; the 'shock machine' had levers up to '450 volts', followed by three more levers marked by large 'X's and 'Danger'. At 120 volts, the 'teacher' would hear the 'learner' complain of pain; at 210 volts, of a 'heart condition', and make repeated requests to be able to get out of the room; and after 330 volts, there was only an ominous silence. On hesitation, the genuine participant received prompts from the experimenter such as 'It's essential to the experiment that you continue' and latterly, 'You have no choice, you have to go on'. How many participants would go 'all the way' to the third 'X' after '450 volts'? Astonishingly, over 60 per cent of the participants did so. The genesis of this series of experiments, was Milgram's reflections on the results of the Nuremberg trials, at which many Nazi officer and soldier defendants attempted to evade their responsibility for their crimes, on the basis of their simply having 'followed orders'. Milgram argued that the views that had developed that 'Germans are different' and that 'the same thing couldn't happen here' were dangerous falsehoods; and in this series of experiments, he demonstrated that 'normal' American people could and did reject or ignore their own feelings of sympathy or empathy for an apparently suffering and dying fellow human being in favour of showing obedience to authority of an experimenter (Milgram, 1965, 1974).

11. This is a principle that Stephen saw in practice in the few Indigenous listening circles in which he has been honoured to have been included. Unlike what is usually the case in the interminably dull meetings which seem to make up so much of his standard working week, in the listening circles in which he has participated, he found there to have been no 'agendas' to work through, in strictly time-limited, linear fashions. Indeed, in such circles it has been enough to show, in one's responses, that one has listened respectfully to those who have spoken; and sometimes, the end point has been that certain decisions cannot be reached without listening and talking some more, or by considering the perspectives of others, both of which might be more possible at a later point. And such outcomes do indeed constitute genuine steps forward; at least, and speaking for himself, they felt that way to Stephen.

12. There are two official written standards of Norwegian: Bokmål, which is used by 85–90 per cent of the population, and is the variety learnt by foreigners (including me), and Nynorsk, which is used by about 12 per cent of the population. As written Bokmål is directly derived from written Danish, the differences between Bokmål and Danish texts are relatively few. However, as a learner of Bokmål, I am more likely to understand a Norwegian speaking in her or his mother tongue than a Dane.
13. The word 'Country' is capitalised to denote traditional lands of a nation or language group. (See Chapter 4, endnote 2).
14. Heartwork is the process of working with and for Indigenous communities that comes from one's heart (Minthorn & Shotton, 2018; Winder, 2015). Heartwork is the purpose and work an individual is called to accomplish with passion and commitment to 'mend soul wounds and healing' (Winder, 2015).
15. See this book, Chapter 7.

References

Adams, D.W. (1995). *Education for Extinction: American Indians and the Boarding School Experience 1875-1928*. Lawrence, KS: University Press of Kansas.

Akande, I. (2018). Decolonization? In the face of racism, neocolonialism, and neoliberalism. Presented at the 14th International Congress of Qualitative Inquiry, University of Illinois in Urbana-Champaign, USA, May 16–19.

Bear, C. (2008). American Indian boarding schools haunt many. *Morning Edition*, May 12.

Caldwell P. (1998). *Person to Person: Establishing Contact and Communication with People with Profound Learning Disabilities and Those Whose Behaviour May Be Challenging*. Brighton, England: Pavillion.

Caldwell, P. (2006). Speaking the other's language: Imitation as a gateway to relationship. *Infant and Child Development*, 15(3): 275–282.

Chrisjohn, R. (2018). The psychiatrization of Indigenous people as a continuation of genocide. Keynote address at PsychOut: A Conference for Organizing Resistance against Psychiatry, University of Toronto, October 1.

Chrisjohn, R.D. & Young, S.L., with Maraun, M. (2006). *The Circle Game: Shadows and Substance in the Indian Residential School Experience in Canada*. Penticton, BC: Theytus Books.

Crow Dog, M. & Erdoes, R. (1990). *Lakota Woman*. New York: Grove Press.

Davis, J. (2001). American Indian boarding school experiences: Recent studies from Native perspectives. *Organisation of American Historians' Magazine of History*, Winter 2001: 20–22.

Eastman, C.E. (1911/2018). *From the Deep Woods to Civilization: Chapters in the Autobiography of an Indian*. New York: Franklin Classics.

Gerlach, W. (2000). *And the Witnesses were Silent: The Confessing Church and the Jews*. Lincoln, NE: University of Nebraska Press.

Glick, B. (1989). *War at Home: Covert Action Against U.S. Activists and What We Can Do About It*. Boston, MA: South End Press Pamphlet Series.

Klein, N. (2013). Dancing the World into Being: A Conversation with Idle No More's Leanne Simpson. *Yes! Magazine*. March 5. Available online: http://www.yesmagazine.org/peace-justice/dancing-the-world-into-being-a-conversation-with-idle-no-more-leanne-simpson [Accessed April, 2019].

Laing, R.D. (1967). *The Politics of Experience and the Bird of Paradise*. Harmondsworth, England: Penguin Books.

Lame Deer, J. & Erdoes, R. (1972). *Lame Deer, Seeker of Visions*. New York: Simon & Schuster.

Marcus, S. (2016). Astounding Archaeology Discovery Places Inland Human Occupation of Australia at 49,000 years. *Sydney Morning Herald*, November 3.

Milgram, S. (1965). Some conditions of obedience and disobedience to authority. *Human Relations*, 18: 56–76.

Milgram, S. (1974). *Obedience to Authority: An Experimental View*. New York: Harper Collins.

Million, D. (2009). Felt theory: An Indigenous feminist approach to affect and history. *Wicazo Sa Review*, 24(2): 53–76.

Minton, S.J. (2016). *Marginalisation and Aggression from Bullying to Genocide: Critical Educational and Psychological Perspectives*. Rotterdam: Brill.

Minthorn, R.S. & Shotton, H.J. (2018). *Reclaiming Indigenous Research in Higher Education*. New Brunswick, NJ: Rutgers University Press.

National Society. (2010). *National Society's Graded Hymn Book With Tunes: Hymns For Children Under Eight; Hymns For Children Between Eight And Twelve*. Whitefish, MT: Kessinger Publishing. Full-text also available online: https://archive.org/stream/nationalsocietys00unknuoft/nationalsocietys00unknuoft_djvu.txt [Accessed April, 2019].

Nin, A. (1961). *Seduction of the Minotaur*. Athens, OH: Swallow Press/Ohio University Press.

Nind M. & Hewett D. (1994) *Access to Communication: Developing the Basics of Communication with People with Severe Learning Difficulties through Intensive Interaction*. London: David Fulton Publishers.

Pauketat, T.R. (2012). *The Oxford Handbook of North American Archaeology*. Oxford University Press.

Russell, B. (1946). *A History of Western Philosophy and its Connection to Political and Social Circumstances from the Earliest Times to the Present Day*. London: George Allen & Unwin.

Snyder, J. (2018). Decolonizing with Indigenous Protocols: Lessons learned from Standing Rock. Presented at the 14th International Congress of Qualitative Inquiry, University of Illinois in Urbana-Champaign, USA, May 16–19.

United States Congress. (1976). *Final report of the Select Committee to Study Governmental Operations with Respect to Intelligence Activities*. Available online: https://archive.org/details/finalreportofsel01unit [Accessed April, 2019].

Wilson, S. (2008). *Research is Ceremony: Indigenous Research Methods*. Halifax & Winnipeg: Fernwood Publishing.

Winder, T. (2015). Heartwork. Tanaya Winder revolution is love and i be healing it through heartwork. Available online: https://tanayawinder.com/heartwork/ [Accessed April, 2019].

Winder, T. (2018). Extraction. Available online: https://therumpus.net/2018/04/national-poetry-month-day-12-tanaya-winder/ [Accessed April, 2019].

Wyler, R. (1992). *Blood of the Land: The Government and Corporate War Against First Nations*. Gabriola Island, BC: New Society Publishers.

Index

Aboriginal and Islander Child Care Agencies (AICCAs) 86–7
Aboriginal and Torres Strait Islander Child Placement Principle (ATSICPP) 87
abuse 1, 7, 11, 38, 55, 77–9, 101, 114, 116, 121, 136, 145–6, 165–7, 169, 176–7, 179–81, 183n8, 197, 199, 209, 212: cultural abuse 116; emotional abuse 177; physical abuse 146, 176–7, 179–80; psychological abuse 116; sexual abuse, 77–9, 101, 146, 165–6, 176–7, 179–81, 183n8
Adams, David Wallace 4, 14n2, 15n4, 16n9, 38–41, 144–5, 197
alcohol and alcohol abuse 83, 86, 101–2, 105, 150, 179
Alice Springs Half-Caste Institution 77
ally 6, 17n18, 191, 215
American Indian Movement (AIM) 14, 19n25, 37, 216n6, 216n8
Amnesty International 209
An Garda Síochána 168, 179
apartheid 8–9, 27
assimilation 2–4, 9, 31–2, 34, 38–41, 48, 50, 58, 67, 74, 76, 79–80, 82, 84, 95, 109n21, 135, 142, 147, 152, 206, 210, 214, 215

Banks, Dennis 36–7, 216n8
Black Elk 15n6
'Black Kitty' 66, 72
Black Panther Party 216n6
Blacktown Residential Institution 72–3
boarding schools, 5, 34, 36; in Aotearoa/New Zealand, 54–7, 61; in Australia, 69; in Norway, 114–19, 121–2, 135–6; in United States, 3–4, 16n13
Brave Heart, Maria Yellow Horse 108n14

'Bringing Them Home' report 83–4
Brown, Dee 44n19
Bubar, Roe 215
bullying 6, 17n16, 55, 172

Caldwell, Phoebe 203–4, 217n9
Camfield School 74
Carlisle Indian Industrial School 15n7, 16n9, 39, 41, 44n17, 144–5
Chrisjohn, Roland 4, 11, 34, 37–8, 43n11, 43n13, 216n7
Christian Brothers (Ireland) 163, 167, 173, 176, 183n11, 184n19
Christianisation, of Indigenous peoples 3, 36, 40, 42n3, 48, 66–7, 69–70, 72, 75–6, 78–9, 82, 96, 118, 143–4, 202
'civilisation', of Indigenous peoples 1, 16n9, 16n12, 32, 36, 39, 41, 48, 49, 66–70, 72–5, 82–3, 144–5, 156
'Colliding Heartwork' 108n14, 143, 150–9, 160n5, 215, 218n14, 218n15
colonisation 1–2, 7, 10, 25, 27–9, 41n2, 41n3, 48, 58, 62n1, 66–7, 75, 78, 83, 86–7, 90n2, 95–6, 100, 105–7, 113–15, 122, 136, 147, 196–7, 200, 208–9, 211, 214; internal colonisation 120–2, 198
Columbus, Christopher 3, 15n5, 27–8
Commission to Inquire into Child Abuse (CICA) (Ireland) 35, 163, 168–70, 172, 174–7, 181, 184n22, 185n25, 185n28
county homes (in Ireland) 168, 174
Crow Dog, Mary 197–200
Custer, George Armstrong 192, 216n1

Dakota Access Pipeline 216n8
Danish national constitution 97–8

Danish settlement in Greenland 96–7
Dawes Act 144, 160n6
deaths in residential schools 15n7, 16n11, 33, 73, 75, 77, 145–6, 182n2
De Beuavoir, Simone 26–7
decolonisation 10, 113, 138
De las Casas, Bartolomé 28
discrimination 3, 6, 17n16, 25, 83, 98, 171–4
disease 15n5, 28, 50, 69, 73, 77, 83, 101, 145–6
Donoghue, Nan 172–3
Dreamtime 69, 90n3

Eastman, Charles (Ohíye S'a) 200
Egede, Hans 96–7
epistemocide 201
Erik Thorvaldsson (Erik the Red) 96–7
eugenics 29, 42n4
existentialism 7, 26–7
'Experiment', the, in Greenland, 95, 103–5, 107, 108n15, 108n17, 109n19, 198

feminism 6, 26, 196
Famine (in Ireland) 43n14, 164, 166, 182n3

genocide 2, 3, 15n5, 16n12, 29–30, 78, 80–2, 84–5, 143, 182n5, 195–6, 200; cultural genocide 6–7, 30–4, 42n9, 43n11, 84, 195–6, 210–13; legal definitions of 30–1, 42n6, 42n8, 80–1, 84; physical genocide 3, 31–2, 43n11, 195–7, 216n5; United Nations Convention on the Prevention and the Punishment of the Crime of Genocide 30–1, 33, 42n8, 80–1
Goffman, Erving 7, 34–8, 43n13, 121
Grey, Sir George 48, 62n1
Grensen Boarding School 127–33

haircutting, of Indigenous children in residential schools 36, 44n16, 142, 144, 160n3
haka 13, 18n22
Hammond, Aleqa 99, 100, 105–6
historical unresolved grief 108n14, 147, 150, 159
Home Rule Act (in Greenland) 98–9, 107n8
Howard, John 84, 85

human zoos 42n5
Hunn Report 53, 63n8

identity, destruction of Indigenous 2, 10, 32, 36, 51–2, 104, 119, 121, 126, 136, 142–3, 148, 150–1, 156, 158, 195, 197, 200, 209–10
Indian Boarding Schools 3–4, 16n13, 143–6
Indigenous, international legal definitions of 24
Indigenous Research Methods 149–50, 207–8
industrial schools (Ireland) 35, 43n14, 163–90
Industrial Schools Act (Ireland) 164
institutionalisation 164, 167, 171, 175, 183n9
Inter Cetera (Papal Bull) 28, 41n2
Inuit languages 96
Inuit people 95–103
Irish Society for the Prevention of Cruelty to Children (ISPCC) 166–8, 172, 179, 183n7, 183n9

Jacobs, Margaret 5, 35, 43n15, 44n16, 44n17
Johnsen, Per Edvard (Molles Piera) 127–35

Keating, Paul 83–4
Kven people 3, 9, 14n1, 40, 109n21, 114–37, 206

Laing, R.D. 199–200, 202
Lakota people 14, 15n6, 17n15, 19n25, 44n16, 108n14, 192, 216n3
Lame Deer, John (Fire) 192–3, 216n1, 216n3
Land Sales Act (Norway) 102
Lemkin, Raphael 30–1, 42n6, 42n8, 80
Letterfrack Christian Brothers School 169, 171, 173, 180, 182, 184n19, 185n24
Levi, Primo 36
Lewis, Patrick 6, 17n18
LGBTQ+ people 6, 196

Macquarrie, Lachlan 66, 70–1, 83
Magdalen laundries 174
Mandela, Nelson 8–9
Manifest Destiny 39, 44n19

Index

Māori people 13, 18n22, 18n23, 41, 48–65, 73, 198, 206, 217n8
Māori language (*te reo Māori*) 49–50, 63n12, 211; biculturalism and 53–4; loss of 51–4, 58, 61; Māori Language Commission 59–60; Māori Language Nests 54; Māori Language Strategy 60; revitalisation of 54, 59–61, 62n2
Means, Russell 14, 17n15, 19n25
Meriam Report 4, 16n13, 145
Mienna, John 122–7
Milgram, Stanley 207, 217n10
Minde, Henry 115–20
Mission Schools: in Aotearoa/New Zealand 49–50, 54; in Australia 73–8
'monitors', in Irish industrial schools 176, 185n27
Moore River Settlement 77
murder 27, 33, 67, 213

national apology to Stolen Generations 83, 85–6
National Society for the Prevention of Cruelty to Children (NSPCC) (UK) 166, 173, 183n7
nation state identity 7, 38–41
native languages, suppression and prohibition of 2, 31, 32; in Aotearoa/New Zealand 49–54, 58; in Australia 66, 90n2, 212; in Greenland 104, 198; in North America 36, 37, 40, 152, 158, 197–9, 203, 214; in Norway 114–17, 118–19, 121–2, 126, 135–7
Native Schools: in Aotearoa/New Zealand 50–51; in Australia 73, 75, 79, 87
Native Schools Act (Aotearoa/New Zealand) 50
Native Schools Codes (Aotearoa/New Zealand) 50–51, 198
Nazis and the Third Reich 29–31, 36, 42n8, 82, 97, 176, 182n5, 185n23, 196, 207, 217n10; concentration camps 43, 176; Holocaust 31, 36, 82, 176, 185, 207
neglect, in residential schools 1, 7, 78, 167, 175–7, 181, 195, 197, 199, 209, 211
Neiden Boarding School 117, 121
neoliberalism 10, 194, 207
Neville, A.O. 77
Nin, Anaïs 194, 210, 216n4
Nordic Sámi Institute 137–8

Norse settlement in Greenland 96
Norwegianisation 2–3, 40, 109n21, 114–20, 135–6, 138

O' Brien, Gerald 29, 42n4, 44n20
orphanages 43n14, 69, 73–4, 177–8
'Other', Indigenous as 7, 24–30, 195–6, 200–201

Pākeha 49, 63n5, 206
Palmater, Pamela 33, 43n10
Parramatta Native Institution 66–7, 70–2, 74–5, 79, 82–3
participatory action research 148, 149, 150–1
Pasifika peoples 62, 63n14
phenomenology 7, 26–7
photo-voice 150
Poonindie Native Training Institution 74–5
Pratt, Richard Henry 3–4, 16n9, 16n12, 39, 144–5
praying towns 143–4
prejudice 6, 17n16, 19n25, 61, 83, 170–1, 174, 213
processes of truth, restitution, reconciliation and reclamation 7, 8–14, 57–61, 82–6, 105–7, 146–60, 177–82, 185n26, 185n29

Qanak, removal of Inughuit people to 97, 107n5

racism 50, 62, 75, 85, 119, 213
rape 11, 27, 33, 69, 177
Reconciliation Commission in Greenland 9, 95, 105–7, 109n21, 109n22; Danish non-engagement with 105–7
Redfern Speech 83
removal of Indigenous children from families 1, 2, 66–8, 73, 76–7, 79–80, 82–6, 105, 198, 213–14
reparations 12, 86, 176, 180–2, 205
reservation system (United States) 39, 44n20, 143, 144–5
Residential Institutions Redress Board (RIRB) (Ireland) 176, 180–2
residential schools in Canada 4, 5, 11, 16n11, 31, 33–4, 43n13, 146, 148, 160n8
Resiliency, of Indigenous populations 141, 147, 157, 159, 213

Index 223

Roman Catholic Church 28, 41n2, 163, 165–7, 175, 177, 181, 183n9
Rudd, Kevin 84–5
Russell, Bertrand 192

Sámi languages 113, 115, 136–7
Sámi Parliament 109n21, 120, 138
Sámi people 2–3, 6, 9, 15n3, 40, 42n5, 106, 109n21, 113–40, 206, 208
Sámi University 120, 138
Sartré, Jean-Paul 26
Sequoyah v, xiii–xiv
self-determination, Indigenous 10, 14–15, 19n24, 63n13, 67, 100, 216n8
Self-Government Act (Greenland) 99–100, 105, 107n9, 108n11
shame 51, 136–7, 182n2, 198, 206
Shelley, Elizabeth 71, 74
Shelley, William 67, 70–1, 87
Sitting Bull 204–5
slavery 27, 41n3
Social Darwinism 29, 39, 42n5, 197
Stannard, David 15n5, 41n3
State apologies to Indigenous peoples 12–13, 85–6; critical views of 12, 86
Stolen Generations 80–7
Sublimus Deus (Papal Bull) 28, 41n2
suicide: by Indigenous peoples 37, 101–3, 108n12, 108n13; by Irish Travellers 171
Szasz, Thomas 35–6, 44n18

Taíno people 27–8
Thiesen, Helene 103–5, 198
Thorning-Schmidt, Helle 106, 108n18, 205–6
Thule airbase 97, 107n5
Thule Culture 96
Tohunga 52, 63n6
Tohunga Suppression Act 52
torture 2, 9, 27, 33
total institutions 7, 34–8, 43n12, 121, 196–201
Transitional Justice (TJ) initiatives (Ireland) 180–1

trauma 1, 51, 76, 78, 84–6, 108n14, 132, 147, 155–6, 159, 177, 210, 212; intergenerational trauma 51, 86, 108n14, 147–8, 154–6, 159, 160n1, 210, 213
Travelling people of Ireland 170–4, 184n19
Treaty of Kiel 44n21, 107n4
Treaty of Waitangi (*Te Tiriti o Waitangi*) 48–9, 57, 62n4, 206; mistranslation of 49, 62n4
Truth Commission in Norway, proposed 9, 109n21, 206
Truth and Reconciliation Commission of Canada 5, 9, 11–2, 14, 16n11, 31, 33, 109n21, 146, 206
tuberculosis 15n7, 98, 101, 108n16, 137, 145, 185n25
Tutu, Desmond 9

United Nations Committee Against Torture (UNCAT) 181–2
United Nations Declaration of the Rights of Indigenous Peoples (UNDRIP) 19n24, 25

Waitangi Tribunal 57–61; assessment of *te reo Māori* 60; recommendations of 60; WAI262 claim 58–9; WAI2336 claim 61; WAI11 claim 58–9
Western privilege 6, 194, 201, 204, 209–10, 212
White Australia policy 80
'white saviour' 5–6, 17n15
Williams, Henry 49, 62n4
Wilson, Sir Ronald 67, 79, 84
Wilson, Shawn 18n19, 150, 194
Winder, Tanaya 213–15
witchcraft trials, in Norway 15n3
workhouses (UK and Ireland) 43n14, 164
Wounded Knee 'incident' 14, 15n6, 19n25
Wounded Knee, Massacre at 3

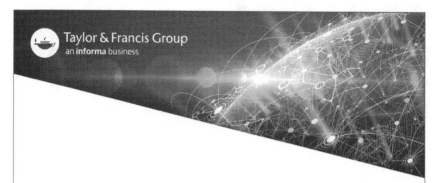

Taylor & Francis eBooks

www.taylorfrancis.com

A single destination for eBooks from Taylor & Francis with increased functionality and an improved user experience to meet the needs of our customers.

90,000+ eBooks of award-winning academic content in Humanities, Social Science, Science, Technology, Engineering, and Medical written by a global network of editors and authors.

TAYLOR & FRANCIS EBOOKS OFFERS:

- A streamlined experience for our library customers
- A single point of discovery for all of our eBook content
- Improved search and discovery of content at both book and chapter level

REQUEST A FREE TRIAL
support@taylorfrancis.com